Constant Disconnection

Constant Disconnection

The Weight of Everyday Digital Life

Kenzie Burchell

STANFORD UNIVERSITY PRESS
Stanford, California

Stanford University Press
Stanford, California

Printed in the United States of America on acid-free, archival-quality paper

Library of Congress Cataloging-in-Publication Data
Names: Burchell, Kenzie, author.
Title: Constant disconnection : the weight of everyday digital life / Kenzie
    Burchell.
Description: Stanford, California : Stanford University Press, 2024. |
    Includes bibliographical references and index.
Identifiers: LCCN 2023057989 (print) | LCCN 2023057990 (ebook) |
    ISBN 9781503632356 (cloth) | ISBN 9781503639799 (paperback) |
    ISBN 9781503639805 (epub)
Subjects: LCSH: Information technology—Social aspects. | Digital
    communications—Social aspects. | Internet—Social aspects. |
    Interpersonal communication. | Interpersonal relations.
Classification: LCC HM851 .B8593 2024 (print) | LCC HM851 (ebook) |
    DDC 303.48/33—dc23/eng/20231227
LC record available at https://lccn.loc.gov/2023057989
LC ebook record available at https://lccn.loc.gov/2023057990

Cover design and photography: Aufuldish & Warinner

For Kelly Jenkins

CONTENTS

PREFACE: THERE ARE REAL PEOPLE HERE

Oh my god, there is a real person here!

—Lena, twenty-seven, model and online retail distributor[1]

Exclaiming with a laugh from her computer—midquest and just twenty-four hours after release of a new edition of *World of Warcraft*—Lena was surprised that she found someone to chat with in her favorite massive multiplayer online game. The other player had apologized for having to step away midgame to check work emails and have a cigarette, at which point Lena recognized that this could be someone her age with whom she could connect, spend time, and maybe even have a laugh in-game.

Lena—one of the first participants in the pilot study for this book—came in to her kitchen from her bedroom, laptop in hand and streaming Korean dramas paused in her browser. She sat down at the kitchen table with me for our interview while her boyfriend set up a new game console at the TV. After outlining how they'll work together using gaming forums to navigate the complexities of a new open-world action game, she goes on to explain that she really does not care for social networks. As she turns her laptop toward me, I can see that Facebook instant message (IM) chats and notifications fill a corner of her screen, interactions that she says she largely ignores. When pressed, it seems that she does IM often but only with a few of her closest friends because the rest of the people "on here" are "useless." Why, then, are some digital interactions not considered "real" interpersonal connections while others are, and what does this say about how our perceptions of digital technology and opportunities for interpersonal engagement limit and shape our social world? What is meaningful connection today if we define it in terms of disconnection?

■ ■ ■

Half in jest, and telling of the everyday tumult and enjoyment of media use, the observations above focus on something that was, or at least should have been, already known. Lena captures a crucial and often overlooked aspect of the everyday experience of using media today, forty years into mobile telephony, thirty years after the dawn of the World Wide Web, and fifteen years since the popularization of internet-ready "smart" phones and the ascendancy of social-media platforms. Her observation is a reminder that will be the first and last note of this book. I'd like you, the reader, to carry that reminder with you as you would your mobile phone, laptop, or other device: to keep engaged and connected to the ongoings of home, work, and current events but also to keep grounded in the interpersonal nature of the communication that constitutes so much of our everyday lives—to consider that when we are connected, we are engaged not merely *to* technology but *with* other people, *real* people.

Panic begets panic.

—Ron, twenty-six, IT support office temp
and freelance scriptwriter

Breaking news alerts, work emails, calendar reminders, social-media notifications, and all manner of messages from friends and family—these are the new arbiters competing for our immediate attention. Pressed for time, overwhelmed by notifications, continually switching between the interruptions of diverse connections, the centrality and glut of networked, mobile, and app- and platform-based communication has become characteristic of the diverse occupational contexts known as knowledge work.[2] This is the contemporary manifestation of "white collar" work today, inclusive of many types of creative, cultural, and digitally oriented labor. Tasks at hand on any given day are often signaled by a ringtone, vibration, or notification that calls us away, even momentarily, from what we are doing. This was evident as Ron checked and rechecked his email over lunch from the conference room that he had booked for our interview while his colleagues in the UK Civil Service rushed out for a bite to eat. With each glance at a mobile phone, every time an inbox is opened or refreshed, there is accompanying concern—if not a degree of *perceived anxiety*—about the interruption and possible contingencies calling for our attention. There is also a real sense of anticipation and delight in the interpersonal engagement of a message or comment, post or thread, email or call. The realities of connection today are as social as they are technological; they are also as professional as they are commercially driven by the platform's decision-makers and associated advertising industries. Connection carries with it both the stressors and pleasures of participating in contemporary everyday life.

Why do I use more media to get away from media?
—Aaliyah, twenty-one, student, production intern,
and self-described social-media influencer

Our mobile devices and computers can feel like Trojan Horses. The intensity and duration of a day's work is punctuated by personal instant-message chats, SMS texts, and personal calls. Social-media feeds, games, and news sites offer palette cleansers among arduous tasks. The pivot to working from home and virtual learning under COVID-19's lockdowns and social-distancing restrictions was for many accompanied by exhausting, vigilant consumption of local news, an exceptional routine in itself, detailed in Aaliyah's media diaries and those of the other college and university-age participants from the Greater Toronto Area. We turn to media use as a salve for—and respite from—our other media practices, whittling away time at home or on the bus by consuming online content and by sharing memes, videos, and articles with friends and family.

These media practices are both alluring and invasive. They are carried into contexts and take root in activities that haven't always been thought of as appropriate for media use. A glance at the phone can ruin a day out; texting can ruin a dinner. Checking email before bed does not bode well for a good night's sleep; catching a single news update can be a slippery slope when shares, likes, links, and comments follow. When we are connected, each notification carries with it the threat of something akin to *communication overload*, a state of perpetual nowness, wherein the present moment is extended through a monopolizing imminent need for attentiveness and responsiveness because, for so many of us, *the conditions for communication today are abundant.* Across the highly connected infrastructures of urban centers and advanced (or post-)industrial economies, many find themselves in a state of near-constant connection, even when not specifically engaged in media use. Defined by subtle degrees of disconnection in everyday life, communication overload is still managed through media use. This is the Janus-faced allure of technological change: it is always the promise, the problem, and the solution.

It is not my job to explain it to them.
—Margaret, thirty, market research analyst

Communication is an interpersonal accomplishment. Connection intervenes—it mediates—and increasingly undoes that work, serving instead to disconnect because not all forms of connection are desirable, mutual, or equitable. Networked digital platforms intertwine our personal as well as professional identities, or, at least, the observable digital traces of how we present ourselves online, by collapsing the distinctions between diverse everyday contexts.[3] In turn, constant connection produces coping mechanisms that are better understood in terms of disconnection. At work, Margaret presents a particular persona, aligned with the workplace expectations and the possible misunderstandings of her coworkers and managers alike yet disconnected from a more casually authentic presentation of herself out with friends, in texts or IMs, or across her social-media output.

Public and private, personal or professional, real as opposed to online life, the distinctions that once helped us understand how to organize and structure everyday life—language that we still use today to navigate constant connection—have been blurred to the point of being inverted and, counterintuitively, idealized in terms of those inherent contradictions. From self-censorship on social-media platforms that celebrate connection to navigating standardized workplace expectations that celebrate authenticity, we craft contours to our communication environment, shifting between degrees of connection and disconnection. For Margaret, constant connection is not a wholesale invitation for social surveillance and evaluation by her industry peers: she does not want to offer the details of her private life to be scoured for inconsistencies or, worse, to turn into a lesson on workplace diversity and gender bias for her largely white colleagues and male managers. There is a normative force that accompanies constant connection because the near-conventions of communication carry assumptions that fit each of us differently: where some commit to the emotional labor of self-monitoring and regulation to avoid interpersonal conflict, they are nevertheless met with the policing of communication practices by others, all under the guise of practicality, common sense, or professionalism determined in terms of communication practice. If the consequences of constant connection are social, the realities of disconnection are changing society.

> **It seems like there's nobody that you**
> **can actually communicate with.**
> —*Farzan, thirty-two, editor*

Users who frequent and inhabit networked platform environments turn to them for information and entertainment alike. We depend on these platforms for the interpersonal dimensions of professional and social life, knowing that others do the same, even if in a slightly different way. We collectively contribute to a shared pressure to keep up with the flow of communication; together we produce and reproduce communication overload. Despite the availability of near-constant connection, of feeling "permanently connected" to others,[4] there remains a real ambiguity about *how* we should connect. There are few stable conventions for how we ought to communicate; or rather, there are contradictory near-conventions based on the multiplicity of our diverging perceptions of technological change. For those who keep their mobile phone within arm's reach, who have lost track of how often they refresh their inboxes and check their screens, there is a worrying ambivalence. Sitting on the curb, a can of lager in hand during our interview, Farzan checked for emails from his boss, who was time zones away in New York, one last time before heading into a club night, unsure about which of his London-based friends had seen his social-media post and would be joining him. Increasingly, so much of users' time, effort, and attention is focused on managing communication practices, keeping up with connection *to* the device, platform, or interface rather than connection *with* others *through* the platform or technology. What does it say about the trajectory of social change if managing constant connection is persistently experienced as a disconnection from actually engaging with others?

This book's reminder, again, feels necessary: *there are real people here.*

Hindsight Is 20/20

Our media have become symbols of social and technological futures that are paradoxically already here—in our hands—while making promises that are paradoxically always just out of reach. Promises of connection and intimacy, convenience and productivity, autonomy, authenticity, and opportunity are accompanied with everyday anxieties about communication overload, online exposure, and the suffocating force of how others feel we ought to communicate. Knowing this experience all too well myself, I ask the question: how did we get here, and what now?

The last four decades have been defined by successive heralds of rapid technological change. Mobile phones and the World Wide Web, smart phones and social-networking sites, through to data-driven platforms, apps, wearables, and toward smart appliances and AI-powered digital assistants—each has become emblematic of a particular decade and the accompanying changes to organization of everyday life that they represent. Such change would be better understood from a triangulated set of perspectives: the phenomenological perspective, which places the experience of everyday individuals and their communication practices in relationship; the materialist perspective of changing media technology, interfaces, and infrastructures that make up our everyday communication environment; and a political-economic perspective that combines the first two through analysis of work and personal life and the surveillance economies of everyday communication technology as they have persisted, diverged, and converged for over a century of coevolution.[5]

In the 1990s, prominent early adopters included techno-utopians who heralded the World Wide Web as an inherently democratizing force, a possible manifestation of the "Global Village" that broadcast and other "electronic" communications had first inspired.[6] Today the intensifying and multiplying roles of media technology are written into so many aspects of everyday life that they have to be reorganized *as* and *through* media practices. In North American contexts, roughly 92 to 93 percent of people were using the internet as of 2020 and 2021, in striking contrast to 2010, when only 76 percent and 79 percent of those in the United States and Canada, respectively, had used the internet.[7] We also have to consider that from 2019 onward, the majority of these users enjoy multiple modes of access—computer and mobile devices—with only 15 percent of users in the United Kingdom and 17 percent of users in the United States dependent on mobile phones alone.[8] Mobile and platform technologies have become facts of life, overlooked and taken for granted but, counterintuitively, having greater consequences both for daily activities and as embodiments of the tumult caused by historical markers of social change.[9] In 2016, the use and misuse of social-media platforms and of algorithmically microtargeted political content and ad distribution, as well as user data sets collected and sold in breach of standard practices, contributed to the polarization of public opinion that culminated in alleged voter manipulation in both the UK Brexit referendum and the US presidential election.

In March 2020, the BBC reported that nearly one-quarter of the world's population was under some form of lockdown, just over ten days into the social-distancing restrictions in Canada and with a strict lockdown announced in India. By April of the same year, the *New York Times* reported that "nearly four billion people—half of humanity—found themselves under some sort of lockdown."[10] For contrast's sake: in 2015, Facebook was being used by more than half of the world's three billion internet users on (at least) a monthly basis, and by 2023, the number of people using Facebook daily had grown to an average of two billion users, a quarter of the world population.[11]

In 2020, everything went online. Correction: everything that could go online did so, and the realities of what work could not be facilitated by communication technology was brought sharply into focus. COVID-19 restrictions on face-to-face social interaction and movement saw a rapidly increased and intensified dependency on communication technologies, an intensification of digital work that has not unraveled in the long aftermath of the pandemic. This included a rushed embrace of numerous video-chat and networked collaboration platforms, as well as an unprecedented shift in cultural, commercial, and professional operations following on from physical separation and the shuttering of many commercial and public spaces beyond the home. Across the entertainment, retail, and personal care services that were forced to shut down and the often over-looked essential services of transport, security, groceries, and health care, there were and still are higher proportions of individuals from Black and Asian ethnic communities facing a greater loss of life due to COVID-19, indicative of economic inequities that could not be blamed on the virus.

Media use adapted rapidly to connect isolated households in order to continue aspects of interpersonal life that had occurred beyond the home: special occasions with extended family, dinners, and hangouts with friends were scheduled among doctors' appointments, yoga lessons, client calls, team meetings, and all-company town halls—all on video-call platforms. Schooling, graduation ceremonies, club nights, live concerts, and late-night talk shows were recorded in basements, bedrooms, and kitchens, streamed live for participation virtually. Until the outpouring of support for Black Lives Matter protests, when marches against police brutality and systemic racism filled public spaces across many cities in-ternationally, masses of people under lockdown were *en masse* only vir-tually. Even so, the tensions felt acutely during these moments of crisis were (and are) symptomatic of long-standing sets of changes to social life being brought into sharp relief.

The sudden halting and reorganizing of everyday life, work, com-merce, education, and entertainment, nearly overnight in many coun-tries, has upended widely held assumptions about the impossibility of large-scale responsive change to the social organization of the status quo. The abruptness of governmental intervention, in tandem with collective social cooperation, has challenged staid conventions and entrenched protocols of our social and economic worlds. But as we learned after the Great Recession of 2008–9, the framing of recovery measured in terms of crisis and an attendant, inevitable return to "normal" belies the lon-gevity of the political-economic tensions and transformations that crisis produces.[12] For many, neither the postrecession trajectory of change nor the prepandemic "normal" are sustainable ways forward.

Over the past decade of my fieldwork, I began to see just how inter-twined practices of everyday interpersonal life are with these wider societal shifts, how our ability to perceive and navigate the changing opportunities for connection on a day-to-day basis offers one of the most promising starting points for negotiating social change and doing so together. How we collectively find value in connection—how we practice communication—contributes to the construction, reproduction, and negotiation of what we expect and accept as our social reality.

The Work Being Done

The pandemic and its aftermath have accelerated social processes of change and exacerbated already existing tensions caused by technology; forms of economic uncertainty have accompanied such change. Part of a longer political-economic history of social reorganization, these changes were spurred by the Great Recession, entrenched in the UK, Canada, and elsewhere by a decade of austerity and economic insecurity, brought firmly into everyday public consciousness under the pandemic's stressors and restrictions.[13] The trajectory of these social changes and the tensions they produce are noticeable within the constellation of interdependent everyday social practices, across sets of people interacting through work and nonwork. For the many who have already been slowly pressed into new, rationalized forms of mediated sociality, these changes are part of a longer reorganization of everyday social life parallel to multiplying opportunities for networked communication: social isolation accompanies promises of individual autonomy; a commitment to the pressured workplace does little to stymy economic precariousness;[14] a compulsion to connect with others produces daily communication-overload anxieties. These are just some of the contradictions at the heart of contemporary Western life, where promises of personal autonomy, choice, and authenticity act as levers for an unbridled drive toward greater economic productivity and the commercial incursion of technology into nearly every aspect of life.

Communication practices involve the interweaving of individual lives. The contradictions of constant connection are most clearly understood through the experiences of everyday life and the social forms of everyday knowledge produced therein. These flow between multiple sets of individuals interacting with each other, seeking better ways to connect and communicate. Day after day, one foot in front of the other, what is often deemed a "society of individuals" coheres in communication with one another, signaling the acceptance, complacency, frustration, and rejection of particular practices.[15] Across diverse settings, norms about how we ought to communicate are diverging, yet conventions are consolidating to produce a new sociality predicated on degrees of disconnection, though communication only succeeds through some degree of mutuality in interpersonal engagement. Throughout this book, I will examine the reproduction and negotiation of these diverging near-conventions in everyday communication. I focus on early career adults in the UK in comparison with Canada, as representative of the Anglo-American West more generally. Across working and personal lives, the communication conventions of these media users are tied to a longer history of political-economic organization of technology use, which after nearly a century has developed into today's platform-based digital advertising economy.

The transformation of working life in the West is a history of communication management. Technologies and practices of workplace organization set the stage for the emergence and subsequent digital transformation of white-collar work across the breadth of communication-oriented work practices across knowledge, creative, and cultural sectors.[16] The widespread embrace of mobile and networked technologies and the ascendancy of platform and data-mining economies represent successive stages in that transformative history of communication management. Alongside the emergence of communication- and knowledge-oriented forms of labor across many sectors of advanced industrial economies, economic crises and neoliberal austerity politics have fostered a series of transformative shifts in everyday social practices.

Communication technologies and their use have become both the needle and the thread of the wider tapestry of everyday life.[17] The Great Recession and the COVID-19 pandemic stand at either end of a decade during which temporal pressures of economic life intensified alongside a seemingly accelerated experience of social life, both amplified by the tools of contemporary surveillance economies. The worlds of work, home, and social life have been colonized. Contours of time and uncertainty shape a new sociality, inextricably mediated by technology. This sociality is a managed, rationalized relationship *to* the communication environment, which at times displaces relationships *with* others through that environment. Yet within these same contexts of constant networked connection, in which conditions for communication are in abundance, *there are practices that are extending what is and can be considered communication*. Forms and patterns of connection are themselves understood and negotiated as expressive acts through which individuals negotiate how communication should and could be occurring in an effort to facilitate change interpersonally. I call these practices of *metacommunication*.

The communication environment of the individual is where the neo-liberal economic policies of the West and the commercial imperatives of platform and data-mining industries meet. It is where the contradictions that they produce can be felt, daily, by citizens-turned-users. The very tensions I have outlined represent levers of political-economic power. The pandemic has shown that these levers can be used to alter the matrices of social organization. The quotidian communication environment offers a site for the continual testing of communication norms: whether or not these norms are justifiably accepted and the related tensions passed on and exacerbated in further engagement with others; whether or not the antisocial and inequitable realties of contemporary society are reproduced and fortified or concertedly examined and displaced. With so much time spent managing and negotiating the pressures of our communication environment, sometimes a reminder is necessary: how we connect and how we communicate matters because there are real people here.

ACKNOWLEDGMENTS

Many people and many meaningful connections have made this book possible. First and foremost, I want to thank my research participants; I have lived with your voices throughout this process and I have learned so much from you. I want to thank Erica Wetter, my publishing editor at Stanford University Press, for her belief and dedication to see this project through to completion. Additional thanks go to Gigi Mark, my production editor, and Joe Abbott for his deft copyediting. I owe a deep debt of gratitude to David Balzer, who proofread this work from its early stages through to its full manuscript form, providing invaluable editing on key chapters with care and patience.

So much of my rigor and love for research was fostered by Nick Couldry, who mentored me throughout my graduate studies in London. At my successive academic homes, Pasi Väliaho, Steve Hutchings, Michael Petit, and Leslie Regan Shade each took up a similar role, helping steer me through so many uncertain points in my career. To my friends at London School of Economics, Goldsmiths, and the University of Manchester, our time together is imprinted on this work. To each cohort of graduate students from my "Surveillance and Identity" class, our conversations have kept my thinking about this work alive, critical, and current since 2014. I would also like to thank all of my friends at the University of Toronto, from my colleagues at the Faculty of Information to all of the staff and faculty in the Department of Art, Culture and Media—the community we are building is something that truly matters.

Though there are too many inspirational people to name, the friendships and community that have grown out of countless academic events have mattered so much, in particular my time with the Mobile Communications Division of the ICA and the Oxford Internet Institute. Rich Ling's early championing of this research and the academic generosity of Illana Gherson came at crucial points in my career. So many insights grew from my conversations with Ruoyun Bai, Maria Bakardjieva, Rena Bivens, T. L. Cowan, Maxwell Foxman, Yi Gu, Andreas Hepp, Lee Humphreys, Jonathon Hutchinson, Asen Ivanov, Anne Kaun, Jenny Kennedy, Youna Kim, Sebastian Kubitschko, Anders Larsson, Peter Lunt, Tim Markham, Juliette de Maeyer, Irina Mihalache, Ryan Milner, Victoria Nash, David Nieborg, Shani Orgad, Jas Rault, Aure Shrock, Jakob Svensson, Son Vivienne, Cynthia Wang, and Sherry Yu, as well as my co-editors Christian Pentzold, Olivier Driessens, and Alice Mattoni and all of our contributors for the "Practicing Media—Mediating Practice" special section of the *International Journal of Communication* (IJOC)—a collaboration that crystallized my thinking on so many issues. And to my dear friend Daniel Knapp: nearly twenty years of constant conversation has painted everyday life with the intellectual intrigue it deserves.

I would like to thank every nurse that I have ever met—for so many people, you are the reason the sky has not fallen. To the medical researchers who trusted me enough to share their decision-making and to those brilliant, caring clinical practitioners who have supported me without fail, year after year—thank you. To my parents, who always supported my curiosities, creativity, and continuing education: thank you for never doubting that I would find—and always was finding—my way. Most importantly, this book is dedicated to Kelly Jenkins. Without his love, care, and support over the last ten years, none of this would have been possible. He made it so that the hardest years have also, somehow, been the best years of my life.

Constant Disconnection

INTRODUCTION

The Disconnected Sociality of Everyday Life

Constant digital connection is the everyday practice of social change. Such connection is how we manage, cope with, and come to influence the changes happening around us—how we come to know the scale, depth, and degree of our mutual participation in determining what it means to be in relation today, both digitally and socially. Practices, however, are not rules.[1] They do not dictate conduct. Communication becomes an applied, interpersonal site for understanding how change takes place and how the practice of social change, in particular, happens. Social practices are always a negotiation. It is imperative to see everyday connection in the same light.

The social world in all its complexity and uncertainty, including the tension between media's contingencies and demands, is at the heart of this book. I explore this world from the point of view of early career adults, situated in their everyday lives. This phenomenological perspective— reflections, interpretations, understandings, and practices—takes lived experiences seriously, as valid, valuable, and consequential. Too often ignored, such experiences are not only a sociological framework for examining the contemporary organization of everyday life; they also lend insight into the social and technological mediation of everyday life.[2] Quite simply, lived experiences tell us what connection means today.

Between social change and reliance on convention, the mundane production of knowledge underpins the "how" of everyday interpersonal interaction. This is lay, practical knowledge, both accepted and contested as common sense, and it has an ordering effect, balancing continuity or coherence of social practices with the differentiation, recombination, and revisability of practices that contribute to social change. The interpersonal connection at the core of my research offers a glimpse into how current economic logics of neoliberalism and the digital-platform economy are reproduced, but also resisted and renegotiated, through practices of disconnection.

Testing the Contradictions of the Era

Talk of social change in terms of revolution is usually misleading. Upheavals rarely produce wholesale societal transformation, with historical ruptures becoming representative of change only in hindsight. Borrowed from astronomy and other natural sciences, the original political usage of the term *revolution*, before the French one, related to the Glorious Revolution in England and carried a different meaning: a return to, or restoration of, a previous order of things after a period of disorderly change.[3] Disconnection is a response to that restoration of control: the closure of generative opportunities for social change amid constant connection.

In terms of economic revolution, sociology often points to the particular ideological ethos of a given era, what, more than a century ago, the German sociologist Max Weber called the "spirit of capitalism."[4] The "spirit" or ethos of an era is tested, crumbles, and changes but, nevertheless, continually restores central tenets that serve to order economic life in terms of what we still call capitalism. These tenets represent sets of contemporary social relations, conventions, and fields of associated practices that are nurtured, reproduced, and intensified by the entrenched political, economic, and social ethos that comes to define the organization of home, work, and personal life. For example, the hard-won post-WWII ideal of lifelong job security, labor rights, and the accompanying expansion of the welfare state currently looms large: it is the economic-social contract foundational to contemporary Western liberal democracy, even though it now stands in stark contrast to the lived reality of many. In such a manner, the revolution from one "spirit" to the next is facilitated through the incorporation of the era's most politically destabilizing social critiques into the economic promises and contradictions of the next. After a decade of crises marked by growing inequality, economic insecurity, and popular protest, it may feel like we are on the precipice of fundamental social change. But the promise of a social contract to be articulated anew seems always just out of reach. Consolidation of the political and economic matrices of power that govern the Anglo-American West intensifies; so, too, do the political tensions and social contradictions at the heart of our economic reality.

Ours is a neoliberal spirit. It is specific to the era of permacrisis and constant connection, and it entails the sublimation of political and social dimensions of everyday life into economic and commercial processes.[5] This ethos, inflected by economic uncertainty and the rhetoric of technological empowerment, singles out the individual as responsible for navigating the pitfalls, tensions, and dwindling opportunities for meaningful employment and responsible for what is valued as social connection. The political role of the individual is not as part of a citizenry, family, or community but rather as an atomized economic actor in service of management and labor. With each passing decade, the social role of the individual is increasingly rearticulated away from colleague, friend, relative, or even stranger and toward media user, in service of data production, for the burgeoning commercial digital economy.[6] Neoliberalization and our growing dependence on media technology are intertwined metaprocesses. Both mutually enforce the longer-term individuation of social relations toward a disconnected sociality—an idealized and typified social disposition amid constant connection.

The infrastructures and prescribed practices of platform and datamining industries—what have collectively been called surveillance capitalism—have long been singled out as agents of transformative social change.[7] Changes to everyday work and personal life cannot be disentangled from the use of mobile phones, social media, and other networked or "connective" platform technologies.[8] In the era of constant connection, social change cannot be disentangled from the commercial and labor-oriented colonization of communication and interpersonal life.

Media users cope with the pressures of constant connection through a diverse array of communication-management practices. Individuals attempt to find balance in everyday life or, rather, to maintain a deliberate imbalance in relation to the industries and institutions that would otherwise capture, mine, and deconstruct forms of social engagement that are still valued as real connection between people.[9] Echoing the critical and pragmatic, though largely predigital, approaches of French sociologist Pierre Bourdieu's (1993) *Weight of the World: Social Suffering in Contemporary Society* and his contemporaries Luc Boltanski and Ève Chiapello's (1999) *The New Spirit of Capitalism*, my research similarly engages with actors who are aware of, and struggle with, the contradictions and tensions inherent in their changing place in Western society.[10] In these important works, the ideological spirit of an era is not a matter of truth or falsehood but of pragmatic, reflexive participation in the day's economic system, which serves both to reproduce existing power relations and to expose their contradictions. Everyday life experientially grounds tropes of fairness and ideals of economic security, as well as the clear disjuncture between such norms and observable experiences—a grounding in individual and interpersonal realities that fosters criticism, ambivalence, and a desire for change.[11]

What follows is a sociological engagement with the justificatory regimes of constant connection: highlighting the role of the individual in the construction and reproduction of a common social world where interpersonal life represents an opportunity for the negotiation of social change through everyday digital practices. These opportunities legitimize and reproduce, constrain and challenge, the trajectory of wider social change, highlighting the incongruous relationship between intensifying political-economic uncertainty and the continued self-interest and commitment of those affected. In traditional sociological fashion, Boltanski and Chiapello sought to "denaturalize" the ethos of the neoliberal era, consolidated in the 1990s as it intertwined with knowledge work and communication practices of economic contexts that praised what they called a "connectionist" ethos of flexible entrepreneurship.[12] In particular, they examined the "ideal" and "typical" character espoused by postwar and 1970s American managerial discourse that had inculcated a generation of *les cadres* into French industry, a loose grouping of specialized knowledge workers caught somewhere between the higher echelons of executives and the less mobile echelons of white-collar supporting and technical staff.[13] Their analysis examines the social character and critiques that contributed to the stability of an era or its transformative renegotiating, detailing France's transition from the political and economic tumult of the 1960s toward a co-opted ethos of the 1990s, where socially oriented promises of self-fulfillment through economic participation were coupled with greater job insecurity. The postwar context of large managerial firms and state policies for economic recovery centered on meritocracy and efficiency, framed by hierarchical planning. While this unraveled, so did the systematic employer support of employee opportunities through long-term career planning, and so did the political commitment to expanding the welfare state. With so much power resting atop state bureaucracies and corporate hierarchies, popular critiques of the time sought a more horizontal and fluid recalibration of meritocracy to foster permanent change as the ideal of career mobility, whereby individual valuation on a project-to-project basis would, according to the ideologically framed market logic, empower those who could manage themselves.[14]

The grammar of any "spirit" is social as well as economic. As a general standard of professional activity, paradigmatic of one's individual contributions, the ability to move from project to project in economic life has been idealized. Nimble professionals foster and, indeed, exploit the economic value of social links across their social network, close and remote alike. There is the investing of one's whole self—one's life project—into the similarly oversimplified goal of a more authentic relationship with one's labor.[15] The stability central to the postwar spirit has been recast as close-minded rigidity, obstructing the potential of individualized innovation. The new model's idealizing of the social potential of trust and involvement with others obscures its economic risk and uncertainty. Interpersonal conduct begins to be reshaped toward this end: enthusiasm, flexibility, adaptability, and sincerity are standards by which individuals and their economic potential can be better evaluated.[16] In theory, the connectionist ideal fosters individual entrepreneurial creativity for collective prosocial benefits: a connectionist spirit, innovative both for the individual and the economy, unfettered by the moribund strictures of managerial power and the corporate rigidity of collective oversight. Unfortunately, the ideal of an era—the model for greatness espoused by popular culture and managerial rhetoric alike—is far, far from the typical experience. Contradictions inherent in the connectionist ethos have incorporated into a new disconnected sociality of constant connection.

The Promise and Pain of a New Sociality

The ethos of an economic era does not persist because of those who attain the ideal. It persists because of the self-interested and ambivalent, if not frustrated, participation of those in particular positions both to benefit and lose from such participation. Today, those people are the burgeoning ranks of young knowledge workers facing diminishing opportunities for economic security but only if they play competitively and by the rules. Unrelenting economic crises fuel pressures, recasting work and social practices alike in terms of productivity. A *disconnected ethos* has emerged—a spirit of constant connection that revolves around the idealization of a particular type of hypermediated management of interpersonal life against pervasive, systemic uncertainty—defined counterintuitively by disconnection and overconnection.

This framework spans the idealized as well as the typified experiences of constant connection. And it fosters diverse sets of socially inaccessible economic actors—*disconnected practitioners*—across an unstable spectrum of those who prioritize a productive mastery of their communication environments, on the one hand, or a commitment to meaningful interpersonal experience, on the other. Sociologists will instinctively reach for what turn-of-the-century scholar Emile Durkheim called the "anomie" of industrialization and urbanization, but this sense of alienation applies only partially: it flows from social change that disrupts the moral horizons for regular action in everyday life, where the known systems of norms and expectations receding into the past have yet to be replaced.[17] But amid constant connection, we are acutely aware of the newly prescribed norms but also their contradictions; we have a perpetual sense of each other's expectations situation-to-situation, but there is a social cost to meeting these demands and an economic cost to resisting them. Some of us are empowered through practices of disconnection that then consolidate those pressures, while others seek to counter the isolation of overconnection by preserving a sense of value in interpersonal life through degrees of disconnection. These are the purposeful, knowing practices of communication management seeking to manage the changing conditions of everyday life.

The subtitle of this book, *The Weight of Everyday Digital Life*, pays homage to a later work by Bourdieu and his coauthors, who probed fracturing, diverging, individualized frameworks for interpreting the changing experiences of everyday life. *The Weight of the World* traces the social negotiation of a new "common sense" specific to the contours of exclusion and disenfranchisement that accompany neoliberal economic change.[18] This individualization of economic risk is central to our socialization as economic actors. We internalize particularly neoliberal ways of thinking about society as composed of economic units rather than of social or political actors. Counterintuitively, this individualizes our shared experiences, detaching our sense of fairness from otherwise institutionalized and collectively experienced economic realities and making many feel personally responsible for their successes or failures, despite increasing economic insecurity and the clear, unmitigated pressures of constant connection.[19]

Sociology must grapple with the tensions of these contradictions from the incongruity of individual points of view.[20] There are unequal matrices of privilege and power in everyday life and, in turn, unequal constraints and pressures to conform to, navigate, cope with, or enforce normative definitions of the social world. My research examines these tensions, with the particularities of the neoliberal, platform era in sharp relief. Bourdieu commented that his increasingly disenfranchised interviewees—from young unemployed men in the *banlieue* of suburban Paris to the multigenerational households of racialized newcomers to France—talked about being socially relegated to particularly limiting and segregated sets of economic opportunities. They framed this exclusion as an obvious condition of their everyday reality. Stratified and disconnected from the benefits of social change occurring around them, theirs was a unique perspective on what Bourdieu called "the order of things"—and "they certainly know what that is."[21] Among the younger manual laborers in this 1990s study, a particular disposition was emerging: the "disconnected generation," always, interminably seeking stable employment, seeing themselves as systematically precluded from social mobility, let alone economic security, and facing persistent denigration by older generations of colleagues and management.[22]

There is much in common here with the popular intergenerational discourse of today. Those who may have never known the same type of early career precarity revel in their criticism of disconnected, disenfranchised early career adults. The more economically secure individuals in Bourdieu's work cited a lack of conformity in the professional comportment of their younger colleagues, criticizing their relative asociality in terms of expected deference to workplace etiquette and, at the same time, pre-emptively dismissing these colleagues as "workers-in-transit" and there-fore not worth the effort that engaging or training them would require.[23] These are forms of economic exclusion reinforced socially, through the denigration of younger peers' personal expressions as "frivolous" con-sumerism, scoffing at fashion choices, and ascribing "addiction" to use of the "new media" of the day. The Walkman of the 1990s represented an earlier individuation of everyday media use that is now commonplace: personal and portable, derided as a distraction in more public settings, where a hitherto unknown "dependency" on personalized media envi-ronments offered some degree of control to these disenfranchised young adults, who managed the degree and form of their participation, or lack thereof, in public interpersonal life.[24] These tensions were specific to the social setting of these economically excluded workers nearly thirty years ago. The necessity of digital work in knowledge and creative economies today sharpens the social and technological contradictions inherent in that connectionist ethos and the disconnected sociality that has emerged in its place. From its emergence, the ethos of disconnection has always been a matter of coping with economic and social uncertainty, through management of one's communication environment.

Intensifying economic hierarchies, increasing precariousness in em-ployment, and the erosion of social cohesion are just some of the neolib-eral tensions that have undermined the connectionist promises of the 1990s and early 2000s knowledge economy. At the same time, there is an intensified focus on the need for individuals to depend on if not be desperate for cultivating opportunities on a project-to-project basis. Eco-nomic and social contradictions such as these are tested, day in and day out, every day. They serve, in turn, as the foundation for a variety of polit-ical critiques, which then fuel sociopolitical change, through practices of correction, incorporation, or resistance, extending beyond the workplace and throughout interpersonal life.[25] By sublimating the tensions of one spirit into the contradictory promises of the next, capitalism proves its historic dynamism, successfully diffusing each era's critiques so as to avoid popular upheaval, despite a continued trajectory toward increas-ing disenfranchisement. As the justificatory regime of the connectionist ethos fails, another emerges, with new ideal types serving as the model for economic participation, resubjugating the workforce with promises belying more typified experiences.[26]

Growing economic uncertainty, inequality, and political instability informed the decade between the Great Recession and the COVID-19 pandemic. There was also remarkably increasing dependence on mobile and computing devices and a proliferation of networked apps and platforms. The sharp intensification of both in response to COVID-19 demonstrates the particular "spirit" of surveillance capitalism today, transformations to social organization of everyday life already heightened in the wake of the last economic crisis. My fieldwork, which forms the empirical foundation of the research presented here, was conducted in the UK and Canada across seven distinct phases, from December 2009 until May 2020.[27] The interviews, media diaries, and other data ground my analysis in the interpersonal media practices of early career adults, who navigate temporal pressures that accompany changing roles and responsibilities in personal and work life against a backdrop of economic and political turmoil. The research participants worked or were seeking work in the wide swathes of economy understood today, variably, as the knowledge, creative, and digital sectors. In the advanced economies of Western urban centers, the uncertain promises for career mobility faced by these early career adults represent the long tail of increasing precariousness, the exaltation of communication-based skill sets, and the related pressures increasingly faced by the connectionist professionals of the early corporate knowledge economy, as well as the disconnected youth within the emerging postindustrial economy.

This book's sociological analysis of everyday interpersonal practices offers new perspectives on the political-economic processes of social change that have occurred over a decade bookended by crises. I fold recent and historical sociological studies into this empirical foundation to better understand how the confluence of changes to particular practices in everyday life is part of wider, interrelated metaprocesses of transformative social reorganization of everyday communication. In the chapters that follow readers will

- Recognize the urgency for the collective negotiation of a new common sense in everyday practices of connection and disconnection—an essential set of political tools for crafting limits to the power of platform and data industries, and a prioritizing of equitable and human dimensions of constant connection.

- See personal and work-related communication practices as increasingly characterized by unmanageable tensions, produced by demands of constant availability and connection and resulting in an increasing sense of temporal scarcity, alongside uncertainties about how one ought to communicate.

- Acknowledge the growing disconnect between interpersonal social life and the individual's struggle to manage everyday communication environments—because of the organizational imprints of employment conditions and media technologies and the commercial imperatives of the platform and data-mining economies that are transforming these environments.

- Place the economic uncertainty that has characterized the decade between the Great Recession and the COVID-19 pandemic within a longer durée of transformative change, from the postwar reorganization of work to the emergence of neoliberalism and knowledge work and the information-revolution-turned-surveillance economy.

- Explore the myriad ways that we, as individuals interacting with each other, are already managing these tensions to repair the everyday domain of interpersonal practices. Despite economic pressures to maintain the status quo, our collective negotiation of social change occurs by taking seriously how we communicate through technology and what those media practices signal to each other.

Metaprocesses of Social Change and Human Connection

There is growing incongruity between trajectories of the user and the platform, the individual and industry, and the citizen and our user data–defined, surveillance-driven society. Understanding technological revolutions is an act of accounting, grounded in uneven realities and the tensions of social change that have emerged in their wake. *Constant Disconnection* is the result of the information-turned-digital revolution, a response to the employment-oriented and commercially attuned trajectories of innovation that are crowding out opportunities for human participation in social change. This revolution has been accelerated by crisis, the controlling mediations of interpersonal life coming into clearer view as a disconnected sociality emerges in response.

Multiple forces are at play when platform and data-mining industries affect mediated practices in everyday life. The term *mediation* helps us understand the rearticulation of particular sets of actions: digital-, al- gorithmic-, and data-driven settings that subsume an ever-increasing number of everyday activities whose social dimensions are, in turn, rearticulated by the form and experiential quality of these technolog- ical settings. So much of everyday life is increasingly engaged *as* and *through* media practices. The necessity of constant connection is taken for granted, and managing one's communication practices is conflated with participation in our daily living.[28] The accrual of these social me- diations contributes to a subtle metaprocess of ongoing societal change. Much like globalization, neoliberalization, and individualization, trans- formative processes that weave change through diverse domains and scales of political, economic, and social life have, over decades, become deeply entrenched across numerous diverse settings and activities of ev- eryday life. This is the metaprocess of "mediatization," a paradigmatic concept that captures how the role of technology is reconstituting social relations and day-to-day activity.[29] Since the early 2000s, the knowledge economy itself has transitioned to digital and communication-oriented labor, subsuming cultural production and the digital economy.

People, practices, and things are enmeshed in a relationship that transcends any simplification based on the design or usability of a hard- ware device, software interface, or connective platform. While mani- fold social practices have been radically reconfigured toward economic integration—depending on constant connection and mediations therein— that very interpersonal quality of human participation includes nego- tiation, persistence, reproducibility, and resistance to change through social practices.[30] To separate these mutually constitutive relationships, we must take into account the dynamic nature of the algorithmic en- vironment in a manner that includes a phenomenological perspective of users. On one hand, platforms respond to user actions through dis- tributed and cascading sets of processes that bring diverse types of user and technical actors together. On the other, there is a durability to the historical trajectories and cultural embeddedness of social practices that come to be recognized as inherent in the interpersonally oriented use and design of platforms and their deployment in knowledge, creative, and digital sectors.[31] Technological change, then, is an opportunity to account for how the asymmetries of commercially driven mediatization crowd out human agency across numerous scales of social change. Today, the ubiquitous pressure and powerlessness of constant connection comes to be redefined in terms of practices of disconnection.

Our impetus toward social connection is a living, growing, and speculative exploration of what it means to be human together: how we come to know, shape, and exploit the tools we have crafted for that purpose.[32] To remove the agency of an individual from this equation, and overlook the unfolding experience of interpersonal life as productive of knowledge, is to impose a particularly limited rationality onto the messiness of human existence. It is also to remove our collective culpability in contributing to, benefiting from, and participating in the reproduction of these very tensions.

While it can be useful—analytically—to isolate particularly overlooked variables, we cannot go too far and lose sight of the goal of sensitizing ourselves to what is hidden from view and difficult to ascertain. The sociologist Bruno Latour famously proposed (and then later critiqued) a similar overprioritizing of the legibility of technological influence in a given situation as if they were agentic actors, decisively on par with human actors.[33] The ethnographer Annemarie Mol qualifies that these are methodological maneuvers: they are not meant to refine, capture, or solidify an overall schema of social relations; the goal is to "generate, transform, translate . . . and to betray" the always-already situated partial perspectives of scholars and everyday actors alike.[34] I want to do the same. We can develop a sensitivity to how we overdetermine technology's role in society today, which in turn underdetermines our sense of how we can and already do participate meaningfully in social change. This tension between over- and underdetermination has grown since the COVID-19 pandemic, from ambivalence to a crisis of constant connection. For this purpose, I ask a particular sensitizing question: what is human about communication today?

Media Connection and Social Disconnection

A disconnected sociality is, of course, paradoxical. It accrues and reacts, is communicated and internalized. It is a frustrated inertia and a nuanced awareness of the situational pressures changing and cascading with media use. For the individual attending to daily communication, this is a *relational domain* of practices where negotiation between disparate forces takes place: technology, human beings, and perceived social and economic transformations lying within and beyond any given situation or set of circumstances. Disconnection is a set of personalized interventions that insist on local, intrapersonal, and subjective experiences. It is our determination to find value in a social—rather than isolated—response to the tensions of constant connection. Today, connection only seems to promise a coherent experience of increasingly automated environments designed to preempt and intervene on collective behavior. Practices of disconnection offer, instead, a commitment to social life through our partial, dissonant, improvised, and unexpected social interventions—by people in everyday life—toward a human-centered communication environment.[35]

As social tools and communication platforms, digital media do afford particularly human opportunities. These are moments of intensity, drive, and momentum, and they may not yet have a particular telos or goal, but they involve a type of social compulsion that counterintuitively drives us toward both connection and disconnection.[36] Thomas Poell and his coauthors define platforms as "(re)programmable digital infrastructures that facilitate and shape personalised interactions among end-users and [infrastructural and service provision partners or] complementors, organised through the systematic collection, algorithmic processing, monetisation, and circulation of data."[37] The responsiveness of this environment supplants the idea of understanding media in terms of the "affordances" of an environment, the latter term defined in ecological psychology as "what it *offers* the animal, what it *provides* or *furnishes*, either for good or ill."[38] Platforms are much more than just technological environments. They are economic and commercial settings accompanied by rhetorical-ideological inflections of what a platform means for society. These computational ecosystems offer commercial opportunities and relationships among the app and digital-advertising industries and a social environment that promises users an egalitarian, aspirational, and professionalized platform from which to speak and gain similar opportunities.[39]

Contemporary users are aware that the affordances of connection require careful tending. There are limits to digital social engagement. Even group chats—nominally private rather than wholly public—are defined by shifting categories of social, conversational, and technical boundaries, necessitating a cautious, disconnective calculus to navigate the indeterminacy that constant connection brings.[40] As danah boyd's early accounting of social-media platforms indicates, they allow social content to be persistent, replicable, scalable, and searchable. Over time, these affordances have translated into the user's reflexive caution in adjusting habits in relation to social surveillance and the personal crises that networked and viral exposure can bring.[41]

Platform mediations on social practice are commercial interventions, specifically seeking the production of data through media use, data that can be sold and, vitally, aggregated with comparable data from competitors across the wider digital advertising ecosystem.[42] José van Dijck delineates the "microsystems" of single platforms and the "ecosystems" of multiple platforms that make up the wider industry. A rudimentary sketch of the industry shows how microsystems are sometimes vertically integrated with other platforms, often providing different media services and owned by or affiliated with a parent company. The wider ecosystem is characterized, on the one hand, by degrees of interoperability among platforms, the web, and other app services, an interoperability that affords some extent of user motility and data sharing across platforms and, on the other hand, a competitive, "locked-in" inoperability that maintains exclusive access to the data produced within siloed microsystems governed amid industry hierarchies.[43] In the West, the dominant actors are Google, Apple, Facebook (now Meta), Amazon, and Microsoft (GAFAM), paralleling in many ways China's Baidu, Alibaba, and Tencent (BAT) and Russia's Yandex, although beyond these transnational clusters or "stacks" of integrated platforms services globally, additional tiers of data-brokerage firms both facilitate and compete among an increasingly balkanized global internet.

There is nonetheless a "syntax" repeated in the protocols across many microsystems that shapes engagement on these platforms.[44] Early social-media sites such as the video-sharing platform YouTube, the text- and photo-orientation of early Facebook, and the original text-driven Twitter (recently renamed X) each offered comparable forms of mentions/tags, starring/liking, sharing/listing, commenting publicly, and messaging privately. Popularized by Snapchat before being competitively cloned through new features on Instagram and Facebook and then superseded by the popularity and recommendation algorithm of TikTok—today, short video posts on social-media platforms afford much more medium-specific functionality in terms of tracking the user's length of viewing, rewatches, likes and comments, shares, and more content-specific elements such as song choice, video subjects, and filter or edit choices. Karin Wahl-Jorgensen calls this the "emotional architecture" of social networks: how the superficially prosocial, positive valance inherent in the syntax of early social-media platforms has spread throughout the internet.[45] In terms of connection, early social media indeed contributed to the spontaneous coming together of "networked publics," where the "affective" and "ephemeral" popular momentum of political movements, often known by their hashtags, increasingly mingled with the interpretive practices of news consumers and conspiracy theorists alike.[46] Today, a multiplicity of shifting, mutable amalgams of user connections is distributed across any given platform—something less than and more diffuse than what we could call a public—occurring alongside the networked persistence of antisocial behavior and misinformation enabled by algorithmic promotion and the opacity of automated advertising networks.[47]

Social media has also afforded a site to participate in, contest, and even hijack the near-ritualized staging of national and transnational participation in "global media events"—those moments when politics, media, and social spheres gather together in celebration, crisis, and protest, when collective identity in its multiplicity coheres, fractures, or undergoes contestation across diverse traditional and interactive mediums.[48] Each of these represents a type of politically expressive act—not just media use—legible in the very form of connection and networked affiliation that represents some sort of collective social participation, however fleeting and fragile.[49] Yet the promises of connection at this global scale are felt only rarely. Each of us is left aware of how this communication environment quickly scales to cross and collapse our local contexts, often rendering the positions and perspectives of any given user's personal experience relatively powerless amid the online multitudes.[50] In an instant, the promises of connection reveal that disconnecting is not merely a set of actions but a relative and constant state inherent in our very relationship with technology.[51]

When we can recognize the asymmetrical power relationship between platforms and users, then practices of disconnection represent a position from which that relationship can be better understood. Disconnection is often an insistence on our right to choose; it reintroduces a flexibility—a fluidity in practice—that responds to the strictures of contemporary economic life, from the economic insecurity that defines so many early careers to the expectations of constant connection and availability that follow. Where social experiences are afforded and constrained—mediated and transformed to produce data-based commodities—the impetus toward socially oriented connection gets hollowed out. Media scholar Michael Petit points to a "digital disaffect" in light of the pressures inherent in constant connection: a "kind of hypnotic, engaged disengagement," something "less than" our drive toward connection, a social-participation mandate that comes to be characterized by "boredom, detachment, ennui and malaise."[52] The media sociologist Tim Markham stresses the need to "inhabit" this experience in a manner disconnected from the temporalities of connection, "to pause, dwell, and reflect on how we feel amid digital environments."[53] The critical sociologist Greg Goldberg sees this as a meaningful disposition toward the labor of constant connection, an "anxious labor" that, instead, constitutes purposefully nonproductive digital work yet is resolutely committed to social life, even if subversively so—a disposition of "the self-involved, noncommittal, promiscuous, irresponsible, pleasure-seeking, antisocial, non-subject."[54] In *Making Time for Digital Lives*, Anne Kaun, Christian Pentzold, and Christine Lohmeier examine how moral imperatives are entangled with the everyday proscriptions for constant connection—an ideological regime of speed and availability attuned to the temporal affordances of connective technology and against which resistance to connection, through practices of "nonuse" and degrees of "denetworking," is not a matter of social inhibition but "a self-imposed choice . . . evidence of self-care or self-determination, not a defect."[55]

Beyond the limits of a given platform, and outside the reach of data-production architecture and capture facilities, further degrees of disconnection give users opportunities to redress power imbalances. In his book *Disconnecting with Social Media Sites*, Ben Light provides an early survey of "disconnective affordances" inherent in the multifunctionality of platforms themselves.[56] Platform giants now allow users, in-app, to choose a "walled garden" experience, rebuffing the embedded connections that link platforms to other games, apps, or services. Users may also provide incorrect or incomplete personal information to disconnect in another way, undermining the circulatory efficacy of their data across commercial platforms and the data-mining industry.[57] While these represent degrees of in-app disconnection, a view of "disconnective power" emerges more fully in the context of the multifunctional environments of internet browsers and device-operating systems.[58]

Where numerous media practices and technologies converge, practices of disconnection find a creative maneuverability among them.
Through the mobile phone, the "metamedium" par excellence, users assert
forms of relationality more attuned to the successive and intertwined
situational contexts of everyday social life.[59] Aure Schrock's survey of
mobile media affordances is instructive, offering a landscape onto which
Kate Mannell's empirical investigation of disconnective practices can be
mapped and demonstrating the manner in which mobile users creatively
and opportunistically exploit metamedia communication environments:
we attempt to disentangle the blurring of social contexts through the
multiple apps and platforms converged onto a single mobile device; we
jam connection by switching off Wi-Fi or mobile signals for a temporary
reprieve; we modulate our constant availability, selecting among types of
connection with particular others.[60] These practices of disconnection are
still only opportunistic, practical tactics, in response to communicative
affordances and intrusions. But where do they take us?

Beyond the metamedium of any device, beyond affordances, is the
social field of metacommunication particular to our everyday communication environment, defined by how we perceive and understand it
via relational, situated practices. The midcentury sociologist of everyday life Erving Goffman called this an "environment of communication
possibilities."[61] Mobile communication scholars Lee Humphreys, Veronika Karnowski, and Thilo von Pape delve into the different social uses
and subjective gratifications of exploiting the commercial-technological
niches of given platforms. Decisive clusters of practices become sets of
mediated actions across apps, platforms, and devices, in a manner particular to a given social situation.[62] We can see this in Mirca Madianou's
study of media practices of Filipina migrant workers in the UK. Involved
in the taxing, embodied labor of in-person care with clients' children,
the migrant workers nonetheless seek to maintain meaningful connections to their own growing children back home. Here is an important
phenomenological finding: the choice of one medium from a range of
media—that is, from the "polymedia" of opportunities for connection,
to use Madianou's language—is a message itself.[63] Choosing among mediums is emphatically expressive, at times temporally framing a message as urgent, or affectively cueing the content of the interaction, and
often relationally particular to the situation at hand. More important, the
choice is meaningful within the context of the relationship. These are

social and technological communicative expressions of a relationship, through intentional decisions, amid media use. How we engage others, how we communicate, defines the interpersonal situation.[64]

Negotiating our communication environment in terms of its mediated and metamediated affordances shapes the particularities of given social experiences and renegotiates tensions beyond our control for meaningful forms of connection. But the extremes of perpetual contact sublimate intimacy into an anxious, overwhelming compulsion toward connection that is at times isolating and exclusionary.[65] We need only look at practices of "mediated tethering" and "tele-cocooning" among teenage friends and young lovers glued to their mobile phones, to the detriment of all other relationships around them, or the deeply felt "fear of missing out" that drives our overattentiveness to social-media newsfeeds, captured by the pandemic era's more anxious portmanteau: "doomscrolling" for crisis updates while isolated under social-distancing mandates.[66] Meaningful forms of connection mingle with a relationally defined individual agency defined by intentionality and self-regulation.[67] Separation and distance from connection is itself productive of knowledge: this is a reflexive, disconnected perspective, from which our sensitivity to and literacy at the level of metacommunication grows.

The Practice Conceit

Communication has not broken down in the era of constant connection. Its complexity and potential to overwhelm have fostered a new intervening layer of social practices. The disconnected sociality of managed and rationalized engagement *to* the communication environment at times displaces relationships *with* others *through* media technologies. This emerging and mutually constitutive set of practices is particular to what media sociologists Couldry and Hepp call "the mediated construction of reality." Building on Peter Berger and Thomas Luckmann's 1967 inquiry into the everyday production of knowledge in *The Social Construction of Reality*, they argue that "the social world is not just a given. We make it, as human beings. . . . The social world is grounded not in ideas, but in everyday action, that is, in practice."[68] By looking to practices, then, we follow the dual character of knowledge produced in the "realization" of social life, both as an understanding of a more interpersonally shared reality and as an ongoing production of that reality in practice.[69]

Practices are what humans say and do, and how we do these things is itself a form of communication with others.[70] Across different social contexts and historical moments, the bases of social practices are still legible and are often immediately recognizable and comprehensible ways of doing things. Practices draw on the shared ways that we feel and assess a situation, on the truth-value of ordinary experience and the social basis for constructing such knowledge—what we often refer to as "common sense," despite the ambiguity of what exactly we mean when we appeal to that shared understanding in everyday life.[71] Earlier disciplinary approaches viewed media consumption by audiences as largely separate phenomena from interpersonal communication between interlocutors, a division that practice-oriented approaches overcome. Practice carries a dual, temporally distinct meaning in the English language: a performative exercise and the knowledge gained through it, and customary and collective practices that accrue overtime.[72] Much scholarship that falls under the label "practice theory" relies consistently on Theodore Schatzki's definition of practices as "centrally organized around shared practical understandings," while other readings subscribe more closely to "specific forms of knowledge ... ways of understanding, knowing how, ways of wanting and of feeling that are linked to each other within a practice."[73] Laurent Thévenot problematizes this sociological position of practices as constituting a "regular and stable" backdrop for human conduct. Instead, he highlights the incongruous temporalities, contexts, and experiences that can come together in any given social situation. In this diverse and changing social world, he asks directly: "Which reality is engaged?"[74] But when we speak about interpersonal practices, it seems more appropriate to ask *whose* reality is engaged, a question of how the normative force of everyday convention eclipses the diversity of experience and knowledge produced in practice. We find an additional dimension of practice by tracing the philosophical foundation of Weber's work up to the critical Marxist sociology of labor studies.[75] Or, as I do below, we can track practice from Weber to Norbert Elias and toward the "pragmatic sociology" of understanding the reproduction of the status quo, asking not "what the relation between the individual and society *ought* to be" but focusing first on understanding "what the relation *is*."[76] Across these German philosophical traditions, practice represents a type of reasoning through experience that fuses with practical know-how toward an imperative for societal transformation through conduct itself.[77] Human conduct is both the subject and object of social practices. Human practices are the site of their own self-transformation.

Practices are already and always social. Communication is only sustainable when there is a coherence of practices between those who are interacting with each other. Although media use is often defined in terms of what connection affords, we might also conceive of it in terms of practices that allow us to engage with emerging, often internalized, and reflexive bases of disconnection. Given the routinized expectations of communication—its definitional engagement with others—social interaction often forces a consistent return to our "infrastructure of repeated interactional patterns," which in turn serve to "anchor" other practices in relation to one another.[78] This has an integrative effect. The complexity of these practices in relation to others is constitutive of the communication that manages so much of everyday life and our relationship to technology therein.[79] When we consider the increasing flexibility, choice, and differentiation in how people communicate across our digital communication environment, there is a degree of conventional interoperability necessary—both interpersonally and technologically—for social practices to cohere. The twentieth-century German sociologist Norbert Elias writes: "As more people must attune their conduct to that of others, webs of actions must be organized more strictly and accurately, if each individual action is to fulfill its social function. Individuals are compelled to regulate their conduct in an increasingly differentiated, even, and stable manner."[80]

Elias refers to the shape of "figurational change" in society: over extended periods of social change, conventional practices and accepted roles in day-to-day life fragment and differentiate. This "to and fro of contrary movements" contributes to a wider, integrating trajectory that, over time, transforms the social environment of personal conduct.[81] He details the inherent interdependency of personal practices across sets of numerous individuals, outlining how we internalize regimes of "self-control" and "self-regulation," which become habitual elements of everyday practices, contributing over time to wider figurations of social change.[82] In this manner, the once "new" and "revolutionary" technologies of the digital era are increasingly woven into the background of quotidian life. Associated practices of "new" media become characterized by a "taken for grantedness," despite their coordinating and ordering role among other practices that serve to structure so many of our daily activities.[83]

This "domestication" of new technologies involves a "double articulation" of media as material objects and practices about which we communicate. We adopt and adapt our use of digital tools to situate them within the temporal flow and social contexts of everyday activities. Yet these media practices are themselves communicative: as we explain and discuss what we are doing and how in daily life, media are enrolled in discursive ensembles of interpersonal engagement and woven into the fabric of routine sociality.[84] As Couldry suggests, however, we must stress a wider and heterogeneous range of "media-related" practices that may be redefining that domain: "how people understand what actions constitute a distinct practice" and "how they categorize what they are doing" to remain open to "practices of avoiding or selecting out" from among established, conventionalized, and therefore more legible practices.[85] Anne Kaun notes that these "negative choices" of disconnected practices emerge in response to, and also embrace, the "responsibilization" of individual citizens and a user's choice to disengage.[86] To participate in social change, we would do well to recognize that our relationships with digital platforms and other media must always be an ongoing, purposeful practice of domestication that includes both connection and disconnection.

Deceptively neutral, practices are malleable vessels. Methodologically, for the sociologist, they facilitate a diverse and telling reflexivity among research participants. Maria Bakardjieva outlines how to employ practices not merely as description but as "sensitizing concepts" for researchers, to trace the social conditions for, and infer the longer-term consequences of, emerging practices.[87] When we reflect on practice, we locate and express ourselves along a spectrum of individualized, relational, and collective definitions of social life.[88] We contort and contest our experiences in ways that reveal the transformative processes and contradictory pressure of selfhood afforded in contemporary life.[89] Agency emerges through social practices, at times frustrated and at times critically hopeful; it is not limited to resistance, and it can world-build.[90]

There is, however, a particular neoliberal currency to the notion of the individual as a practitioner, which includes the platform era's disconnected practitioner. Instead of a type of "craftsperson" honing skills through engagement and experience over time, the ideal neoliberal practitioner is an amalgam of interchangeable skill sets—practices—attuned to, called on, and evaluated by changing market needs.[91] The market places responsibility on each individual as a free economic actor, and

platforms instrumentalize these actors as media users—wholly independent, autonomous, and strategic. Any considerations beyond market calculations and an emerging neoliberal media literacy are individualized
spaces of accepting risk.[92] In its ideal type, the disconnected practitioner
speaks to neoliberal notions of manageability and self-regulation, the
instrumentalization of one's communication environment to productive
and economic ends. But disconnected practices are more typically used
as a bulwark against these pressures. Recalling Georg Simmel's century-
old essay on the urban dweller's "blasé" comportment amid the bustle
of the metropolitan boulevard, disconnective practices offer a similarly
"protective organ" against the "profound disruption" caused by "shifts
and contradictions in events," the "fluctuations and discontinuities of the
external milieu," and the "thousand individual modifications" of one's
actions necessitated by the clash of occupational, social, and commercial
life.[93] In their more typified manifestation, disconnected practitioners
do not conceive of themselves as neoliberal practitioners, but they understand the order of things. Media anthropologist Ilana Gershon points
directly to how we facilitate our participation in today's economy: we
fragment our sense of self in terms of what is marketable yet putatively
authentic. This "manageable" self produces insurmountable paradoxes
when we begin to denigrate what remains as an "irrational, unmanageable neoliberal self."[94] Goffman warns of the moral and political vacuum
produced when individuals are aware of such definitional pressures:
concerned only about meeting standards by which we are evaluated, we
begin to approach socioeconomic life as performers disconnected from
identifying with the particular roles involved.[95]

Structure of the Book and Chapter Summaries

Constant Disconnection offers a timely and unique engagement with
communication management in working life and with the experience
of interpersonal communication at the heart of the platform and data-
mining economies. I ground these dual political-economic analyses in
the qualitative empirical data collected across metropolitan areas that
are home to burgeoning knowledge, creative, and digital economies. I
engage with the complexities of the aforementioned *phenomenological*
perspective—a sociological analysis of everyday life as it is experienced.
This perspective permits a better understanding of the institutionalized

economic realities of knowledge work and the platform industry in relation to *everyday practices of managing one's communication environment* and the *longer-term, socially negotiated processes of transforming
the communication environment* in which these practices take place.

My data come from multiple times and places from over a decade of
sustained fieldwork. They are organized around my unifying, distinc-
tive thematic focus on practices that seek to negotiate communication
as a central facet of day-to-day life. I hope to provide empirical, theoretical, and historical analyses of contemporary political-economic change,
from the perspective of individuals living together in connection and
disconnection. Key to this research was the careful development and
triangulation of qualitative methods to facilitate reflection among 122
research participants, including open-ended interviews, media diaries, and related workshops, including sets of reflective tasks that draw
from both Human Computer Interface (HCI) and Clinical Psychology
approaches.[96] Between 2010 and 2020, I engaged early career adults in
the UK and Canada to examine and follow their changing experiences
of managing media use and interpersonal communication. The various
norms of how one ought to communicate are diverging, but communication only succeeds when we can engage with one another. Throughout
this book, I will examine these early career participants' (re)production
and (re)negotiation of those diverging near-conventions, which are also
tied to longer histories of political-economic organization of technology
use in work and personal life.

How does it feel to live at the pressure points of intersecting economic realities? This book offers an answer through lived, phenomenological perspectives. I begin by locating the economic realities and
historical particularities of working life and surveillance capitalism in
the Anglo-American West; chapters 2 and 3 investigate empirically how
our sense of *time* is mediated and reorganized and how we, in turn, mitigate constant *connection* for types of meaningful engagement afforded
by practices of disconnection. In chapters 4 through 6, I examine how
we facilitate, participate in, and reproduce tensions inherent in social
surveillance, tensions that, in turn, contribute to the performativity and
policing of *authenticity* in our communication practices at work and in
everyday life. Taken together, these elements reveal an extending field of
communication procedures in which patterns of practice have become
expressive, intentional, and intelligible interventions in how we ought

to communicate—practices of *metacommunication* that have come to re-shape today's disconnected sociality, while also affording opportunities to negotiate with a more reparative, ameliorative, prosocial relationality.

"Time," "Connection," "Surveillance," "Authenticity," "Metacommuni-cation"—each empirical chapter addresses different forms of political-economic control as relational levers of disconnected power amid interpersonal practices. Each chapter also represents a site at which disconnected sociality emerges, in response to the political-economic contradictions particular to constant connection. Each chapter's theme speaks to the reflexive interpersonal regimes that test the "spirit" of jus-tifiably participating in—rather than challenging, contesting, and dis-connecting from—the economic pressures and technological promises of constant connection. Some readers may prefer to focus on these chapters for their close engagement with the voices and experiences of everyday individuals, while this introduction, chapter 1, and the conclusion con-stitute the book's wider analytical arc, exploring that sociological work through the trajectories of political economy and social change.

Chapter 1, "Economies of Communication Management," asks readers to consider the historical context of mobile and networked platform com-munication and the decade of interest here (the Great Recession to the COVID-19 pandemic) through the preceding reorganization of everyday work and personal life under forty years of concerted neoliberal policy. Changes to everyday labor and managerial practices have, incrementally, converged with the designed communication pathways for platform use. The adoption of American industrial organizational strategies in postwar Europe and the ascendancy of communication, knowledge, and creative sectors have shaped emerging forms of economic labor since the 1970s. I situate historical and sociological vignettes relating to the reorganization of economic and social life over the last seventy years within histories of technological change to examine the larger metaprocesses of chang-ing everyday interpersonal communication, and of social life itself, still under way today.[97]

Chapter 2, "Managing Time," explores the motivations for, and social implications of, managing everyday life. Idealized practitioners embrace the reorganization of social life in terms of a hypermediated manage-ment of communication tasks, but the typical experience is communica-tion overload, an anxious expectation of the uncertainty, interruption, and contingency of constant connection. There is a fragmented reorga-

nizing of communication into discrete temporal units of platform opera-
bility and a recasting of social life as finite and interchangeable tasks to
be completed.[98] In the decade following the Great Recession, economic
austerity and increasing precariousness of work have exacerbated the
need for early career individuals to juggle multiple roles, moving from
project to project. What happens to individual autonomy if acquiescing to
workplace pressures, increasing flexibility, and a porousness of personal
boundaries are joined with economic precariousness and anxiety related
to communication overload?

Chapter 3, "Managing Connection," examines the manner in which
near-constant availability has dissolved so many distinctions between
the times and spaces of work and personal life. In this context, managing
degrees of disengagement and disconnection emerge as sets of practices
themselves. The practice of managing one's communication environment
has led to distinguishing between ever more nuanced *degrees of networked presences and networked absences.*[99] Like the embodied autonomy in media use explored in chapter 2, the temporal tensions produced
by the communication environment and the benefits afforded to manage
one's availability are not equally accessible; this condition further complicates the temporalities of, for instance, caregivers and transnational
family groups. Where knowledge work is increasingly organized on a
project-to-project basis, in contexts where freelance work is preferable
if not a necessity, there is a desire to foster particular atmospheres free
of communication overload and a necessity for many forms of emotional
and creative labor.

Chapter 4, "Practicing Surveillance," examines the social-surveillance
practices that contribute to the management of everyday communication
environments. What are digital traces of user practices today when defined by mutually reinforcing but contradictory uses, both as the digital
fabric of interpersonal connection and as an advertising-oriented commodity, driving the platform and data-mining economy? Surveillance
is central to online life, where patterns of media use are made visible
through engagement with mobile devices, apps, and platform architecture. A disconnected sociality emerges in the ways that we turn to additional layers of technological mediation to manage our relationship with
the communication environment. This contrasts a more relationally attuned approach to interpersonally engaging with others based on shared
needs—the prosocial motivation at the heart of our social-surveillance

practices, assessing how to ease the burdens of constant connection for others, in connection with others.

Chapter 5, "Practicing Authenticity," examines practices of exposure and control alongside the policing of identities through norms of conduct—both professional and online—that are neither objective nor equal. Many individuals are faced with the dual challenge of role segregation for particular audiences and discrepancies between roles when milieus of personal, social, and work life blur. For members of the LGBTQI community, those with physical-ability and mental-health challenges, or those whose social lives include expression of ethnic and religious communities that may be marked as different from the norms of particular work settings, managing disclosures and divisions is a distinct type of emotional and relational labor, another dimension of neoliberal responsibilization of the individual.

Chapter 6, "Practicing Metacommunication," examines everyday decisions and patterns of communication as distilled forms of social expression, an ongoing discourse-in-practice that negotiates interpersonal relationships and their mediation by technology. What is the role of reflexivity in relation to changing social practices? How do individuals recursively express and negotiate changes when communication platforms promote particular forms of connection? At the level of metacommunication, so many of our practices are intelligible and communicative, even without us knowing it. When we engage our communication environment to constrain or correct the communication practices of others, this is an antisocial prioritization of our individual agency at the cost of the agency of others. This mutual negotiation of connection enacted through everyday media practices, rather than communicated explicitly through speech or content, occurs through the field of practices that I call metacommunication. As a form of negotiation through everyday practices, metacommunication does not occur through any one mode of communication but rather through multiple forms of connection across a range of communication platforms, defined in practice and in changing relationships between one another. A particular type of knowledge is produced from the experience of interpersonal life; it is a legible and recognizable dimension of those practices. Acting on this—what we can call social knowledge—is intertwined with and instrumental to the metaprocess of social transformation. It stands in contrast to the types of knowledge produced from detached observation, data collection, and statistical correlation: social knowledge is a collective well of understanding that can only be derived from the act of participating in social life, from the experience of interpersonal connection itself. Our communication practices have become fields of daily moral and political negotiation through practice itself. However, the scales are tipped, technologically, by the commercial imperatives written into design and, habitually, by the increasingly fraught dependence on media technologies for participation in everyday economic and social life. Metacommunication offers opportunities to foster a collective ethos of care, a desire to repair what is lost to the rationalized sociality of disconnection.

My conclusion, "To Count and Be Counted," reengages with the long view of data production across governance, economics, and communication to challenge the presumed infallibility of the neoliberal market and the big-data promises of surveillance platforms. This closing chapter ties together how the management of time and connection meets practices of surveillance and authenticity, which taken together reveal the social field of metacommunication, becoming sites for negotiating social change despite also being sites of data-driven and labor-oriented interventions into everyday interpersonal life. Where Western neoliberalism and surveillance capitalism mutually reinforce a particular trajectory of social change, how much power do we—citizens as users and users as citizens—have to repair and manage the continual reorganization of everyday life?

A successor to the Great Recession and antiglobalization rhetoric of contemporary populism, the crises of COVID-19 and the subsequent destabilization of global economies clearly demonstrate our entrenched dependency on the platform economy. This book highlights the need for national and supranational regulation of platforms. But this cannot be done in earnest unless there is greater scrutiny and amelioration of the social and political-economic contradictions at the heart of the neoliberal endeavor. Without deeper understanding, the social life of knowledge-oriented and surveillance economies, and the politics of crafting limits to the platform and data industries, may continue to overlook the fact that there are real people here.

ONE

Economies of Communication Management

Understanding how we live with constant connection means paying attention to a setting's social definition and human experiences, despite its economic and material determinations. We are not mere objects or commodities. We are actors. Living sets of forces shape our changing relationship with each other and technology. These forces also, I argue, shape our participation in the trajectory of social change. When institutional actors from economic or political domains face the complexity of social life, the greater the indeterminacy found, the greater the desire for management and control.[1]

For this reason, a political and economic history of communication management is essential. We must also remain open to other forms of relation—to each other, technology, and the definitions and conventions of social life. This chapter explores how ideologically inflected types of political-economic analysis have obscured the production of such knowledge within the longer durée of social change, in tandem with technological innovation and workplace management.

The Ideological Mediations of Analysis

Metaphors for technology cannot fully capture human experience and the social organization of conduct. The history of these metaphors offers a perspective on their always-already politicized nature, demonstrating how they are deployed to validate and justify ideological interventions, as well as their contradictions in practice, and disconnections from experience.

The natural sciences, for instance, like any discipline or industry, are subject to ideological biases and blind spots. In 1863, the biologist and artist Ernst Haeckel coined the term *ecology* to refer to an interconnected "system of active living forces." Despite the paradigm-shifting "dual hypothesis" of lichen as a single yet symbiotic pair of organisms shortly thereafter, the nineteenth century resisted and even derided the concept of "symbiosis" as a romanticized, politicized, and even anarchistic stance. Ideological bias undermined the embrace of empirical realities, which were further reinforced by institutional divisions separating the different domains of scientific expertise, such that questions that would eventually prove to link their isolated objects of study were overlooked.[2]

Privileging the analysis of technological settings of media use represents a comparable analytical myopia, subject to vast oversimplification. Affordances, as noted, are what an environment "*offers* the animal what it *provides* or *furnishes*," but the remainder of Gibson's definition is often truncated: "for good or ill."[3] What types of social knowledge do those outcomes produce? What are the social implications of such experiences over time? Taken up in earnest by media studies in the 2000s and increasingly interrogated in the changing field, necessitating its continual rearticulation, this concept was considered a radical shift in the study of behavioral psychology because it outlined a way in which the perspective of the individual actor—and indeed the socially articulated values and meanings of a given setting—could be inferred by an external observer through an assessment of the material environment alone.[4] Still reflected in the thinking of industry actors, this behaviorist accounting reduces opportunities for exploring human agency by systematically overlooking the social knowledge produced in collective practice.[5]

Computational metaphors themselves are similarly ideological and disciplinary: economic, sociological, and media-centered attempts to understand social change. The economist Fredrich Hayek, an early champion of what would become known as neoliberalism, relied on cybernetic theory later in his career to explain the invisible hand of the market.[6] The sociologist Zygmunt Bauman used the metaphors of computer hardware and software to contradistinguish old and new forms of economic-social relations, the latter conceived of as "liquid modernity"—contemporary capitalism as an underdefined lightness and fluidity of local, situational human connection, disconnected from the global forces that structure economic relations.[7] Media sociologists Lee Rainie and Barry Wellman look to the always-availability of mobile and platform connection as the "new social operating system" manifesting relationships between sets of networked, interacting individuals.[8]

These metaphors, which emerge from distinct fields of thought, overlook the unique nature of knowledge production amid practice and the compelling social interdependence of individuals, whose self-regulation is at the heart of communicative practices; thus, they risk obscuring the political-economic rationality of today's disconnected sociality. They may cause us to internalize the contradictions of wider social life and see them as failures in our own practices of communication management.

From the user's perspective, the reflexive production of social knowledge is qualitatively different from the automaticity of commercial-platform database processes. The history of political-economic rationality in tandem with changes to communication management practices are only analogous in a metaphorical way to the digitalization of knowledge work and the recent shift toward platform-based communication management. When we speak of recursivity—that is, the production of information from available information, for reuse and reapplication in a comparable setting and process going forward—the recursivity of social practices and the recursivity database processes are fundamentally different.

Sociological and linguistic definitions of recursive learning, linking individual social life to collective change over time, share little with computational notions of recursivity. Echoing the statistical enumeration of probability over the nineteenth and early twentieth centuries—what Ian Hacking called an "avalanche of printed numbers"—computational recursion represented, as the sociologist Tim Jordan argues, a key innovation that drove the late twentieth-century shift from information scarcity about social life to information abundance, in which "the flood produces its own effects."[9] Recursivity is a product of the formalized, programmatic separation between sets of rules (algorithms) and data-structures (to effect a program) and the application of those rules within and across components of that program (or subroutines), and it "defines parts of [those activities] in such a way as to transform them so that they can return to be absorbed and put to work within the same activity."[10]

Computational recursivity determines sets of successive iterations of change within the confines of an algorithmic and machine-learning process acting upon itself.

For the last decade, the increasing centrality of platforms has led to a concomitant transformation of the production, distribution, and circulation of cultural content. News, gaming, marketing, and social-media consumption are increasingly governed as platform economies, inflected by the recursive nature of database processes. There is a widespread penetration of economic and infrastructural logic into what media economists David Nieborg and Thomas Poell call the "platformization of cultural production."[11] There is also a comparable and related "datafication" of social processes linked to data-dependent governmental and commercial interventions in everyday life. Taken in tandem with the algorithmic and database-to-database governance of platforms themselves, and the flow of data between intermediaries and across the platform ecosystem, this leads to what Nick Couldry and Andreas Hepp have warned is a process of "deep mediatization": data-oriented infrastructural processes increasingly constitutive of, but far removed from, everyday individual user experience and opaque even to digital-knowledge or platform-oriented culture workers involved in their production.[12] App-studies scholars highlight the multisited nature of these mediating processes. Individuated renderings of a given user environment—a responsive interface, that mediating bridge of so much of our professional and personal lives—depend on the "infrastructural situatedness" of various constituent platform and app intermediaries, or infrastructural and service provision "complementors."[13] These complementors work together to dynamically render the content for given users, at given times, to "enable specific, embodied, and often context-dependent" opportunities for user practices.[14] From the mediation of particular practices to wider metaprocesses of mediatization, the interrelatedness of these scales and depths of change represents not only the extent of technological infrastructural change but also the need to reenvision the role of individuals in social change.[15]

A Relational Manifold of Knowledge Production

The knowledge that comes from practices of connection and disconnection speaks to what it means to be human together, of how we come to know, shape, and exploit the tools crafted for that purpose—this is what I mean by social knowledge. Before the recent scholarly conceptualization of mediatization and platformization, technologist and media theorist Tiziana Terranova pointed to the all-encompassing digital environments of everyday life as an informational milieu that "supports and encloses the production of meaning" but also "exceeds and undermines the domain of meaning from all sides."[16] This milieu demands a reassessment of communication not only as a site for engaging with social change but also as a site through which new forms of social meaning are produced.

Couldry suggests that this complex web of practices occurs across something like a referential system, extending beyond our changing repertoire of platforms: a "media manifold" comprising the "connected range of media" that users can navigate, migrate to and from, and explore across a competitively expansive reserve of options, through which "we actualize social relations."[17] Our engagement with the media manifold "can seem to be everywhere and nowhere in particular: we are just embedded in it to varying degrees."[18] Derived from the Proto-Germanic for "many folds," *manifold* expresses the complexities and possibilities of interrelated, constituent elements—a topology—in which relationships among a multitude of dimensions are expressed through a descriptive abstraction, an approximation using only a few dimensions that are, therefore, easier to grasp.[19] This echoes practice-theorist Theodore Schatzki's definition of the relationship of individual everyday practices to social convention and social possibility, by situating the practicing body as the meeting point of "mind and activity and of individual activity and social manifold."[20] That is what I am seeking to accomplish here. I focus on a manifold of communicative practices through the openness of defining social practice in terms of both connection and disconnection.

The possibility held in the plasticity of practices, both social and mediated life *in practice*, holds promise for our purposeful participation in the negotiation of social change. But how we think about communication management constrains and mediates those very possibilities. Multiplied across so many overlapping modes of communication and intensified by the relentless pressures of working life, the cacophony of available information related to a given social or professional situation has implications for how we orient ourselves. Past experiences, the present situation, and future expectations can be continually reordered for reinterpretation.

This reordering can leave an individual to assess how to be and participate in everyday life on a situation-to-situation basis. Writing in the

early 1990s, Kenneth Gergen saw a dramatic multiplication of the range
of relational cues within a given situation, whereby the complexity of
modern life gave way to a "relational self" saturated in realities, reasons,
and attitudes of social, political, economic, technological, and even imagined dimensions of any given moment.[21] Twenty-five years later, in his
book *Social Acceleration,* Harmut Rosa picks up where Gergen left off, arguing that the individual's highly relational assessment of a given social
situation already constitutes temporally oriented practices, pressed into
the real time of our economically and technologically accelerated present: "the duration, sequences, rhythm and tempo of actions, events, and
relationships are first decided in the course of their execution, that is,
within time itself."[22] If we can accept that a pressure of constant connection and the disorienting experience of information overload contribute
to a frenetic experience of everyday life, then the situation-to-situation
experience of the present is itself intensified moment-to-moment: an accelerated and relational temporalization of practices amid practice.[23]

In this relational tumult of the present moment amid constant connection, disconnection fosters a deeper understanding of our relationship to
connection and to each other. It exposes a reflexive reserve of possible
practices for the production of social knowledge, a relational manifold
for rearticulating the basis of social and media practices alike. The trajectories of these cognitive and social changes have occurred, intertwined
with economic conventions and technological mediations. They are part
of a longer history of industry-led interventions into the practices of communication management, revealing the predigital history of neoliberalism and mediatization.

Wartime Economies and Coca-Cola Imperialism

The history of innovation is also a history of the stratification of opportunity through the division of labor. At the heart of the colonial-industrial
revolution, the UK has undergone a steady reorganization of workplace
practices through technological rationalization for more than two centuries. The management of communication and information involves a
particular type of labor, which has changed how workplace practices
are themselves organized. Today, this includes the labor of managing
connection and disconnection. There is a lineage here, from the "cult"
of efficient domesticity in the late 1800s to the auditing and reorgani-

zation of assembly lines in the early 1900s and then to the continual redevelopment of information reproduction and retrieval technologies— first analog, then digital.[24] Even the recent proliferation of digital platforms for communication and task management draws from forty years of development: the first mobile telephones of the 1980s; the laptops and Personal Digital Assistants (PDAs) of the 1990s; internet-ready mobile phones extensively adopted after c. 2005; to the platform-dependent forms of cultural production and monitoring.

There is widespread belief that organizational systems and communication technologies universally enhance workplace productivity, with productivist rationalizations extending beyond work to everyday life. The reality is more complex. The benefits of technological change are always inscribed within circuits and hierarchies of political-economic power, but at times, it can be difficult to step back from the harried pace of day-to-day existence to see the political-economic relations of our communications environment. Greater efficiency, greater convenience for particular activities, whether at work, home, or elsewhere, means the imposition of greater control through the systematization of other activities. Flexibility in some domains comes with rigid structures and codification of practices in others. Who has access to these conveniences? Who reaps the benefits? These are matters of political economy, questions that come to define social relations within a society. As the science fiction writer William Gibson (who coined the term *cyberspace*) famously quipped: "The future is already here—it is just not very evenly distributed."[25] Turning first to the past, then to the future, helps frame a set of possible answers.

Over the first half of the 1900s, Britain's industrial development was plagued by the costs and disruptions of two world wars. WWII spurred state-led industrial organization and the subsequent embrace of an American-style managerial ethos in the reconstruction that followed,[26] leaving an indelible mark on British society still evident today in strident forms of economic ideology, particularly Anglo-American neoliberalism. The last half of the twentieth century oscillated between Keynesian economics of increasing government spending to quell recessions and the austerity economics of this neoliberal monetary policy, which saw unfettered market forces as the prevailing method of economic correction.[27] The consolidation of postwar welfare states in Canada and the UK stands in contrast to the United States, decentering analysis from the excesses of American inequality. While neoliberalism embraces market rationality as an evaluative mechanism both for individuals and practices of social life, even its early proponents such as Milton Freidman and Fredrich Hayek argued that this could only function through equality in education and public health, as well as competition and job-market regulation.[28] Changes to American and British economic policy in the postwar era would have reverberations for the structure of trade globally, but, much like the policies following the Great Recession of 2008–9, they would also affect everyday working life—changes that have compounded over the decades and have intensified alongside technological innovations up to the present day.[29]

Wartime Britain embraced the strategy of state-led economic intervention alongside massive budgetary deficits in order to maximize widespread industrial output. Academic economists were enlisted to develop statistical models, inform long-term planning, and determine changes in fiscal and manufacturing priorities on a national scale.[30] These types of emergency state-led economic interventions would not be seen again in Britain until the nationalization of banks following the Great Recession and then a decade later in the nationwide income-support and furlough schemes of the COVID-19 pandemic. The austerity of wartime Britain involved massive increases in taxation and a squeeze on civilian and civil-service spending that would reshape public life in the postwar period. The 1950s and 1960s saw a broad context of full employment and no major recessions, though there were four distinct "stop-go" fiscal squeezes of slow economic growth.

Notably, however, the wartime interventions would have another effect. Both private businesses and private individuals alike had been expected to contribute to the war effort through income- and corporate-tax hikes. Additional wartime taxes took the form of postwar credits to be paid back after the war. While these repayments were expedited for businesses to stimulate the economy, they were not required for individuals until the 1970s, when inflation had eroded their worth. The administrative deference to economic efficiency at a macro level would become foundational to British neoliberalism from the late 1970s onward, and it was accompanied by prioritization of business-oriented stimulus plans over individual economic security.[31] Another pillar of this economic ideology would come through successive waves of American interventions in European industry and the accompanying managerial techniques for inculcating and nurturing a spirit of productivity in the very relationships and character of the British workplace.[32]

Following the war, American corporate ideology became a very real presence in Europe, reshaping the future of economic life for millions of people. From the Marshall Plan to the European Productivity Agency, large-scale policy interventions to rebuild Europe involved the establishment of numerous "productivity institutes" across the continent, while industrial leaders undertook "productivity missions" to the United States. These were pilgrimages to study the emerging paradigms for the corporate and entrepreneurial workplace of the future. Economic policy sought to shore up European political stability through a culture that fostered more competitive and dynamic forms of capitalism across national economies.[33] Often derided as "Coca-Cola imperialism," this policy was meant to instill generations with a "revolutionary faith" in free enterprise. Across European nations, where emergency-state intervention had tended toward nationalization of key industries to manage economic crisis, this emerging transatlantic ideology was meant to stand as a bulwark against both fascism and communism.[34]

The Dissolution of Career Certainty

The supposed golden age of the postwar welfare state was accompanied by the corporate behemoth of industry and the sprawling bureaucracies of the public sector. This largely Keynesian era—idealized as benevolent interventionism that worked toward full employment (however punctuated by neoliberal austerity politics)—would persist in the UK until the mid-1970s, after which it would be steadily dismantled into the mid-1990s.

The scale and complexity of contemporary working life is a relatively new phenomenon, but this extends beyond workplace organization. The social complexity of a working life over time has become the management of one's career within a particular field or sector, characterized today by networks of shifting relationships and opportunities. Even the word *management* did not come into widespread use until the 1950s, and its contemporary definition—controlling people and things, overseeing or having the responsibility of oversight—only emerged in the middle of the 1800s.[35] Management by the owner-entrepreneurs of the prewar era was a day-to-day management of operations, with little support staff or expert evaluation to review operational reporting and other available metrics or statistics. The lives of employees, and the livelihoods of entrepreneurs and often their families, were so intertwined with the enterprise itself that economic risk and long-term planning was, in a manner, life planning.[36]

In the era of corporate behemoths, focus shifted from the rationalization of manufacturing processes and manual labor that had dominated the prewar era to the reconfiguration of corporate and bureaucratic life. The original goal was a more egalitarian model of what would become contemporary office culture. In stark contrast with the prewar era of small-scale "owner-manager" oversight, vast multilevel corporations and their public-sector corollaries highlighted the growing need for advancements in workplace organizational structures and communication practices.[37] In the United States, the science of business management had incorporated a vocational sense of an individually oriented "calling" or devotion to one's work, a modern echo of the "spirit" of capitalism that Weber had originally framed as the "Protestant work ethic," within a wider systematic approach to workplace training and career management.[38] The resulting workplace culture would, in theory, collectively inspire dedication to one's own advancement through a competitive climate where entrepreneurialism was rewarded.[39] This extended beyond mitigating the traditional conflict between management and labor. The new managerial culture sought actively to identify, train, and socialize an ever-expanding segment of "white-collar" employees across management, sales, and technical workforces, while fostering opportunities for the growing echelons of an administrative and clerical workforce.

An individual sense of responsibility over one's career and its trajectory was supposed to offer a new engine for productivity, yet this subsequently allowed for businesses to retreat from caretaking roles for employees in an effort to more shrewdly respond to changes in the market. What had been training and career mobility for a booming postwar economy became the individualization of economic risk and insecurity in the austere economic climate that followed. Workplace cultures in North America and Western Europe of the 1950s and 1960s had an unfaltering belief in the stability of large organizations and in the utility of clear-cut hierarchical divisions between specialized, often executive, roles and the work of support staff who often specialized in other, more systematized, forms of labor. Following the unparalleled expansion of

Western economies in the postwar period, the economic stagnation that triggered the 1972–75 recession primed Anglo-American governments for a retreat from managing the economy.

In the UK, a very different form of strategic economic intervention replaced government planning: a small, strong state to manage policies of economic deregulation. Framed as a noninterventionist approach to labor laws, economic deregulation would bolster businesses vis-à-vis the market at the expense of employees vis-à-vis their employers.[40] In light of the 1970s recession, organizational stability was reframed as restrictive largesse, unresponsive to market changes. Bureaucratic sluggishness was blamed; more agile approaches to workplace organization, and flexible regimes of employment, emerged. Deregulation of employment laws allowed for a neoliberal sleight of hand touting market supremacy: the competitive "going rate" for employment incomes was replaced by the lowest "market rate," eroding the hard-won collective bargaining that had previously protected job security, worker safety, and lifetime employment.[41] But this was not just a matter of conditions; the very nature of work was changing.

Mediating the Knowledge and Creative Economy

Theories on neoliberalism suggest its tendency to replace traditional manual labor with "human capital"—that is, an increased reliance on entrepreneurship as an engine of commercial knowledge production and creative innovation rather than the production or exchange of material commodities.[42] By the mid-1970s the American sociologist Daniel Bell had already plotted the emergence of what he called the "post-industrial society," an early thesis signaling the shift of a majority of urban workforces into new knowledge-oriented service economies.[43]

What has become known as the "knowledge economy" involves diverse forms of information-, knowledge-, and communication-based processes as commercial products and services. These have emerged alongside the more traditional cultural production of public- and audience-oriented media products in the arts, advertising, and design. Two decades prior to Bell's thesis, the term *knowledge worker* had already been coined by the Austrian management consultant and scholar Peter Drucker, while what has now been dubbed "knowledge work" was emerging through sweeping organizational changes to corporate enterprises and public-sector organizations from the 1950s onward.[44] In both the private and public sectors, the greater size and complexity within postwar organizational structures gave way to a stratified managerial class—venerated for its prowess at interpersonal communication and professional relationships—and the standardization of other communication-management practices as additional layers of support from below. This early organizational bifurcation tellingly signaled the increased value accorded to the social aspect of economic life. Workplace codification of communication-management processes represented an analog precursor to the digital platform literacy necessary for many contemporary careers.

Today, work across knowledge economies and related cultural and creative media sectors is often understood as "immaterial labor" that supplies forms of communication, knowledge-based process inputs, cultural products, and services.[45] The immaterial character of these practices as types of paid employment or work stems from value derived from the transmission, interpretation, or application of knowledge. To varying degrees, the breadth of cultural and creative work often understood to be part of today's knowledge economy enlists the use of language, imagery, emotional experience, and degrees of technical, niche, or aesthetic know-how.[46] The incorporation of numerous cultural and creative sectors into the wider knowledge industries began in the late 1990s and early 2000s alongside the digitalization of these previously disparate forms of work.[47] The aesthetic and cultural experimentation that constitutes creative labor is driven by unique experiential practices of organization and innovation that exist outside codified processes and some of the repetitive translations of knowledge acquired through specialist skills and technical systems.[48] The absorption of some forms of more readily commercialized creative labor within wider market trajectories has left a number of other creative practitioners, from hobbyists to professional artists, struggling outside of paid, established employment yet still socialized with a personal obligation to produce opportunities for success through online reputation management and promotion.[49]

The idealized craft of the knowledge worker is sociable and entrepreneurial, professionally adaptable to new ways of working but with an interpersonal agility for moving among peers within the industry to network, collaborate, and identify the next opportunity. This craft is always a balancing act: demonstrating competence in sector-specific skills—whether process-based, technical, or creative—and those necessitated by any given project, while contributing to the common good of colleagues, collaborators, and clients involved. These, when taken together, are the essential building blocks for one's professional reputation, opening doors to future opportunities and, over time, constituting a cobbled-together career from project to project, position to position.[50] While these characteristic approaches to interpersonal practices are indicative of the promise of entrepreneurial autonomy, in more precarious working situations the lure of networked availability and flexible schedules quickly shifts toward work-life practices characterized by compulsion and control.[51]

"Entrepreneur" came into common and recognizable usage in the sixteenth century. Derived from the old French *emprise* and then *enterprise*, *entrepreneur* describes a person who undertakes a project within which risk is implied. This particular type of risk, however, is an economic hazard related to "exchange and time": over the length of time it takes to execute an economic endeavor, often under some sort of contract, the entrepreneur exposes themselves to the uncertainties of intervening events.[52] These uncertainties lie outside of reducible, calculable financial risk; they are the contingencies that, according to the economist John Maynard Keynes's general theory of employment, drive the "animal spirits" of individuals within a marketplace economy. This is the foundation of the Anglo-American conception of entrepreneurship as employed from the 1900s onward. The social, creative, and innovative craft of the entrepreneur is the generative locus of human industriousness, embracing uncertainty and therein able to intervene, resist, and exploit the rationalized and calculable risks of economic and market activities. Even in these early days of the term, however, the promise of venturing into such uncertainty was motivated by the acquisition of relative independence from the upper classes of land or industry owners, on the one hand, and the restrictive conditions of working for subsistence wages, on the other. These political-economic assumptions in Anglo-American thinking continue to this day—a legacy of stratified opportunities for economic and career autonomy. Neoliberal policies and discourse celebrate such individualized framings of economic uncertainty and entrepreneurial opportunity, which on close inspection are also written into the promises and uses of digital practices and platform technologies.

The Political Economies of Dividing Labor

In the West, "white-collar" office work is a historical by-product of corporate expansion and the types of early workplace reorganization that sought to increase autonomy for those whose technical prowess, entrepreneurial intuition, and creative vision were, rightly or wrongly, lauded as the primary engine of commercial success. The protection and preservation of time for their particular craft meant redefining their domain of executive work, excising the more mundane practices of operational management from their workload to protect their time to create a reserve for those celebrated skill sets.[53] Operational elements of their workloads that could be reorganized as systematic and codified processes were identified and deferred to others, outsourced, or delegated downward within the hierarchy of the organization.[54] New echelons of administrative and support staff emerged alongside intermediary levels of near-executive employees, a precursor to middle management, bureaucracy, and the wider office culture that still persists today. Sara Ahmed reminds us that "if the freeing up of time and energy depends on other people's labor, we are simply passing our exhaustion on to others."[55] These are not merely organizational schema; they are institutionalized enactments of political and economic social relations: mobility is a lever between connectionist autonomy from hierarchy and disconnectionist relegation of labor to others in order to work in contexts where social affordances provide for professional advancement.

Whether intern, trainee, or another form of junior probationary role, entry-level positions across the numerous sectors of knowledge and creative work today are characterized by day-to-day lack of autonomy, so much so that working life is an ordeal to which you are subject. This lack of autonomy is amplified by the reach and constant availability of connective communication platforms that in turn foster forms of managerial surveillance and the proliferation of practices centered on accountability. The pressures of postrecession economies echo the types of uncertainty faced by the new executives and intermediary management positions that marked the emergence of the knowledge economy in the 1980s and 1990s: "where everything from the job title to the job description itself is ambiguous and shrouded in uncertainty, even the smallest action becomes difficult and fraught with anxiety: the individual tends to see the outside world as an ordeal to which he must subject himself."[56]

In the aftermath of the COVID-19 pandemic, there has been a lot of debate around the expectation for workplace presence that was previously explicitly mandated by employers, but the benefits of a more remote and casualized workforce are among just some of the ever-changing prescriptions from management responding to the vagaries and pressures of the market. Employees respond to these shifting priorities and the insecurity of their own positions through steadfast practices of self-monitoring and self-improvement, resulting in a necessary mutability of how to manage one's communication environment, which in turn frames how one's professional self is presented and viewed.[57] Such explicit expectations are accompanied by implicit but uncertain opportunities for promotion, with promises of eventual inclusion within upwardly mobile ranks of more secure, autonomous conditions of employment as the prize.

While traditional hierarchical forms of managing employees or being managed at work are still the status quo today, an increasing number of knowledge and creative workers are managing a diversity of working relationships, collaborations across project teams, and thereby diverse opportunities for contract-to-contract-style career progression. The contemporary equivalent of both an entrepreneur and a highly skilled service provider would be a freelance software developer, media producer, or marketing specialist—with one foot in the knowledge economy and the other in the service economy, selectively taking on contracts with teams for the adjacent sectors in between their own projects. In her study comparing unemployed tech workers following the burst of the "Dot.com Bubble" in 2001 and after the Great Recession of 2008–9, Carrie Lane saw a growing ambivalence to this freedom over the following decade: job security was not a matter of keeping your current contract but preparing for the next before it disappears; indeed, company loyalty was demonized as "deficiency . . . as stagnant."[58] This is an augmentation of the traditional freelancer in the project-to-project makeup of the gig-style economy, whereby individual working life is managed as a business of one. Short-term contracts involve temporary collaborations that can occur in a networked manner or with project teams coming together within the client organization or a coworking space. When the project is complete, the collaboration dissolves, but the accrual (or loss) of reputational capital and social connections within that sector is carried forward in the search for the next collaboration. This is where the connectionist promise idealizing flexibility, adaptability, and constant mobility between jobs gives way to the disconnected era's reality of vastly increasing the number of life moments when dramatic, downward mobility is a genuine possibility.[59]

Ethnographic accounts from creative sectors and media industries remind us that such conditions foster difficult, capricious, demanding, and antisocial behavior that serves to privilege those at the height of "winner take all" hierarchies while also excusing behavior that marginalizes subordinates and in doing so reinforces the very same hierarchies.[60] Even early forms of well-honed restraint in the West—the Renaissance strategy of *sprezzatura*—idealized being "less self, more sociable."[61] By the 1970s, Bell's account of knowledge-oriented industries already described it as a competitive "game between persons."[62] In her examination of self-help literature, popular media, support groups, and dating websites, Eva Illouz unpacks the emotional landscape of contemporary capitalism to reveal "cold intimacies" of contemporary sociality in economic life, where networking, relationships, and reputational management within the world of work fall short of what we often consider social relationships—a diminished interpersonal sociality lacking empathy and intimacy.[63] Today, this sociability is a disconnected sociality: a protective, rationalized field of interpersonal practices that shields the individual from the waves of social stimulation of constant connection or the uncertainties of working life.

The Platformization of Communication Management

Where technologies permit observation, measurement, and analysis of communication-based work, they deepen and extend knowledge-intensive forms of work but also serve to recursively produce information about those processes, information that can then be packaged and repackaged as additional commercial outputs.[64] Across the knowledge economy today, there are layers of industry-specific accounting for our work that have preceded what we can call the *platformization of communication management* and the datafication of productivity: evaluative processes intertwined with technical mediations and social transformations of how and what we know.

Where particularly held knowledge sets, creative-process skill sets, or technical understandings are applied in the production or transformation of knowledge or communication-based products or services, decades of sector-specific standards have mediated these processes in terms of project-management conventions: from reporting and auditing standards to the conventionalized "best-practice" reliance on particular software and platform packages even within more loosely defined professional fields. The political economy and labor studies scholars Catherine McKercher and Vincent Mosco point to this commodification of communication, knowledge, and creativity through the technical entanglement of evaluative oversight within the commercial production and transmission of knowledge. As early as the 1980s, surveillance studies economist Shoshana Zuboff was examining the forms of workplace automation that preceded the platformization of communication management in large corporate settings: the use of new "smart machines" involved the automating of some workplace practices, also "infomating" those practices by producing data to assist management in future, recursive interventions toward greater and greater productivity.[65]

Something akin to disconnection lies at the heart of this accounting and oversight, whether it's the disconnection of data for management from the practicing individual or the individual's reflexive detachment needed to review. More than a century ago, a productivity and self-monitoring "cult of domesticity" sought the rationalization of household activities through a practiced disruption to—and deliberate reflexive retreat from—the social flow of practices "necessary for calculating the merits of activities in relation to a greater cause" that continues to this day in types of "efficiency thinking," normalizing degrees of a disconnected sociality. Anthropologist Melissa Gregg links the anchoring and ordering role of these managerial practices to the mediation of connective apps as part of the political-economic "productivity imperative" at the heart of our era, in which the individual is responsible for a greater intensity of communication management, informed by a longer historical recognition that such "media ideologies" (to use Gershon's term) have inflected both the personal and professional domains since their emergence.[66]

This responsibilization of individuals to rationalize and manage their interpersonal knowledge work through additional platforms for communication management accompanies the greater casualization and increasing precariousness of the knowledge workforce, on the one hand, and the consolidation of horizontal ecosystems of platform ownership and technical integration, on the other. From Salesforce, Microsoft, Facebook, and Google, extensive suites of workplace productivity platforms and client management systems have competed in company acquisitions of, respectively, Slack, Skype, WhatsApp, and Dropbox and in the mirroring of each other's innovative functionality. After its acquisition of the VR headset maker Oculus, Facebook was restructured to facilitate its rebrand and launch as parent company Meta, part of a pitch for the future of working life through their virtual-reality platform, the Metaverse. The French economist Yann Moulier Boutang argues that ascendant sectors and emergent forms of work in contemporary advanced economies rely on a more entrenched precursor to the platformization of knowledge work through standardized software suites and workflows, suggesting that technical systems have been increasingly simplified to be defined by (at least pockets of) interoperability. Here, new forms of cognitive labor are prioritized, to be produced within industries but, more important, between spheres of economic production, which previously have had little interaction—what Boutang describes as "cognitive capitalism."[67] These wider metaprocesses offer a useful precursor—and contemporary parallel—not just to the platformization of cultural production for more public-facing knowledge products across the creative, cultural, and digital sectors but also to the platformization of knowledge work and communication management itself.

Despite the infrastructural interoperability connecting platform industries and knowledge work alike, the global supply chains of numerous digitized sectors are marked by their sociopolitical discontinuities. Globalized transnational hierarchies of knowledge work are inscribed with economic and racialized divisions of labor through the "offshoring" of more routinized forms of communication work to other regional and national workforces.[68] A proliferation of internationally recognized training certifications in office, enterprise, and data applications has extended the transnational interweaving of the knowledge sector and its stratification of opportunity across a wide variety of labor contexts. Digital-economy scholar Ursula Huws points to the increasing dependency on this global reserve of labor within the hierarchy of advanced Western economies over the last fifty years, coinciding with the "long and slow unravelling" of labor standards, job security, pensions, and other rights for the digital economy's "privileged core workforce" in Western nations.[69]

A transnational perspective on the platform economy highlights additional forms of "gray labor," specific to categories of nonelite knowledge workers. This is a form of work between the knowledge production of "white-collar" work, still representative of information processing, and "blue-collar" work, traditionally defined as manual labor and materials processing. Gray-collar work involves the repetitive labor of transforming and processing digital objects, such as scanning analog books for online repositories or moderating social-media content.[70] By 1962, Austrian-American economist Fritz Machlup was already proposing that emerging conceptions of knowledge work should be understood to encompass additional echelons of nonelite workers, such as mail clerks and technicians—today, device manufacturers, repair people, and platform-support services—who still contribute to the knowledge economy through a more manual or technical labor.[71] Gray laborers are today's overlooked workforce, sustaining and propelling the information revolution toward the new intensities of constant connection.[72] Across the globe, the cost of constant connection also reveals itself in terms of resource extraction, manufacturing, and assembly.[73] Given the material and extractive needs of constant connection, mediatization is intertwined with another defining metaprocess of our era: the degradation of our natural environment. Our climate emergency is the ignored externality of our knowledge, platform, and data economies.

Extending Economies of Control

A curtain has descended between the citizen consumers, knowledge workers, and cultural-producers-turned-platform-users and those economic actors who gather new proprietary data sets of everyday media use that are then commodified for purchase, sale, circulation, and aggregation across a wide range of digital advertising, platform, and data-brokerage industry sectors. Yet the data produced is not like traditional marketing data. Rather, it is disaggregated, granular, and thereby has questionable commercial viability for future applications, meaning it must be aggregated with larger and diverse pools of data about audiences-turned-users and users-turned-probabilistic populations. A political and ethical conundrum emerges, separating and distinguishing who, even among commercial actors, has access to this data and for what purpose.[74]

The interoperability of the platform and data-mining industries hinges on commercializing each technological revolution, a competition for—or cloning of—innovations for greater user engagement. Connecting the productive potential of a given platform or device and the data captured therein is foundational to the data-brokerage and digital advertising sales sector. Social media and other connective platforms have long sought to extend their influence throughout online spaces, beyond their primary web domain or apps, to ensure that data produced across the remainder of the web is "platform ready" for integration into their wider economic model.[75] In stark contrast to the openness and freewheeling innovation for which early personal computing and web development was celebrated, the contemporary user environment, devices, and operating systems are remarkably closed to tinkering, adaption, and reprogramming. Instead, they are opaquely governed by the interests and commercial relationships determined by dominant industry actors.

The future-oriented use of these immense pools of user data is both opportunistic and speculative, which itself speaks to longer trends in understanding technological innovation. By 1977, Langdon Winner had conceived of the "function creep" of new technologies for use beyond the applications of their original design. Alongside Clive and Norris's theory about the "expanding mutability" of surveillance infrastructures in 1999, Haggerty and Ericson outlined a reactive and functional coming together of heterogeneous infrastructural and data processes, attending to new uses and novel situations, what they called the "surveillant assemblage" in 2000.[76] Mark Andrejevic sees greater permeability emerging, whereby data collection processes have a "framelessness" extending beyond particular platforms, devices, and infrastructures, from metamedia relationships among types of media use to our physical environment and physiology but also extending data collection beyond preselected criteria and thereby beyond our sense of what and how future application will model, predict, and intervene on behavior.[77]

We need only look to the commercial imperatives of seeking to extend and intensify forms of media use to see the functional mutability of platform design. By intensifying and extending the productive nature of user engagement, platforms create positive externalities for future commercial use—those unexpected socially driven innovations in media use that no programmer or venture capitalist could have predicted. Predicated on novel disconnected practices that were already emerging among young privacy-conscious users on other image-sharing platforms, Snapchat's limited-duration video posts—designed to disappear after twenty-four hours—represented an innovation that fostered new intensities of user engagement, by disrupting an early affordance of social networking platforms—that is, the persistence of content. Quickly cloned across

Meta's Instagram and Facebook platforms, this competitive edge has become an industry standard for encouraging greater spontaneity in embodied and visual performativity from video-producing users, increased diversification of engagement types in a single multifunction platform, and, therein, the foundation for developing the present state of facial recognition software and related data production.

Whereas communication management in the last century may have been defined by the migratory corporate know-how of "Coca-Cola imperialism," today it is increasingly defined by technological competition and the resulting "platform imperialism."[78] Messaging service apps such as WhatsApp have extended their purview to welcome the group chat and broadcasting functionality precluded from early SMS texting, while extending into the realm of e-commerce and user-to-user payments. This functionality has led to the widespread uptake of WhatsApp in India, where Meta's largest userbases can be found. These are competitive and innovative extensions that can be traced to the Twitter-like microblogging platform Weibo, from the Sino Corporation in mainland China. Similarly, Tencent's internationally facing WeChat and its parallel platform for mainland China users, Weixin, have grown into mega-apps—multifunctional platform ecosystems and economies in their own right—integrating e-commerce, messaging, voice, and video calls, alongside a "Moments" feature comparable to Snapchat. More interactive elements for largely text-based platforms, such as up/down voting, commenting, and variations of "quote tweeting," have been remediated for more complex audiovisual forms that involve sharing clips or remixing—for example, TikTok's "duet" and "stitch" features. Real-time comments or reactions have additionally been integrated into the flow of audio or video tracks, exemplified by the "bullet" comment subtitle system that visualizes reactions and commentary over videos and livestreams, known respectively as "dànmù" and "danmaku" on Chinese and Japanese video-streaming platforms. Even though they are competitive, platform and data-brokerage industries have many horizontal linkages, facilitating flexibility in user actions across the communication environment. These complex hierarchical relationships are defined by forms of economic and infrastructural dependencies, a "platform governance" that sets the stage for emerging forms of "data colonialism" between regional and transnational economic actors.[79]

Industry Conventions of Mass Personalization

For app and cultural-content developers alike, the degree of dependency on the most entrenched market-leading digital platforms is increasing. This dependency alters fundamentally the very practices of cultural production, which are subject to emerging forms of infrastructural and economic "governance" by platforms.[80] From blogging and news to multimedia content and interactive gaming, the products and services circulated through digital platforms are also informed by (and therein contingent on) forms of data-driven feedback processes: "they are malleable, modular in design, and . . . open to constant revision and recirculation."[81] This means that the very forms of cultural production—news, entertainment, music, shopping, fashion, sports—are being tailored in relation to platform-oriented user data.

The metrics of social-media platform use, however, are qualitatively different from the types of metrics journalists and editors need to better understand news literacy or that entertainers and designers need to understand the lifestyle needs of their audiences and consumers.[82] The distribution of these cultural products has shifted to platforms where new data-driven rearticulations of how best to produce engagement with those cultural representations of our world provide a sense of the first layer of Couldry and Hepp's concept of "deep mediatization." The additional layers of deep mediatization come from increasingly data-driven and machine-learning processes, articulating the outputs of multisided interplatform industry relationships, and the additional degrees of data processes between Big Tech and data-brokerage firms at the apex of the digital advertising industry.[83]

Despite the proliferation of personalization and microtargeting technologies, the value of individual users and their communicative experience is disaggregated into moments of advertising "impressions" during use. The US Federal Trade Commission and the UK's Information Commissioner's Office have consistently called for transparency and accountability for the data-brokerage sector, in particular as ad-tech developments lead to the automated real-time auctioning of "user impressions" across vast sets of digital advertising networks.[84] Impressions are the monetization of media use in terms of economically framed definitions of attention, recognized only by industry discourse in the aggregate: "personalization at scale," "mass personalization," or "eyeballs" in industry parlance, the price measured in blocks of thousands or in Cost Per Mille (CPMs).[85] These are not just technological and economic mediations but also ideological disconnections between commercial life and the multiplicity of everyday social experience, discursively collapsing a one-thousand-fold prism of situational moments into infrastructural blocks to evaluate advertising success.

Linear models of communication—information transmission from user devices to platform databases and back—fail to represent even remotely the infrastructural reality of the platform ecosystem today.[86] Multiple forms of continual and automated communication occur between the databases of distinct companies, each serving diverse content and data-processing needs, while responsively shifting among multiple nodes of networked architecture.[87] The computational database itself—an "algorithmic totality" of rules-based programs, data structures, and subroutines—is perpetually incomplete, constantly interrupted by multiple events, users, actions, and other database-to-database communication.[88] The output or a result from a database process is not the end point. Database-to-database communication represents continual deferral of possible end-states of information, a processual "black box" where only the program-structuring inputs and outputs are accessible, and process itself is obscured.[89] Here, the multisited "infrastructural situatedness" of processes mediates user practices involving numerous discrete components, each responsive in different ways to a diversity of variables that inform the conditions for their processing or for their state of engagement within a process.[90] Any conceptualization of media use must take into account the radical variety of user experiences, shifting any analysis mapping isolated communicative settings and the social mediations therein toward a multiplicity of processes that mediate the diversity of a distributed individuated connection *en masse*.[91]

What Comes after Crisis?

Without disconnection we lose perspective on the differentiating and integrating pressures of communication management—which may be traced through economic interventions spurred by crisis. The accompanying recoveries after eras of crisis offer historical hinges, whereby the everyday citizen—altogether, the public—internalizes responsibility, both to accept and effect change within everyday life, in parallel with the

intensification of other political-economic and social changes already
under way, far beyond their control. There is a common narrative in governmental and media messaging during these times that serves to intensify the sense of individual responsibility without much thought about
what comes after the crisis.

This future-oriented myopia involves the "periodization" of economic
crisis, as if it were a limited historical juncture, and belies the continuity
of social changes and their long-term effects. In the late 1920s, as well as
the 1970s, economic instability was accompanied in the UK by electoral
turbulence similar to what followed the Great Recession, which in the UK
saw widespread student protests against austerity measures in 2010, nationwide riots against racialized police brutality in 2011, and protests for
racial equality on both sides of the Atlantic that reached a critical mass in
2020 at the start of the COVID-19 pandemic.[92] In the decade of austerity
between the crises, the stay-and-leave voting patterns of the Brexit referendum in 2016 followed a map of economic disparity in Britain. Similar
to the aftermath of WWII,[93] following the Great Recession and up to the
beginning of COVID-19, a cascading set of crises exposed contradictions
inherent in political-economic life, leading even the staunchest market-
oriented Western governments to embrace extraordinary measures, not
just for the return to political and economic stability but for the maintenance of the continuity of public participation in the spirit of the era.[94]
Whereas Google employees protest their employer's military contracts,
workers at Amazon fulfillment centers protest for humane working conditions. In 2020, UK students protested their algorithmic-deduced final
grade assessments during the COVID-19 cancellation of exams. In 2023,
Hollywood writers and then actors protested streaming services and the
imminent threat of AI to their very occupation. Across social and political life, there is a disenfranchised and disconnected well of social
knowledge, testing the economic spirit of constant connection.

What links each of these recent crises, however, is a persistent sense of
self-responsibility for economic recovery, despite their national or global
nature. The sociologist Richard Sennet speaks of a staunchly American
sense of individualism noticeable after the Great Recession; similar sen-
timents were found by Stephen McBride and Sorin Mitrea in the UK and
Canada during this same period, where applying a "non-individualistic
lens" for understanding austerity was perceived as avoiding personal responsibility for managing one's own economic insecurity.[95] Bourdieu ob-

served the "obviousness" of economic realities as they are experienced in everyday life, which translates to individualized, subjective responsibility amid unequal yet collective disenfranchisement—the "destiny effect" of internalizing self-stigmatizing forms of economic isolation.[96]

Precarious employment continues to be understood by many as an individual problem: self-blame, on the one hand, accompanied by reduced expectations, on the other, and, during crisis, forms of individual sacrifice underpinned by the hope of a collective ameliorating of the situation. Following the Great Recession, personal resilience through reduced consumption and tightened domestic budgets was framed as contribution to collective recovery.[97] COVID-19 has seen something similar. Government messaging and social-media users alike frame collective recovery with messages about individual responsibility, with individuals in turn performatively demonstrating how they have changed their everyday practices to cope and keep collectively safe. Disenfranchisement translates to an individualized sense of despair, underpinning our disconnected sociality amid the pressures of constant connection.

Across these half-century periods, from the Great Depression to the 1970s recession to the Great Recession and the COVID-19 pandemic, the erosion of hard-won social protection and the retreat of private-sector responsibility has left individuals feeling largely responsible for their fates, even among states with relatively strong welfare and public health care traditions such as the UK and Canada. This matrix of uncertainty and working life matured in the information-era 1990s and 2000s but metastasized in the platform era of the last decade, contributing to an intensified fragmentation and routinization of activities that provide entrepreneurial autonomy for some and anxiety-ridden burdens of individual responsibilization for others. These tensions lay at the intersection of economic uncertainty and communication overload. The political and economic realities of encroaching disenfranchisement translate to an individualized sense of despair underpinning our disconnected sociality amid the pressures of constant connection.

TWO

Managing Time

Deluged, anxious, overwhelmed. It takes time to check and recheck our phones, to keep up with the constant flow of social-media posts, and to manage the inboxes that increasingly represent our professional "to-do" list. This is the time it takes to manage our communication environment. Technology, however, has a more meandering, promiscuous way of inserting itself into the human experience than many expect or can casually account for: networked platforms intervene and reorganize how we keep track of time, not by minutes, hours, and days of everyday life but by the mediated flow of communication that fills screens with notifications and floods inboxes with new tasks to which we must attend. Managing communication always involves practices of managing time, but how we connect to others is rearticulating the content of communication in such a way that time is a message of its own, legible in the communication practices of others.[1]

Most days, all day, Chris sits at home in South London in front of his laptop, immersed in his academic writing or editing work but without his email or web browser open. Chris, forty-six, is at the upper age limit of participants I interviewed. In contrast to the early career adults at the heart of this book, he began his professional life before owning a mobile phone or having broadband internet at home and has some steadfast rules about managing connection as a way of managing productivity and protecting his few evenings off from his night job. He is the first to acknowledge the consequences of not being permanently online, being acutely aware of the pitfalls of avoiding constant connection.[2] He schedules when he will "put the email on," but he knows that he is failing to persistently chip away at the growing list of unread messages in his inbox: "It . . . really *built up* and it became a bit of a 'thing.' . . . I ended up with this huge number of emails . . . becoming *a burden* in itself and it made me *suffer* because it felt like something I ought to be doing."

For Chris and many others, freelance work means a continuous effort to chase, develop, and manage collaborations on a contract-to-contract, project-to-project basis in order to make ends meet. After a particularly stressful winter, Chris recognized that he was simply unable to accommodate the continual flow of online communication. Since then, any accumulation of unanswered emails causes him anxiety and makes him adjust his workday accordingly, around his inbox. But this takes time away from his primary work responsibilities rather than helping him to fulfill them.

Zaina rolls her eyes and scoffs at the idea of being able to resist distraction and responsibly manage communication flow. As a twenty-eight-year-old tech-sector journalist, her next story must be better than her last, so she knows the value of staying on top of industry trends and the opportunities that can come from the blurring of the social and the professional: "You just get totally *warped into this world* where if you miss a status update about so-and-so's job, or so-and-so's gig, or so-[and-]so's event . . . it's like *overload*, you know? . . . It feels like you're just not on top of things. Honestly, the best thing for me to do sometimes is just drop out and tune out."

She gives examples of hypothetical interpersonal interactions and event announcements, all fleeting opportunities. The ephemeral quality of such phenomena and their associated social-media promotion is built into the design of many platforms and their newsfeed algorithms. This distorts a sense of social obligation, compounding the experience of communication overload with feelings of urgency and loss. Like Chris and nearly every early career adult I spoke with, Zaina tries to qualify her desire to better control the situation: "No, I do seriously: I tell myself just don't check it anymore. I have to say, 'That's it. You've got nothing to share over the weekend.'" While constant connection comes at a price measured in time, disconnection is measured in social and professional terms.

In the first few weeks of Canada's COVID-19 restrictions, Hannah found that after virtual university classes, her evenings in isolation blurred late into the night, with each evening blurring into the next. Her typical media practices became exaggerated and tinged with more frustration than usual: "Watching, well partially watching, [a streaming TV comedy] again. I more so have it on in the background, occasionally glancing at it. I've seen every episode at least 3 times now . . . for familiarity and comfort and to fill silence because I hate it. My actual attention was on my phone, which I have not put down in 2 hours even though I don't want to be using it. But I am, because I'm bored out of my mind."

Flipping between social-media platforms, watching and rewatching videos, reading comments, and clicking through links to pandemic news items keeps Hannah awake until 1:00 a.m. nearly every night. She adds, "I don't even enjoy it and I was very tired, but for some reason or another I feel like I'd be missing out on something if I were to go to bed early. I feel like a moth attracted to the light of my phone." Hannah laments, "It's not even a decision or choice to use my phone, I genuinely feel like there's nothing else to do so my hand just reaches for my phone." She once again flips between apps before typing another note into her diary: "Get me off this phone!!!"

There is a speculative, cumulative sense of risk that accompanies connection. It is not always a specific fear of missing out but rather the compounding force of numerous habitual media practices that contribute to the compulsion to be constantly connected. Our compulsion for connection is characterized by degrees of habitual automaticity in practice—with each furtive check for notifications or of inboxes—yet there is an intentionality that regulates one's practices of maintaining connection in relation to perceived social and economic pressures. This is not to be confused with more popular mental health considerations of social-media addiction or an individually disordered experience of compulsivity.[3] It took the urgency of a global pandemic and the isolation that social restrictions brought to many to make the monopolistic qualities of digital connection so clear.

Our vague yet stubborn drive to connect is not always to connect with others: often it only amounts to connecting with the device and platforms themselves, providing that initial social disconnection at the foundation of everyday communication management practices. The interchangeability of multiple overlapping communication practices across competing apps and other modes of communication provides fodder and fuel for this perceived need. There is now popular criticism of Big Tech's manipulative tactics to manage our attention, but this distractedness is not solely a matter of cunning design.[4] This chapter explores how the temporal composition of everyday life—how we meter and regulate our activities in general and our interactions with each other in particular—is changing.

Modular Platform Mediations of Everyday Time

Time is social.[5] Time is not above and beyond everyday life but rather performed in ways that are inescapably entangled with it. Despite what conversational expressions suggest—"to determine the time," "to time something," or even to "take one's time"—time is inherently instrumental and communicative in contemporary life, organizing and ordering so many other practices: Norbert Elias argues that "time above all is a means of orientation in the social world, of regulating the communal life of human beings."[6] In *Time: An Essay*, Elias teases apart these two distinct social functions in terms of "time meters" and "time regulators." Clocks represent just one such meter through the observable "sequences of physical events"; the social dimension of time is represented by "common features of observable sequences which people wish to grasp by referring them to a standard sequence," shifting standards for regulating our own practices in time relationally with the world around us.[7] We may manage our communication environments in highly individualized ways, toward diverse sets of actions, but this differentiation comes amid the normative force and expectations of constant connection. Though Elias wrote during the midcentury spread of mass broadcast communication, not in an era of individually networked, mobile, and data-driven platform communication, his analysis of social change captures a greater sense of fragmentation among everyday practices than the collective timing standards of his era might suggest. In that context Elias asked, "What do clocks really show when we say they show the time?"[8] I ask something similar about platforms and constant connection: what do our screens really show when we say they show connection?

We no longer turn only to the clock to tell time: the fragmented, observable flow of communication tasks—relationally, anxiously, and imaginatively—intervenes as new sets of meters setting the pace of constant connection. Technology mediates these forms of social coordination, though, as the sociologist of science and technology Helga Nowotny notes, "technologies do not manufacture time, any more than clocks do."[9] Media technologies do intervene, however, reconstituting the ways in which we experience time and timing, organizing new temporalities of digital practices, and orienting social practices toward a particular utility—data production.

External to and independent of human activity, nature offered the earliest sets of time meters that allowed for practices to be organized, while also providing the basis for cooperation and coordination between sets of individuals. Today, the US Naval Observatory Master Clock, which itself depends on the aggregate accuracy of numerous atomic clocks, keeps the internet, cell phones, GPS devices, and numerous other digital platforms collectively in sync: "Time is the most accurately measured quantity that humans have come up with."[10] As a society, we have developed technologies that measure human performance to such a degree of temporal accuracy that they not only outstrip any human capacity to observe but also exceed the capacity of the technology itself to guarantee its measurement outside of a laboratory setting. Consider, for instance, the ambiguous evidence of photo-finish technologies in sports, from sailing and horse racing to swimming and sprinting.[11] These are the measurements afforded by technology, institutionalized within infrastructures and processes but disconnected from our everyday experience.[12] The technological "instant" has been disaggregated far beyond our own subjective sense of time, yet in social life, the "now" of synchronicity, or coordination of interpersonal practices, is always defined in terms of how we define, meter, and regulate delay.[13] Temporalities of connection are relationally attuned to experiences and practices of disconnection.

Human cognitive faculties—including comparison, assessment, and (re)orientation—are inextricably linked to communication practices in a manner that complicates the experience of time. Rather than a single linear timeline from past to present and toward the future, multiple temporalities are cognitively invoked in everyday life: individuals draw on diverse past experiences to assess and act in the present, with consideration of possible outcomes in the future, while bringing distinctions between multiple observations to possible future actions.[14] This is true even when those practices are not specifically focused on scheduling, duration, speed, or another explicitly temporal measurement. With the tracking of past events, human activity in the present becomes similarly observed and interrupted, with the sense that the future can be both assessed and influenced. Even the earliest mediating tools for tracking changes in nature and recording information about simple forms of economic exchange represented an extension of the human ability to synthesize and compare. Past-oriented observation and interaction, "activated and patterned by human experience," informs decisions in the present and plans for the future.[15] Similarly, degrees of control are exerted by individual, bureaucratic, and commercial actors alike comparing past accounts and behaviors with those in the present, with the hope of influencing the future.

Time is written into that synthesizing and calibrating capacity of the individual, but platforms intervene among the temporalities and chronologies of how we connect with each other socially. The limited storage capacity of earlier mobile phones meant, for example, that for the first time in human history, the bulk of written communication being produced was designed to disappear.[16] The past of SMS chats was lost, making space for incoming texts and prioritizing flow over permanence. Two separate studies of Facebook Groups dedicated to various generational media memories and cultural nostalgia found that algorithmic interventions not only constrained but frustrated user and community management of their timelines. In terms of digital content posted or produced by users, Anne Kaun and Fredrik Stiernstedt found that fresh content is prioritized so that a more continual flow of posts and comments perpetuate further user engagement, itself an opportunity for the production of new posts, comments, reactions, and interactions by users.[17] Christian Pentzold and Manuel Menke found that users could not figure out a way to produce searchable online archives of their own digital content or simply maintain linear chronological histories of posts in their group.[18] In their place, other users (and uses) began to dominate the online communities. By soliciting comments and enticing interactions among other users, particular types of posts maintained a higher degree of visibility, bumped to the top of group pages and newsfeeds through more performative relational practices attuned to the particular algorithmic functionality of the platform.

Across so many social media and connective platforms, algorithms intervene, ordering the display and accessibility of their posts—anchoring the possibilities of social practice within particular mediated temporalities of platform design. The "recency" or "time decay" of online content is just one form of algorithmic weighting that can be used to determine the importance of a search engine or social-media content vis-à-vis the platform's functionality. Taina Bucher mapped such weightings in her study of the "programmed sociality" of Facebook.[19] Degrees of affinity between the user who is posting and other users additionally and differentially determine a post's immediate visibility across the wider social network and its persistence of visibility in the short-term in relation to other content. These weightings determine who sees what within the social-media timeline or newsfeed, refracting the timelines of content availability in diverse ways and resulting in a different algorithmic curation of content for different moments of use and users.[20] On screens and social-media feeds, the past is stale and the present is an extending horizon, perpetually refreshed, across which multiple parallel temporalities of the new, the now, are served in different ways at different times to sets of different individual users *en masse*.

Since the mid-2010s, Twitter (now X), Instagram, and Facebook have each introduced greater algorithmic management of user-content on the primary feeds of the platforms' landing pages, in contrast to the previous chronological listing of all relevant content from a particular user's group of "followed" accounts or "friends." These algorithmic platform interventions pale in comparison to the recommendation engines that drive more recent video platforms of TikTok, its mainland China version *Douyin*, and other short video platforms. The algorithmically curated "For You" TikTok page evaluates users (and use) in terms of preference and personality metrics, location and device or operating system environment, and indicators of user interests, while the "success" potential of each video draws from content evaluations using Natural Language Processing and Computer Vision Technology.[21] TikTok programmatically disconnects the user from navigating among options of recommended videos, only permitting them to swipe further into the automatically curated stream. Tech journalists and industry insiders have commented that this is a more "algorithm-friendly" design oriented toward media consumption, in contrast to the "user-friendly" interface of more socially oriented social-network platforms.[22] This is not lost on TikTok users, who, Ignacio Siles and colleagues have shown, develop not just an "algorithmic awareness" sensitive to platform mediation but have translated that literacy into concerted, intensive practices seeking to "train the app" so that its personalization algorithms are better attuned to their preferences.[23]

Disconnected and Disoriented

Every morning there is a "fear of missing out" for Joshua, aged nineteen: "FOMO . . . I insist to scroll through EVERY story and post on Instagram, I insist [on] checking EVERY snap on Snapchat." Martina, twenty, echoes this common refrain among participants of reaching for her phone first thing in the morning. "Since I had just woken up, I feel the need to keep myself in the know." She equates this habitual practice of checking social media to the continuation of her social world and the messages it has accrued "in the eight hours I've been asleep." In March 2019, when Facebook, Instagram, and WhatsApp suffered widespread outages due to server-configuration issues, users were confronted with an unsettling form of disconnection.[24] During the server outage, she found herself "annoyed" and "uncomfortable" with "nothing to check while I am on my phone." Rather than turning to other platforms or enjoying the break from social media, she decided to "check the issue by using both [my] phone and laptop to try using Instagram [and] I decide[d] to check the app almost every hour until it works again." Writing in her diary about the same server outage, Filipa points to its central effect on her social life at eighteen years old: "Not being able to use Instagram is a big deal. It's the main source of communication between my friends and I." She continues by outlining just how collective the experience turned out to be: "I spent a lot of the day checking Instagram, deleting and reinstalling the app even sending emails to see why this was happening. Honestly, I completely freaked out having been disconnected from my friends. I felt isolated and I wonder if they were also dealing with this. When Instagram finally started working, we all went straight to the group chat to talk about it. Funny enough they did all the same things I did during the period Instagram was down."

Without the metered, regulating engagement with constant connection in our day-to-day life, we can become somewhat unmoored and adrift. Time-regulating practices involve not just observation but the exertion of control using an independent set of changing reference points, useful because of their distance from natural events and human actions and interactions. The simplest example of this is the hourglass or clock. Such tools have steady, standardized units along an observable set of sequential changes, providing a rigid meter that acts as a portable backdrop against which other processes are assessed. A manifold of uses and applications, some mutable, stem from the design of such tools. The hourglass or clock can be used at will to measure and regulate two or more sets of practices or processes that the human user wants to compare, contrast, or analyze.[25] In this manner, time metering can compare simultaneous processes in the present, memories and records of which could be drawn from the past, in order to plan for the future. Time-regulating practices allow for the assessment and comparison of temporal processes in relation to one another. The length of time it takes for an hourglass to empty, or the stop-and-go of seconds and minutes on a stopwatch, offers a modular, independent timing system that mediates the ways in which humans reflect on and interact with each other and the world around them.

This is not to say that our email inboxes, TikTok and Instagram stories, and push notifications crowding our mobile phone screens are akin to a sunrise or sunset or that they are explicitly designed to be timing devices. But maintaining constant connection across numerous platforms allows us to observe the flow of external processes that constitute social life: the dawn, midday, and dusk of social and professional connective platform interactions—meters for our personal senses of responsibility in everyday life. A common refrain among my research participants, which many readers may recognize in their own daily lives, is reaching for our phones the first thing after waking and only putting them down at night, moments before going to sleep. Maintaining connection to communication platforms offers the pace, rhythm, and differentiation of temporal metering. Against this backdrop, discrete interpersonal activities coalesce for comparison and management as much as for distraction, enjoyment, or camaraderie.

Media is also something that we consume, and in doing so, we produce and reproduce "temporal arrangements" of use and consumption: like all forms of consumption, there are traces and patterns of practice, those "sticky footprints" produced by media use and communication practices alike and that in their digital form are increasingly referred to as traces.[26] Among other social cues, these digital traces are compared, fragmented, multiplied, and ordered in time as part of our cognitive and social capacities for temporal orientation.[27] Human attention has thresholds, however. Degrees of certainty in the interpretation of these signals and arrangements can be lost or replaced by the grasping unintelligibility of information overload.

It is not the flow of communication itself that acts as the rigid temporal regulator but rather the perceived potential for communication, a near-compulsive need to maintain connection. Hannah laments that "when I do nothing, that's when I feel shitty," admitting that when she scours social-media platform after social-media platform, she "wasn't really fully paying attention to anything I was doing, sort of going through it as if on autopilot. . . . I'll be actively thinking about how I do not want to be scrolling through this useless content, but I am doing so anyways." In her diary, she digs deeper into the lingering fear behind this: "I guess it's a fear of missing out (FOMO) . . . wanting to always be doing something, talking to someone, getting information about something or another even if I couldn't care less about said information." Opportunities for social engagement and commercial interventions by platform technology mingle across our everyday communication environment, vying for our attention in a way that contributes to the push and pull of temporal regulation in everyday life.[28]

Our Conflict with Overconnection

Yichen's pizza was not the only one burned during the course of this research; a number of participants were left with overcooked dinners after being too preoccupied with their screens. He complains about a group IM chat with his friends from the university: "The conversation they had was really big, so I have hundreds of unread messages on my phone. This annoys me a little bit. . . . While scrolling through messages, I got too into it, and I forgot I had pizza baking in the oven." In workplace contexts, being overwhelmed by an unexpected deluge of messages was a common enough occurrence to be persistently anticipated. But how does the flow of platform communication itself, as well as that of a given interaction, contribute to communication overload?

Recognizing our perceived need for constant connection involves learning to manage time amid the pace of notifications and the lure of multiple algorithmic temporalities; this can easily become a question of managing one's communication environment or of being managed by it. Both of these outcomes produce a disconnected disposition to constant connection. Our communication platforms represent new types of time-metering and time-regulating tools, which mediate practices that are interpersonal though also individualized. The interpersonal nature of communication platforms is inflected with the temporalities of others, of their observable digital practices and the pressures we associate with our relationships and responsibilities to them. The individualistic nature of platform use and interface design contribute to a further responsibilization for each of us, individually: there are few agreed-upon limits on the expectations for maintaining constant connection and little literacy in how best to self-regulate the seemingly endless opportunities to connect with others online.

Onscreen notifications interrupt and distract, while numerical notifications of unread messages on an app or in an inbox offer a quantified symbol of the mounting pressure, the often-felt sense of communication overload. Zaina teases that she feels a parental urgency toward any new message—"Really, I feel like they're little children crying, 'Look at me, I need this attention'"—before stating more succinctly: "You don't understand; zero inbox means zero responsibility." Yichen feels the same pressure to attend to each and every message in his group chat with friends, at the cost of other tasks. "I ended up finishing the messages, but the pizza is completely burned."

Clocks and calendars, transport and broadcast schedules, in addition to the once-conventional division of a typical workday from free time, have long been accepted as providing a fixed temporal scaffolding for everyday life. Such tools offer conventionalized temporal meters against which the scheduling of diverse and numerous activities could be individualized without forfeiting the possibility of social coordination between individuals and groups. These predigital time-metering tools are based on a collective acceptance of how time will be organized: coordinating with others in terms of twenty-four hours to seven days a week, nine to five except on weekends for many, and firm trust in scheduled departures and arrivals, as well as the predictability of morning and afternoon rush hour. Such normative realities are temporally regulating, whereby commonly understood units of time allow for the coordination of practices between individuals.

Today, forms of temporal regularity in everyday life, such as our minute-to-minute maintenance of constant connection and the persistent infrastructural availability of networked platforms, are often obscured by our individualistic focus on the unexpected, disruptive, and contingent day-to-day experiences of these platforms. Cognitive sociologist Eviatar Zerubavel outlines how the longer-term normalization of more consistent collective temporalities provides the field of possible divergence among shorter-term sets of individual practices.[29] This individualized flexibility depends on the "rigidification," to use Zerubavel's term, of other temporally oriented practices as expected conventions across wide sets of individuals, often including those who do not benefit from the flexibility that those conventions bring to others. Platform and device interfaces, from push notifications and inboxes to social-media feeds and chat windows, offer new layers of temporal metering atop the self-regulating practices and collective influence of the clocks, calendars, and schedules of the predigital era.

The Temporal Divisions of Labor

It wasn't until he got to the top level of the double-decker bus that Scott, thirty-three, realized his phone was not connecting. His morning commute across London stretches to almost an hour most days, and so, as an account manager in communications and social-corporate responsibility, he uses that time to start checking in on clients and addressing emails. Scott writes in his diary, "[Mobile phone] wasn't working on the bus this morning for some reason, so I couldn't access my emails. I feel like I was behind all day because of it." Checking and rechecking platforms may maintain connection, but it is in and of itself a time-consuming task, and even a brief loss of connection—one hour—has left Scott feeling out of sync for the remainder of his day.

Everyday anxiety finds its affective basis in the experience of uncertainty and, therein, represents a cruel adjunct to our desire for control. Etymologically, the term *anxiety* relates to Romantic and Germanic words for "narrowness" and "tightening" and has been linked by existential philosophers to the suffocating angst that cannot be grounded in a particular fear or reality.[30] Much like the economic relationship between calculable risks and the ineffable "cunning of uncertainty" in economic life, fear and anxiety represent an individualized social experience of a distinctly different quality.[31] Time, however, is still implicated in any relationship between uncertainty and a desire for control. The famed (and infamous) psychotherapist Sigmund Freud argued that anxiety comes from a compulsive demand best characterized as "a particular state of expecting the danger or preparing for it, even though it may be an unknown one."[32] Internet scholar Annette Markham points to the affective response that digital detoxes and other forms of disconnection provoke among young adults: they could not locate themselves "in the world . . . in their larger social networks" without the call and response of being connected and interpreting the observable connection of others.[33] In many ways, anxieties around constant connection are symptomatic of our struggle to constrain the possibility of the indeterminate world around us and the plausible futures just before us.

In its idealized type, the disconnected practitioner is one that seeks to control the flow and contingencies of constant connection. Scott's inbox, with its waiting emails and flow of new messages, is a time meter that allows him to measure and plan his work throughout the day. His ability to engage with, reply, ignore, or otherwise act on each email, in relation to wider, shifting sets of calls, emails, and meetings, represents his personal communication-management practices, which temporally regulate how and when he engages with particular clients or colleagues and determine how much work he will allow to bleed into his personal life. Early career adults often describe their defensive posturing, where constant checks allowed them to keep ahead of anticipated deluges of emails.

Despite the emotional and often psychological overtones of the words used to describe media practices, such as *anxiety* about incoming messages and *obsession* with checking notifications, inboxes, or social-media updates, these are matter-of-fact descriptions that outline an everyday experience of communication-management practices. From nine to five, Ron works in IT support for a large public sector bureaucracy, outside of which he works in the theater, writing and putting on plays with a changing roster of collaborators. In his diary he describes a typical nine-to-five workday:

> So that won't go away, so if I have 50 emails that I haven't answered at some point there will be 100. I can't change the way that that system works, I am subject to it.
>
> Panic begets panic. I checked my emails on my phone twice during lunchtime, somehow afraid that, because I'd received so many emails at [work], I must have been *deluged* on my [personal] account as well.

If we accept that practices of overconnection have spread from workplace media behavior to personal media behavior, we now see the panic and anxiety of workplace *communication* spreading to personal communication. These are neither exceptional moments of crisis nor failures of individual responsibility. These everyday crisis scenarios stem from accepted norms relating to everyday practices of managing one's communication environment. There is another embodied contour of political-economic control manifest between particular types of media practices: Ron had to wait until his lunch hour to check personal communication. The durational nature of his schedule, working on a computer to provide IT support from nine to five, involves a prohibition of nonwork-related communication. Even when such prohibitions are not explicit, in many workplaces, there is a sense that one does not want to be seen on a personal phone or with social-media sites open. The simple reality of physically sharing a workspace with colleagues and superiors represents a setting of peer-to-peer, as well as managerial, surveillance.

In a clear contrast to the degrees of autonomy afforded to those whose time and schedules enjoy privileged protection for interpersonal, entrepreneurial, and creative work, rigid rules or expectations about what types of technology use and media practices are appropriate during work hours often define the working regime for the various echelons of employees undertaking supportive, administrative, or assisting practices. Miki is a twenty-five-year-old hairstylist who apprentices under a master stylist at a salon and works as a social-media intern at a PR company. When she is at the salon, greeting and prepping clients or tidying up, she is not allowed to use her phone. While the same is true for her desktop-based work at the PR firm, she can sometimes excuse being on her phone to check the social-media profiles and posts that she manages. Outside of these roles, however, her career will depend on developing a client base and other potential contacts for work on photo shoots as a professional stylist. She considers promoting her portfolio and networking online a necessity. In a more traditional service setting of a café, Henry, twenty-three, sneaks to the washroom to use his mobile phone in between waiting tables. After having felt incoming email notifications buzzing in his pocket, he can finally check in case there are urgent edits on his latest freelance commission as a music journalist. In her study of media practices among high- and low-wage workers across a number of American cities, Julia Ticona reveals a divide between the autonomy gained by higher-echelon knowledge workers and lower-status service workers for whom the use of personal mobile and platforms seeks to resist, in a manner, their highly controlled working conditions. This is often, in part, a matter of filling those "in-between" times of nine-to-five schedules

or shift work with the distractions and pleasures of interpersonal communication, social media, or games. These furtive moments, switching
between work-mandated practices to personal media consumption and
communication practices, are chances to wrest some control over one's
day and, through communication practices, to manage emotional states
by elevating boredom and checking-in on loved ones.[34]

Joanna is a thirty-year-old finance account manager, Farzan is a thirty-
two-year-old editor for a well-known cultural magazine, and Sydney is
a twenty-six-year-old manager at a large London entertainment venue.
Despite the diverse and contrasting working schedules they keep, with
managers and colleagues in North America and clients from around the
world, they wake up every day to a backlog of overnight interactions.
The perpetual functioning and availability of platform databases affords
these forms of "connected asynchronicity," whereby access to an email,
voicemail, or social-media platform does not necessitate simultaneous
engagement between sender and recipient—unlike, for example, a video
or telephone call.[35] Despite the reality that those emails will still be waiting for them in the morning, Sydney and Farzan both routinely check
their email in the middle of the night, hours before their alarm clocks
go off. Sydney reviews late-night intake reports after the close of his
venue, and Farzan keeps track of requests and reviews from editors in
other time zones. In her media diary, Joanna describes something similar: "Couldn't sleep last night so was light in waking up. Woke up before
alarm and checked [phone] for time (mistake!). Had 10 unread msgs [sic]
which made me wide awake and got up 30 mins earlier than usual. . . .
Checked [phone] as was getting morning coffee at local coffee shop. Normally check and respond to emails and texts if I am waiting around."

These work-oriented media practices, again, seem to migrate to the
times and spaces of personal life, translating practices of constant connection into habits of monitoring and keeping ahead of any potential
messages or updates and spreading from more work-oriented media practices to personal communication and even entertainment media. Joanna
surfs channels and websites, while scrolling past messages and keeping
an eye on her email inbox and text messages in case her boss is trying to
get in touch. Sydney and Farzan similarly admit to checking their social-
media accounts moments after they review the emails that have come in
overnight. Eugene, a junior lawyer at a television production company,
still checked his personal mobile phone during our interview, though he

was only obliged to monitor his work phone. Whether it is midweek or a Sunday evening, the persistent availability of networked platforms, from SMS to email and social networking, generates an uncertainty of what could come next that underlies the potential incoming flow of communication. Even if these individuals are not always on, the schedules of their disparate clients and collaborators, time zones of industry, and network availability remains 24/7.

In contrast, Evelyn, thirty-three, was a career executive in marketing until she had her first of two young children, at which point she shifted into a freelance-style relationship with key clients so that she could work from home while the children were young. Her husband, David, travels quite a lot for work and consistently talked in interviews about "rising above" the flow of communication by constantly managing his long client roster, day or night. Evelyn has found that her opportunities to connect with others, whether for work or otherwise, have been configured around morning park times with other young mothers, planning lunches, and naps. "We don't have time to go on email, check back and forth," she says, explaining that she can only really sit down at the computer in the evening if her husband is home and can take care of dinner, or once the kids are in bed. For everything else, "It's text-based . . . so it's always—are you going to Monkey Music this morning? Are you going to the [thrift shop]? Okay see you in a half hour. You know, do you want to come back to ours for lunch after? That type of thing, all by text." While still characterized by flexibility rather than mere employment and economic autonomy, this freelance approach to being a business-of-one comes from having to attend to other responsibilities, which would be difficult in many traditional, fulltime employment positions.

Task-Based Units of Communication and Time

From analog file folders to the digital interfaces of apps, with their notifications and inboxes, practices of managing a communication environment are often defined by temporal utility and temporal scarcity. Like all time-metering and regulating technologies, observable units of time or activity frame our engagement with the technology itself and with others through that technology. In comparison to the clock, which once again serves as a useful metaphor, "the physical device is so arranged that it can function as a transmitter of messages and thereby as a means of regulating behaviour."[36] This holds true for the material design of filing systems that were so central to managing communication in the past and to the interfaces of our contemporary communication platforms today. If the clock communicates that thing we call time, then our interpersonal platforms communicate a great deal about how connection today is assessed and organized in daily life.

Peter is twenty-seven and works in computer and network architecture. His morning ritual begins with a scan of the platform interface. He checks his email to better understand the day ahead of him. "Because typically if I get an email, it's asking me to do something and typically the thing it's asking me to do involves a computer so, yes. So I go and sit in front of the computer, maybe I'll put the kettle on and I read my emails and try to, like, figure out what I need to do today." In the context of his work, addressing these email interactions represents engaging with and possibly completing tasks for his colleagues or a client. These tasks make up his everyday activities.

For the same reason, Hannah declares her "extremely unhealthy fear of checking my emails. . . . I don't even really get that many, but for some reason I cannot bring myself to do this on a regular basis." As an eighteen-year-old student managing some of her first career-related work experiences while trying to keep up with assignments, Hannah knows that avoiding "these adult things . . . is unreasonable, so I simply need to do it." The practice of assessing the day's tasks as a series of interactions extends for many beyond the work context to include scheduling social plans or household and parental responsibilities, among other tasks: the phone call that needs to be returned; the coffee with a friend that is long overdue; the errand; the playdate; a doctor's appointment that needs to be rescheduled owing to the busy workweek ahead. The varied rhythms of maintaining constant connection, and the leisurely personal-communication platforms that are comparable in format and interwoven with more productivity-oriented interactions, reinforce processes of learning to manage time in one's communication environment.

There is a mediating syntax to the practices of maintaining and managing connection that orders opportunities for and practices of disconnection. As the clock divides the day into minutes and hours, the organizational syntax of platform communication divides everyday connection into discrete units of communication. Emails and messages, posts and shares, reactions and comments, phone and video calls, stories and moments all represent similarly discrete, "focused" units of interaction and are displayed as such on device interfaces—in contrast, for example, to the buzz of a busy street or a crowded bar. Intelligible in their own way, these forms of "unfocused interaction" structure the potential for purposeful "focused interaction." Goffman defines unfocused interaction in face-to-face situations as the "fully shared basis of unfocused" engagement between all of those who are copresent, in contrast to the multiple "partially shared bases of focused interaction" when specific mutual interpersonal engagements occur.[37] We are exploring the mediated equivalence of unfocused interaction of maintaining constant connection—that background from which degrees of disconnection emerge to efficiently manage successive sets of focused interactions. Once again, I turn to a theoretical account of time as a synthesis of observable events, unfocused and focused interactions or otherwise: "To perceive time . . . requires focusing units (humans) capable of forming a mental picture in which events A, B, C, following one after another, *are present together* and yet, at the same time, are seen *clearly as not having happened together*; it requires beings with a specific potential for *synthesis* which is *activated and patterned by experience*."[38]

On a given platform's interface, individuals' emails, social-media comments, or even notifications from different apps on a device home screen are present together yet clearly not produced by the same sender or commenter. Kaitlyn, twenty-one, outlines her habitual assessment of diverse notifications at the start of her day before college and the end of her day after her evening restaurant shift:

> I wake up around 5:30 a.m. . . . [and] the first thing I do is check my cellphone. I go through all my notifications, respond to text messages and emails, and scroll through social media, specifically Instagram, to catch up on anything that happened overnight.
>
> When I get home from work after a closing shift I am tired and all I want to do is get ready for bed. I try not to focus too much on using media because it will take up too much time and I try going to sleep as soon as possible. I use my phone most efficiently at this time, just answering important notifications quickly and avoiding wasting time scrolling through social media.

Her engagement with the glut of device-level notifications and app-specific interactions represents that moment of synthesis, when communication-management practices group, classify, and tease apart priorities relating to blocks of discrete interactions. The asynchronous flow of interaction is mediated toward single, legible units of digital communication, demonstrably separated as such across sets of notifications, unread messages, or missed calls. Much like a single paper file of the vertical filing cabinet, any given digital interaction is framed by the particular and explicit affordances of the communication management platform and its user interface.

Managing Communication as Separate and Separable

Eugene complains about the meandering conversations among his colleagues that reduce the filing-like utility and accessibility of particular client correspondence stored by an email platform: "The thing is [that] the important emails get lost between the chain of fifteen emails where they're talking about some picture or something. And then when a client sends something it gets lost in between and it's very annoying." The word *file* comes from the Latin *filum*, denoting the earlier filament on which separate documents were threaded in chronological order for storage and future access.[39] Scholars point to the organizational characteristics of paper documents, in particular their ability to be discrete units unto themselves or bound together, both "separate and separable."[40] Where our professional and interpersonal correspondences mingle, the facility of our filing-like communication platforms is reduced, often requiring greater upkeep and management or greater proficiency in using the platform's search functions.

Today, we see the proliferation of platforms in order to separate the internal chatter among colleagues from formal client or contact communication. These tools represent the platformization of staged performativity and less staged interpersonal conduct. This echoes the "dramaturgical" approach that Canadian sociologist Erving Goffman developed to improve interpersonal practices in both personal and workplace roles by considering everyday communication in terms of performance teams and backstage and front-stage roles.[41] Among a team or with clients, this goes beyond making the invisible aspects of one's efforts visible: a considerable amount of time and energy is expended to divert attention to the myriad activities involved in fulfilling one's role. In many ways, cc-ing team members and managers on project email threads becomes a stage for performing accountability. Email as a platform is the site for performing a committed attentiveness to incoming messages, thereby meeting expectations of near constant availability with an immediate reply. Across today's multiple mobile and networked platforms, managing the flow of communication practice represents a "front stage" of performing to colleagues, clients, and superiors, in contrast to the numerous types of "backstage" communication when and where such performances are less necessary. Under the social-distancing restrictions of the COVID-19 pandemic, Christoph Bagger and Stine Lomberg found that the "forced disconnection" from copresent opportunities for interpersonal communication had the effect of reinforcing "the ideology of connectivity" and the performative rabbit hole of greater and greater "optimization of self, work, and life."[42]

On the one hand, workplace productivity apps that combine thematic instant-message channels and task- or goal-management tools allow teams to enjoy a productive backstage for collegial coordination and interpersonal communication.[43] On the other hand, database platforms are geared toward Customer Relationship Management (CRM). They are used across a wider variety of industries to ensure up-to-date and easily accessible profiles on external partners, clients, or collaborators, with details of the relationship and past communications for a given user that may have to connect with a client or otherwise engage with a project, even if just to return a single email or phone call. In today's platform-mediated gig economy, we see the fragmentation of this customer into the real-time management of singular, ad hoc interactions between available contractors and clients online. The history of past performance is reduced to platform metrics and reviews for both parties, but the management of such assessment is removed from the purview of any given user, to be automated by the platform itself.[44]

As with the file and the memo, treating fragmented representations of digital communication as discrete interactions organized along a platform interface involves a contextual temporality created by how the user engages, first, with the platform and, second, with individual interactions. This gives way to a task-based perception of communication but also to a task-based perception of time, somewhat disconnected from clock time. A task is something that needs to be engaged to be completed. This engagement is not determined solely by clock time but rather has a task- and context-specific duration. This notion of task-based time has been associated with preindustrial societies where agricultural labor was a matter of doing tasks as needed until they were completed rather than spending an assigned amount of clock time on a given activity.[45] The latter is more attuned to an industrial setting, where labor continues only until the end of the workday and then continues when the next shift "clocks in." As I have written elsewhere, these distinctions contribute to divergent temporalities around which much of everyday life is organized, where interpersonal communication becomes increasingly defined as

> fragmented, quantified, and temporally limited actions to be completed ... lending itself to seeing communication not simply as activities of engagement between individuals but as practices of managing the communication environment. . . . With individuals attending to communication as tasks and to the constant actions of maintaining connection, there is a partial displacement of attention away from the quality and content of interaction. . . . Practice drifts towards and fixates on the need to maintain networked connection alongside interface-level practices that seek to manage the potential quantities, tasks, and patterns such connection introduces to each day.[46]

Ways of communicating and, for our discussion here, of managing one's communication environment do not emerge from a vacuum. They are part of a constellation of social contexts, societal changes, and the multiple trajectories of technological advancement. The "task" has emerged as a particular unit of communicative practice. Much like earlier forms of organizing communication, such as the letter, the report, the memo, and the file, the communicative task emerges from within relationships of multiple communication channels and interlocking systems that provide for the production, storage, and access of communicative content.[47] Tasks highlight the way in which particular activities are temporally organized: units through which we have begun to perceive and manage our connections with each other. This task-based ordering of communication is central to the asynchronicity of platforms, written into the syntax of their interface design but intertwined with the twenty-four-hour persistence of internet availability, platform databases, and the accessibility of content.

Taking Control through Asynchronicity

The temporal pressures of constant connection—of being overwhelmed and deluged—have seen practices of asynchronous communication management migrate to colonize and reorder our preferences for "live" interaction: individualized adjustments among one's repertoire of media practices are translating once synchronous modes of interaction to more individually timed, editable forms of asynchronous interaction, a temporal shift in practice toward the disconnected sociality of constant connection.

Marco states bluntly, "I am not really a phone person . . . I don't really like to *just* use my voice to communicate . . . because if you're saying something I want to *see how you say that*." The twenty-five-year-old lab assistant moved to the UK from Italy for work and studying. He is quite dismissive of the phone as a mode of communication because it is a "*muted environment*, muted from direct contact." It brackets out his "poses" and stops him from literally seeing "what's going on, on your face, what are your expressions." It is aurally embodied but not visually embodied. He does not feel as comfortable on the phone as he does in person. He continues with a comparison to text messages: "You can't really express everything in a text, but a text saves you from that moment of awkwardness, kind of, silence or waiting because it's already there, it's all there what I wanted to say to you, it's there. That's what I said, you read it, if you want to reply to me something, then you do. You do *reply on the basis of what is written.* . . . It is just like very, very—how to say—simple, you know. So, it's just there."

Outside face-to-face interaction, where conversation benefits from the full range of body language, Marco prefers to limit connection to an asynchronous medium, to simply and directly craft and present his side of the conversation: "it's there." Seeking a degree of temporal control is at the heart of this. Marco is avoiding an ongoing, staggered messaging thread, preferring a single interaction that includes everything that he "wanted to say," avoiding the lulls and uncontrollable silences of a phone conversation. Each form of communication is managed, ordered, entwined vis-à-vis each other to confer practice-negotiated temporalities between diverse mediums and platforms—a relationship anchored by the relative temporalities of connection and degrees of disconnection to focus on and achieve mutual engagement.

At the end of a day studying and taking research notes on his laptop, interspersed with social-media use, Park began texting a classmate to meet up: "I sent so many pictures on Snapchat to friends in Vancouver, but in the evening I text and then phone my friend to say I will be late meeting her downtown." After dinner, he shifted from the immediacy of sending "Snaps" to friends on the West Coast to a collaborative in-person photo session: "we were taking some pictures together, edited them and uploaded them to VSCO." In contrast to Instagram or Snapchat, VSCO (Visual Supply Company, originally called VSCO Cam) is a creative mobile photo-editing app and sharing platform, with a competitive priority in the platform industry on attracting creative users. While there is horizontal integration to share its content to microcontent-themed communities or other mobile app platforms, there is an opacity to the social-networking affordances of connecting with others through VSCO: programmatic preferences keep users focused on content—favoriting and reposting—without the social-interaction options of messages or comments.[48] Park shifts his social and relational impetus to produce something "more than" just a Snapchat photo but something edited, something collaborative, something to circulate online but in a different way. After dance practice on campus, Ruomei similarly took the time to edit digital content, selecting from among her repertoire of platforms but for a more programmatically social experience: "We shot video for our performance and after doing postproduction, we posted our dance video on Bilibili." Though the morning saw Ruomei on Weibo reading about domestic politics in China and the evening saw her video chatting through WeChat with her parents, she chose Bilibili, a Shanghai-based video-sharing site, for the "dànmù" or bullet-screen comments overlaid and screaming across the screen. By evening, the video had "received about a hundred clicks and several comments." In terms of media practices, constant connection contributes to these sorts of relational reordering of one's communication repertoire with shifting situation-to-situation preferences for particular, expressive temporalities in how we connect with others.

Christina is a twenty-seven-year-old civil servant who volunteers for local political campaigns. She assesses different modes of communication by the amount of control she has in each: "I text a lot, like, I like to write long texts [on my phone]. . . . I like email because you have more room to express yourself than in a text; you can go back and edit what you write. Really! You can go back and check for mistakes in a way that when you're talking on the phone you can't. . . . So yeah, with email you have a lot more—God I sound like a control freak—you have a lot more control over what you write and yeah, you can write properly."

Christina is unequivocal that she can express a more authentic version of herself in text-based, disembodied modes of communication, than in embodied, live forms of communication but with an additional preference for editing control based on the degree of asynchronicity involved—the "instant" message quality that some texts can take in contrast to the longer letter-like qualities of some conversations. For users like her, email is perceived to allow for the most purposefully crafted interactions. It is text-based and asynchronous, so she can edit, reread, and carefully check the message. Each message becomes a composition of her self-presentation in contrast to live speech. Though confident in her communication preference, Christina worries she may come across as a "control freak." She contrasts voiced and partially embodied interaction with the control of editing texts, which allows her to communicate "properly," implying that less-controlled phone interactions are somehow less "proper" forms of self-presentation. This, however, is not always the case: "It depends who it's with. With my parents and a couple of close friends, it's pretty much the same [as email]. *It's just very fluent* and I can talk for a long time and I don't have to kind of think about what I'm saying or think of things to say. . . . [With other people, I'm] not so good. I get very self-conscious and I start thinking excessively about what I'm saying all the time and my voice."

Christina often worries about what she is saying and how she is saying it. She mentions something similar when leaving voicemail messages: "I lose control of the syntax and it *turns into [a] rubble of words* and I want to reset it and I can't." The liveness of the interaction is clearly stressful for Christina; she concentrates on the disarray of her self-presentation, one that does not apply to the full presence of face-to-face interaction.

George explains flatly, "If I type, I feel more natural than when I speak." He works, ironically, in radio. Our interviews took place on his coffee and lunch breaks during the workday, as he spends his evenings with Tania and their young daughter. He is a sound engineer, presents a bimonthly radio segment, and writes on a few blogs, consistently updating his four online social-media profiles. Throughout the day, George is likely working on a few things at once: a radio piece, a few admin emails, or a blog post, listening to music while he does this but chatting with his colleagues throughout. In the evening, both he and Tania (also in this study) are on their separate laptops. With their daughter fast asleep, they can finally prioritize platform communication above their intimate face-to-face time as a family.

"I'm more a typist when it comes to communicating," says George. He believes that there is a "general move in that direction," with more people recently adopting text-based forms of communication, and he surmises their collective viewpoint: *"I'm communicating more now, I guess, because I can type."* He reminds me that English is not his first language: "I mean my gut feeling is something to do with me not being *quick-witted* enough to come up with responses while I'm speaking. And the *speed of thinking* catches up with my *typing speed.*"

Time plays an important role in the controlled interactions of disembodied modes of interaction. Text-based communication is not only a *self-realized* interaction, detached from the body, but is also detached from the *embodied time* of live interactions. Communication-management patterns show a clear preference for *either* the intimacy of *fully embodied encounters* with close friends and family *or* the control of *fully disembodied interaction*, but the pressure of constant connection has interceded and disrupted the simplicity of this binary. Even George's work in radio reflects this notion of authenticity that comes from the purposeful realization of what he wants to communicate: his radio segments are all prerecorded so that he can edit out pauses, coughs, and stumbles. His radio work more closely resembles his blog entries than his telephone calls: edited, reviewed, and perfected. I barely recognize the man I hear on air only a few hours after sitting with him face-to-face.

The Lure and Pace of Platform Persistence

We glance at our screens to register the number of unaddressed message notifications; we scan emails to ascertain what unexpectedly may interrupt our day. The pace and organization of these tasks are coconstituted by the numerous others with whom we communicate and the design of the platform interfaces that make up our everyday communication environment. But these communication platforms are not neutral tools. They are products, a mix of entertainment and utility, governed by the commercial imperative of attracting users and maintaining their engagement to the platform for the purpose of producing data on users themselves.

This in turn allows for production of further data through the mining of complex relationships between sets of users' practices. For many, the practicality of managing the communication environment has been replaced by the gamified quantification and programmed reciprocity of social life amid the lure of algorithmic content curation.[49] These constitute the basis for new forms of highly mediated social expectations. From comments and messages to tags and mentions, and from streaks to moments, an ever-growing number of platform features are centered explicitly on enticing and enrolling other users into engagement with each other but through a more concerted maintenance of engagement with the platform itself that requires a particular timing and pace.

When Savannah, nineteen, does not have time to scroll through her social-media newsfeeds, there is a particular hierarchy of social-media engagement that allows her to triage what's most important. While late for class, she says that "I usually check my Instagram and Snapchat in the line while I wait to get coffee, which isn't a lot of time so it's pretty purposeful, and I just really check my notifications." Those notifications signal a direct interaction with one of her posts, a direct message, as well as when other users "tag" or "mention" her account by name, within a post or comment. "My German friend tagged me in a video that was related to a meme she and I thought was fucking hilarious last summer. I got the notification and stopped scrolling as I usually do when I get a notification, but it was weird because I'd sent that same video to her four days ago and I knew she saw it then. It was still nice of her and I laughed but it was a weird situation."

Notifications distract from more passive engagements with the platform and motivate many to engage more directly with a specific interaction with another user, even when there is nothing new, content-wise, to be consumed. Savannah laments that "I checked all my social media and nobody's really messaged me and I've been feeling really bored with Instagram, so I didn't really spend that much time on social media other than quickly browsing through Twitter." Wenzhuo, twenty-two, similarly toggles between modes of communication across apps, musing, "Is there anything new or fun happening around me? I first checked WeChat and my email boxes. And then I keep refreshing my friends 'moments' on WeChat till the latest one." Our compulsion to maintain connection with social-media platforms is sometimes a search for something to carry our attention away, a digital interaction with which to engage. Presented as limited actions, sequentially ordered along the platform interface via in-boxes, notification lists, and feeds, connection provides us with tasks to organize and complete. The self-isolation and social-distancing restrictions during COVID-19 exacerbated this compulsion. Wenzhuo points out: "My friends take pictures of traditional Chinese cuisines and share [them] via their 'moments' even during their self-isolation period. I keep refreshing . . . till the latest one." With her in-person classes now online and her workplace shut for the moment, Zeynab notes how the pandemic has exaggerated our habitual connection practices: "I have realized that being at home has increased the distractions I experience due to media. . . . Since people are mostly [in] their homes, they have more time to share stories and posts on Instagram. Therefore, I check Instagram for updates more often." These are task-based units of interactions, accessibly maintained on platform servers and readily available on any given check of a platform. Our desire for a sense of connection is refreshed with each swipe of our screens.

"Instagram, Snapchat, WeChat etc. . . . I am focusing on reading through particular messages that someone might have sent that I missed," explains Lillian. She is touring each different social-media app, searching for something to do, someone to engage with, despite having addressed all her notifications—just in case. This is a degree beyond the fear of missing out; it is a platform-mediated set of opportunities for engagement, which expire. Lillian spends the first few minutes of her morning "sending out snapchats to friends by taking a picture with the caption 'early mornings.' I am focusing on keeping the snapchat streak . . . between the contacts who I have the most streaks with. . . . I don't want the streak to break." In a very perfunctory and matter-of-fact way she explains that "[I] send out snapchats for the main purpose of keeping streaks, which basically are the number of consecutive days you and another user have contacted each other. The higher the streak, the more you make sure not to break it." Xin explains the lure of maintaining a streak: "I send a streak to everyone who has a Snapstreak with me to keep the little emoji [notification]. Otherwise, it will disappear if I or my friend do not snap each other over twenty-four hours." Snapchat's cache among early users centered on the temporary availability of the image-based messages, specifically their expiration and subsequent inaccessibility after twenty-four hours. While often framed in terms of privacy, this ephemerality drives a sense of urgency to keep up-to-date and was quickly adopted by Facebook and Instagram as time-limited image-based "Stories," with Twitter testing out something similar in 2020 under the time-oriented moniker of "Fleets." Snapstreaks are a gamification of the persistent maintenance of time-limited messages, rewarding users who maintain contact with each other with visual indicators of that daily commitment to direct, focused, mutual communication. The fear of missing out has moved beyond the sense of social opportunities. It is now mediated by the interface: FOMO is a platform feature.

Distributed Engagement across Platforms

It is difficult to separate our desire for distraction from the search for some sort of social connection. A meandering tour from one platform to another forces us to consider the wide temporal management of our entire communication environment, where the repertoire of media practices and opportunities for communication is more expansive than just social media. After exhausting her social-media feeds, Lillian continues through to other apps on her phone: "[I] check CBC and CNN. . . . As I was scrolling, I realized it is mostly the same news that has been making the headlines for the past few weeks and quickly [to] email—my email notifications are overflowing, so I decided to take the time to check and go through them to clean out my [inbox]."

Her cross-platform perusal of social-media and messaging apps leads to news apps and only then, finally, to forms of communication she associates with work and university. An overflowing email inbox represents the degree to which she avoids the forms of connection that represent unfulfilled work-related tasks, despite a slow and concerted tour of other media platforms beforehand. Bowen's tour of messaging apps and news sources similarly demonstrates a succession of bundled media practices that draw from the domain of interpersonal communication and entertainment to more information-seeking behaviors: "Replying to some messages on [Tencent's message app] QQ and WeChat. . . . Browsed the [Tencent's] Qzone and WeChat moments section (sections resembling Facebook pages) and learned about the meltdown in NYSE this morning. Checked Twitter (specifically the CNN account) for further details and updates." His tour across east Toronto while running errands points to the wider contours of an everyday media environment:

Briefly read *Sing Tao Daily* (one of the two prominent Chinese news-
papers in Toronto) at the newspaper booth at the Chinese supermarket, sifted through the first several pages, mainly read news about
COVID-19 outbreak worldwide. I just read . . . at the booth but never
buy them.

There was a long queue at the cashier at the Chinese supermarket,
so I decided to read a feature presented by *Southern Weekly*'s official
WeChat account while I wait. It was a long article, so I hated reading
it in parts with fragmented time (a main reason why I don't read news
articles on the move very often). The queue moved fast[er] than I expected, so I didn't finish before it was my turn.

The way we organize digital communication and media consumption
has the effect of similarly ordering and organizing nondigital actions.
Whereas others schedule phone calls and face-to-face interactions as
tasks to be completed in and among a succession of platform-based tasks,
Bowen's perusal of newsstands and news apps while at the supermarket
demonstrates the bleed of task-based management of media consumption from digital to analog. Just as Bowen skims social-media newsfeeds,
he sifts through the headlines of a print newspaper without necessarily
committing to the deeper engagement of reading an entire article. In the
checkout line, his engagement with an online article is interrupted, the
task left uncompleted, to his dismay. What happens, however, when he
chooses to engage with print publications? "Picked up the latest edition of
[the university campus magazine]. . . . The contents about Black History
month and the championship of the [university team] caught my eye, so I
took a print [copy] home for further reading later. Although I had always
planned to do so, I hardly ever reread them because there are so many
other 'prioritized' things to do; so they're just piling up on my desk."

Whether it amounts to an overflowing inbox, unaddressed notifications on a mobile screen, or past issues of a print magazine cluttering the
corner of a desk, our media practices are consistently broken down in
terms of temporally limited task-based units of activity. These are made
accessible through rigid practices of maintaining connection, amounting
to a temporally consistent backdrop of scanning, skimming, and sifting
through larger sets of possible tasks with which we have only cursory
engagement.

Disconnected Time

The increasing differentiation between our highly idiosyncratic, individualized schedules and patterns of media use are made possible through the rigid, integrating temporal practices of participating in and maintaining constant connection. Against this backdrop of unfocused communication management practices, focused practices of attending to, managing, and anticipating a deluge of successive tasks emerge. This is our contemporary compulsion toward connection: we struggle against communication overload as much as we do the fear of missing out and the lure of cleverly designed platform features that seek to hold our attention.

Our autonomy, flexibility, and control in the pace, patterns, and form of social interaction are made possible through an increasing embrace of the common denominator of constant connection: asynchronous communication management practices. In the early 1900s, Norbert Elias outlined how time consciousness developed as a central coordinating aspect of collective social life. Melissa Gregg has similarly traced the century-old cult of productivity in the management of home and work life as having inculcated the contemporary notions of time mastery and its concomitant professionalism.[50] Speaking across very different points in recent history, both scholars note that the observable contours of our social life provide meters for the external measurement of our conduct and that of others. In everyday decision-making, sensitivity to time is internalized and reproduced through sustained self-restraint, self-scrutiny, and self-regulation of how and when to maintain connection. This amounts to the temporalization of everyday communication practices. Elias reminds us that "whatever else they may be, timing devices are always transmitters of messages to people."[51]

The mediations of connective platforms serve to focus our attention on managing the "now" of potential communications, an economization and efficiency in managing one's communication environment disconnected from the situational realities of each relationship. This is the "just-in-time" ideology of neoliberalism applied to the flow of everyday communication, but these practiced degrees of disconnection take work, and, indeed, disconnection takes time.[52] Through its fragmentation of interpersonal life into sets of limited and quantifiable tasks to which we must attend—filed and visually displayed across app, platform, and device-level interfaces—our communication environment translates the flow of everyday communication into observable temporal meters.

Notifications, stories, moments, comments, reactions, messages, emails, and calls have partially replaced minutes and hours of the day as go-to signifiers for how successfully we are managing time in terms of how we are managing the flow of communication. Ilana Gershon argues that the neoliberal practitioner is never "in the moment," always faced with a rationalized distance onto themselves as an actor—the project of self, consciously projected through the reflexive management of both "our abilities and alliances," a social manifestation of engagement with the market.[53] This amounts to the transfer of both economic and platform uncertainties into sets of flexible coping tactics, an individuated and isolating enterprise of communication management. Drawing on the phenomenological tradition of Edmund Husserl, the sociologist of everyday life Maurice Merleau-Ponty argued that such reflexive and intentional actions are not wholly individualized but are instead always relational; they are not limited to the decisive horizon of an immediate present but fragmented and deferred.[54] In the flow of our communication management decisions, we are processing the momentum and plasticity of social opportunities amid a multitude of modally structured metadata, among more ambiguous social cues, and the uncertain outcomes that together they proffer. The result is an intentional drive for mutual engagement that is increasingly attuned to the degrees of asynchronicity afforded by platform interfaces and constant connection in tandem.[55] We are primed to wait for the SMS "read" notification or the potential response; we refresh inboxes; we await the notifications and alerts for the plurality of engagements that can occur on social networks. This is the metering capacity of views, shares, comments, and the streamlined emphasis through clicks of each emoji. Amid moments of concerted and focused asynchronous engagement, we are expecting but not witnessing the outcome—mutual engagement mediated in time by technology. In phenomenological terms, the "retention" of the immediately fleeting moment is preserved and held on to—"drawn along in the wake" of intentional practices, while the "protention" of expectation and accomplishment of mutual engagement is in a state of perpetual asynchronous deferral.[56] Platform mediations represent a management of everyday communication skewed to an overwhelming need to attend to flow of communication in the present—in preparation for crisis, in anticipation of intervening contingency, in the imagined next message or notification.

New forms of social knowledge emerge in relation to the metering and regulating of everyday life through interpersonal communication. When this form of reflexivity coalesces with the temporalities of constant connection, myriad degrees of social disconnection emerge in practice, forging a perspective from which we begin to shift from decisions about any single interaction toward the patterns and practices of metacommunication. At a certain point, however, any certainty in the interpretation of these social cues, of these temporal arrangements of practice, can become the unintelligibility of informational overload. While Elias contends that "time . . . is a symbol . . . of socially learned synthesis,"[57] I suggest that practices of disconnection are a socially learned synthesis seeking to mitigate the temporalities of constant connection. In the next chapter, we will explore how when we manage our compulsion for constant connection through practices of disconnection, we are able to reorder and renegotiate our communication environment in a manner that affords us the socially defined—rather than technologically managed—atmosphere for intimacy, entertainment, or different types of productivity.

Time consciousness today is better understood by problematizing the disparate experiences of connection and its mediations on our participation in everyday life. The implications of temporal scarcity in terms of communication overload characterize the practices of communication management explored throughout the remainder of this book, a characteristic that reproduces the neoliberal tensions of working and personal life, while simultaneously offering opportunities to repair what is wrong with connection today.

THREE

Managing Connection

Managing connection is the practice of disconnection. Engagement in one way often means disengagement in many others. Opportunities for constant connection across multiple modes of communication ask us to determine our presence and absence at any given time—in person and online. Our attention and time are finite. We struggle to manage being present for ourselves and others, while practicing degrees of absence—of disconnection—from the other ways in which we might connect.

Elisabeth, twenty-five, has just passed the probationary "trainee" period in her current role as junior lawyer. When we sit down, she turns off the ringer on her mobile phone, explaining her frustration with people who don't give others the courtesy of their full attention. She demonstratively puts her phone away in her purse. "There! Now I'm ready." I could see, however, that Elisabeth took mental note of each buzz from inside her bag. Another incoming text, another email? When I turn off the recorder at the close of the interview, she immediately excuses herself, reaching for her purse to scan for urgent work emails. During our second interview, a long vibration from her mobile phone set to silent signals a telephone call. I can see the conflict between connection and disconnection on Elisabeth's face when she finally and apologetically reaches for her bag and steps out into the hallway. It could have been work, but in the end, it was her mother. In either case, she says, she needed to answer.

Personal or professional, face-to-face or digital, synchronous or asyn-chronous, communication in everyday life is a series of numerous, dis-crete flows teased apart, attended to, and intertwined. As the preceding chapters outlined, the demand to maintain networked connection re-quires constant, time-consuming effort, and so do the practices of dis-connection that I will explore in this chapter. Even passively scanning notifications, emails, news feeds, and threads is stymied when trying to complete a particular task—drafting an email to a client, perfecting the timing for a TikTok video, or even spending time with family, whether in front of the TV or on a video call.

Aaliyah muses that "perhaps it is just my inner battle not to be as consumed and addicted to social media as my peers." She manages con-nection through several concerted practices of disconnection: "All my notifications, with the exception of phone calls, are turned off so I am in control of how often I check my phone. I am aware that turning off my notifications does not minimize my use; however, I am not literally alerted to take my attention elsewhere if I am focusing on something."

Against a background of constant connection, there are degrees of connection and disconnection, or rather degrees of engagement with and disengagement from platforms and modes of communication. These are central to understanding the management of time but also the multiple forms of overlapping networked interaction that have come to define the platform era. What does it mean to be present with others, for others? Aaliyah answers by describing a visit from her sister-in-law's family: "I am choosing to stay away from my phone and be a good host. . . . I am trying to make the guests feel comfortable, as they are not close family and we do not know them that well. Making sure to listen, laugh, and engage with them is the reason it was so easy to disconnect and unplug."

Being physically present with others allows for connection not always defined by technology. In face-to-face contexts, engagement is often clear, but there are networked equivalents to this. Degrees of disengagement and absence from one type of communication can promote more atten-tive presence in another. This can be a matter of care, intimacy, fun, or professionalism.

Aaliyah is the first to admit that sometimes disengagement is neces-sary in different ways, for different reasons. While working on a univer-sity assignment, she explains: "I have decided to put my phone away so I can focus." But she is still online to recheck course materials, conduct

research, and check definitions. Distraction includes all sorts of interruptions: "There is endless commotion in my house right now. My mom
yelling, calling me, the doorbell ringing and my dad putting together a
barbeque. I am choosing to focus on my schoolwork and literally blocking
out all the noise." To engage with the task at hand, Aaliyah disconnects
from some mediums, but not others, and withdraws from her situated
environment.

Often the task at hand, whether for work or entertainment, entails
many moving parts, a flow of both interpersonal and digital practices.
The multiplicity of this engagement provides a distinct quality of managing degrees of heterogeneous, competing forms of engagement. Lian provides a snapshot of just such engagement at an extracurricular campus
event: "Our club held a debate contest [from] 6 to 8 p.m. that day. My
job is to stay in the preparation room with the debaters, and the contest
is happening in another room. Thus, we communicate and update new
information via WhatsApp. Throughout the event, there were flurries of
messages, and I need to pay extra attention to the messages which were
about my job so I will not mess up the event."

This is the hard-to-define pressure to be "on," fully engaged in situ but
with a divided, distracted, and ambient attentiveness, purposefully set in
multiple directions, anticipating all sorts of possible contingencies. But
to be on in this way means being off in others, absent from nearby conversations and personal IM threads, disengaged from Instagram and TikTok.
These are the concerted contemporary practices of managing presence
and flow across multiple types of platform communication through degrees of disconnection. Our constant engagement with digital platforms
embeds us in a "hum of activity" that itself represents a social "displace-
ment," suspending our focused, decisive enactment of media practices
that seek some sort of determinate outcome.[1] Constant connection promotes these displacements—a deferred process of social action that is yet
complete, insisting on a disconnected sociality to feel more immersed
in the unfolding uncertainty of particular situations. Counterintuitively,
we also practice degrees of disconnection to steep ourselves in the flow
of connection, to clamber and explore haphazardly without distraction.

Division, Disassociation, Disconnection

To assume that these are wholly contemporary conundrums would be a mistake. For well over a century, such issues have been central to sociology, an academic discipline that—at its emergence—sought to better understand the social complexity that accompanied shifts toward mass industrialization and urbanization in the late 1800s and early 1900s, including new environments for connecting alongside new practices of disconnection.

Managing one's engagement through practices of disconnection was a central facet of interpersonal communication and media use before the rise of digital networks. The French sociologist Emile Durkheim examined changing forms of solidarity when urban living began to displace smaller, tightly knit communities. New divisions of labor among increasingly large sets of individuals largely unknown to each other resulted in new types of proximity and interdependency. These changes constrained the ability of a given individual to understand the complexity and scale of the personal and the economic: the "systemness," in Durkheim words, that cannot be ascertained in a "single thought or glance"; the nature of an organization, including its many, underpinning norms that are distinct and separate from everyday individual experience, what Durkheim called the "life-world."[2] Where Durkheim saw a detrimental breakdown of norms, and therein the basis of social cohesion, other scholars would see opportunities that diversity and a lack of convention would bring.[3] In the US in the 1960s, urban centers became dense and diverse, with unexpected connections and disrupted conventions, providing what Richard Sennet celebrated as creative disorder, a divergence from norms in favor of multiple experiences necessary for individuals to adapt, learn, and negotiate a changing world.[4]

Much earlier in the 1900s, navigating the chaos and cacophony of urban life was already predicated on disconnection, captured in what Georg Simmel called the "blasé" comportment of the city dweller, where a practiced state of "dissociation" secured one against the gazes of others and the attention-grabbing lights of advertisements on the crowded urban boulevard.[5] At the height of midcentury postwar society, Goffman similarly observed the numerous "traffic relationships" urban dwellers endure, opportunities for engagement with copresent others who are persistently met with practices of "civil inattention," exemplified through the conventional silence of a crowded elevator.[6] These sociological accounts from different eras and diverse contexts are not refusals to interact but practices of managing one's communication environment: practices of self-regulation by means of internalizing shifting, diverse social pressures and squelching the abundant clamor of opportunities for communication with others.

Acknowledging or ignoring an opportunity to connect is a practice that limits and shapes the contours of our social lives, both in the immediate situation and over time.[7] Gergen examines the "absent presence" of how others in a room perceive, for example, an individual reading a book.[8] They are physically copresent, but their attention is monopolized, resulting in a degree of disengagement despite the opportunity for face-to-face conversation. Analog and digital devices that provide for communication at a distance—whether landline telephone, desktop computer, mobile phone, or laptop—are similarly designed for individualized use, resulting in a physical copresence that Gergen suggests is "virtually eradicated by a dominating absence."[9] In his examination of how mobile media are increasingly intertwined with our experience of urban spaces, Scott McQuire argues that "every situation is increasingly experienced as lacking 'full' presence," as possibilities for attending to and interacting with numerous copresent others is persistently redirected and extended toward the "fluctuating and discontinuous pressure of the generalized 'elsewhere.'"[10]

How can we understand the diversity of presences and absences in our current management of connection and disconnection? Goffman provides a starting point with his definition of the "full conditions of copresence": wherever and whenever an individual can "sense that they are close enough to be perceived in whatever they are doing, including their experiencing of other, and close enough to be perceived in this sensing of being perceived."[11] If this predigital understanding of presence hinges on corporeality and one's perceived proximity to copresent others, then its digital-era iteration rests on awareness of one's visibility by others. Physical copresence is just one type of copresence, existing alongside the myriad of connected or networked forms of copresence that communications technology facilitates.[12] As I have written elsewhere: "These constituent elements of perception and presence allow for distinctions between a perceived presence and another actual presence that may or may not be perceived. This implies possible degrees of presence along a spectrum from the 'full' conditions of presence towards a perceived absence and then finally to the actual 'full' absence."[13]

Absence, or the lack of shared presence, also rests on notions of perception and visibility. The absence that matters to Goffman is perceived rather than actual, again suggesting there are degrees of absence we can attend to and engage with across the multiple mediums we use for constant connection. Engagement, then, involves a concerted coordination of interaction, made reciprocal by the perceived degree of shared presence acted on. Consider verbal communication. Whether in person, over the phone, or on a video chat, each of these is additionally facilitated by degrees of disengagement or absence from other possible interactions. Forms of networked absence provide for the focused nature of opportunities to engage with others—defined by how, when, and to what degree it is mutually achieved.

Disconnection itself has become a lens through which platform and metamedia can be understood. The rhetoric of digital connection and the affordances of platform participation sketch out idealized framings of constant connection central to the business models of the digital advertising industry—so much so that disconnection represents more than just a lack of engagement, or nonparticipation; it is evidence of how we negotiate the changing spaces of possible communication.[14] Tero Karppi states that disconnections are "tools to think about the outside," to think about what is beyond connection: practices that challenge the "totalizing images of the connected world, showing that there are cracks everywhere through which the outside will get in."[15] As I will explore, practices of partial disengagement while maintaining constant connection allow for different degrees of presence to be separated, refracted, and overlaid, for different types of relationality in social life to emerge.

Reciprocity and Engagement

Our management of mediated connection with others, no matter how intimate, is closely related to the qualities and characteristics we give to relationships with individuals or sets of individuals. When two or more individuals engage, "openly . . . maintaining a single focus of cognitive and visual attention—what is sensed as a single *mutual activity*"—this is often understood, according to Goffman, as a type of "preferential communication rights" expressed in face-to-face practices.[16] Today, however, our cognitive and affective attentiveness can be distributed across the plurality of ways we can connect yet still lead to a sense of sustained and intimate engagement. This helps us understand the allure of the hypermediated digital environment: connecting in numerous overlapping ways can seem "more real" for its very multiplicity.

In contrast to the immersive "immediacy" of stereo systems, movies, books, or TV—media that sought to erase any distance between the audience and content—digital "hypermediacy" is defined by how media noticeably organizes our experience in multiple, heterogeneous ways: from application windows across operating systems and the World Wide Web to the information-laden screens of video games, the value of the metamedia and multimedia experience is the visual separation of multiple modalities and information flows.[17]

Hannah and her two best friends are seldom offline and are in near-constant contact. Even while together in person, they participate in a cocoon of perpetual online engagement, mutual attention, and interaction. In the morning, Hannah explains in her diary, she messages a friend to confirm plans, including a few Snapchat photos of their faces, before getting ready:

> [In the] afternoon, my friend and I got together and sat on our phones in her car for probably 2 hours. We did pretty much what I had assumed earlier and made funny videos on Snapchat, tried to learn some TikTok dances, and scrolled through our various timelines together, showing each other things we found funny, shocking, strange, or worth sharing for some reason or another.
>
> We sent some videos to our third best friend that lives [an hour east of Toronto] to tell her we miss her and update her on our life. We do that A LOT. Rather than texting each other, the three of us for the most part communicate everything that happens via Snapchat videos.
>
> This makes it feel more personal and face to face, I guess. We've done this more than texting for the past three years. It's also easier to grasp emotions and whatnot through these videos.

There is an intimacy to these types of constant connection—one predicated on continual exposure, the sharing of mundane rituals (and the emotional states that accompany them), and a commitment to a particular type of ongoing and mutual engagement through social media. This extends beyond the necessities of microcoordination by text or phone call among couples, families, and roommates, which nevertheless may continue throughout the day, with check-ins, grocery lists, and last-minute adjustments to plans.[18] Mobile studies scholars have long been interested in the manner that moments of monopolistic mutual engagement occur alongside degrees of less constant, less intense "tethering" between clusters of friends, family, or coworkers. These interactions contribute to what Ito and Okabe call the "ambient accessibility" and "peripheral background awareness" in mobile use as well as to Crawford's degrees of "background" and "delegated listening" of unfocused social-media scrolling alongside more focused practices of "reciprocal listening."[19]

Today, the lure of platform algorithms, the gamified pace of maintaining message streaks, and the perceived pressure and anticipation induced by message-read notifications, all contribute to a greater mutuality inherent in the compulsion for connection in real time. Considering the finite resources that we have to attend to in our communication opportunities, these continual forms of engagement contribute to the maintenance of existing, strong ties, which likely mean less time and attention spent interacting with others. When constant engagement becomes a defining feature of relationships, the finite nature of our attention translates to an insularity in how we overconnect with some by failing to connect with others; disconnection is predicated on the compulsion for connection itself.[20]

The Intimacy of Mutual Engagement

Committing one's time and attention to being present, in person, with others, has become a decisive act. After finally reaching for his phone to post about lunch with friends on Snapchat, Jun considers the cost of always trying to share what's happening on social media: "This is great but we have to be careful. Sometimes we get too caught up in displaying our special moment online instead of really enjoying it." To assert and manage absence from platforms becomes a task in itself, ensuring a particular atmosphere for face-to-face communication.

For Ayanna, celebrating the Sabbath means taking a day for family, church, and the community. This begins in the morning, "speaking with my mother while . . . doing my makeup and doing my hair, since I'm getting ready to go to church." She is "trying to refrain from going on to social media because in my religion . . . we shouldn't be taking any part in secularity, since Saturday . . . is our holy day of rest." It isn't just mass but morning routine with family and engagement with the wider congregation that gives Ayanna a chance to feel closer with her parents' wider social network, the Caribbean community in Toronto. When she meets with the young-adults church-planning group, Ayanna decides "to keep my media devices out of sight." Yet media technologies and practices still seem essential for many face-to-face contexts: "During church I access [a website-building platform] to show my church congregation a website that I have been working on for the church . . . displayed through a projector onto a larger screen. . . . It is still [a work] in progress." When connecting with family is the motivation, and technology contributes to this engagement, other media may continue to distract: "I get home from church; I facetime my sister who lives in [the southern United States] who [is] also an active and practicing [Christian denomination]. Whilst talking to her my attention is split in half between her and a show that is playing on television. I [decided] to call and talk to her since we did not communicate with each other all day. . . . We were both at our respective churches."

Many users shift seamlessly back to constant contact with social media each morning, or after the workday. Ayanna also reconnects: "my attention is fully on my cell phone since I had not been on it all day." She turns to her social-media accounts, "Instagram, Snapchat, and Twitter. . . . [I] look through my feed, direct messages from friends, and snaps from friends, as well as the activities of the public figures [who I follow]." Aaliyah has a similar, albeit more casual, way of prioritizing time with family, without a scheduled shift at her part-time job: "I am currently off work, so I spend the first half of the day sitting in front of the television with my parents, watching a Bollywood comedy show. When I am hanging in the living room, I do not take my phone with me because I want to [be] present with my family, rather than refreshing my Instagram feed every few seconds to aimlessly stimulate myself."

She outlines the uniqueness of this atmosphere—"it's nostalgic and reminds me of my childhood sitting around the TV watching shows with my family"—which needs to be managed and maintained for those limited windows of being copresent. Otherwise, as she explains, "all of my shows are either consumed on my iPad or laptop"—which she would more often than not watch alone.

For others, like Savannah, similar practices of managing disengagement are central to intimate time catching up with friends: "I didn't really use my phone this afternoon as I was hanging out with a friend. I only see her about once a week so I try not be on my phone or engaged with anything else when I'm with her." Of course, media are part of contemporary social life, however, whether for community organizations or family-friendly movies. For Savannah, sharing social-media content is a dimension of her friendships: "She's on a social-media cleanse as well, so the only time I used my phone was to show her some memes I found on Instagram that I knew she would find funny."

The ordering effect of one communication practice on others is evident here, whereby "cumulative media practices create an affective milieu that orients people towards or away from the presence of others," thereby changing the very "quality of time" spent in each other's company or alone. As Sarah Cefai and Nick Couldry further discuss, intimacy and social belonging are "closely linked to the temporal organisation of people's media practices."[21] The inverse can be said about the vigilant awareness of online activity maintained by near "permanently online and permanently connected" users, demonstrated by the growing number of studies on the antisocial nature of "phubbing" or phone-snubbing people in one's immediate vicinity.[22] Media use is intertwined with engaging others, even in person, offering a socially legible expression taken as characteristic of relationships among the wider disconnected sociality inherent in constant connection.

A Compulsion for Connection and Other Autonomy Paradox(es)

I've not been waiting long when Augustine, thirty-four, strides up the station stairwell at Tottenham Court Road in Central London. With a quickly raised eyebrow, she signals for me to wait a moment while she finishes typing an email to a client on her phone: "I know there's no signal down there, but it is [a] great time to draft a response without interruptions. . . . And send!"[23] With the dramatic press of a button, she gives me her full attention. As a PR professional, in fact as the founder of her firm, Augustine leads the conversation, even though it is supposed to be me asking the questions. Within minutes, her casual demeanor defuses the stiltedness of my academic interview techniques. She always keeps her mobile phone within reach, and the screen is always within view. A few instant messages (IM) have come through in an open chat window. She sends a quick response and sighs, "You know some clients, even big ones, are friends now. It's Sunday evening, and I can't tell you who, but I'm chatting away with the last winner of a certain reality television show!" Augustine knows how to keep my attention even while instant messaging with someone else. She knows how to build rapport. She has built a career out of it.

So much of the entrepreneurial ideal today, whether as a self-employed freelancer or a small-business owner, is contingent on maximizing mobile, networked technology to attain maximum flexibility through always-on availability. This is simply not possible for many. When we talk about labor, bodies at work, and mobility, this is also always a question of time, as the temporal anxieties of some are more often than not intertwined with the "temporal sovereignty" of others.[24] For "mumpreneurs," working from home is seldom a matter of balancing work and care practices but rather of creatively finding a way to fit work into spaces and paces of home life.[25] Being able to work anywhere and being available at any time isn't simply a matter of having a home office, nor simply the right phone, laptop, or even data plan, when other responsibilities intervene, such as the need for a child to be changed, held, fed, in essentially time-consuming and embodied ways.

The difficulties of working from home as a parent became acutely clear during the COVID-19 pandemic. Parents managed workspaces and schedules alongside partners who may be doing the same, while also caring for young, school-age children. A recent survey of opposite-sex partners in the UK and their balancing of paid work and domestic responsibilities during lockdown outlines the difficulty of this challenge and the disproportionate impact on mothers. In a situation where both parents are still working, but now from home, mothers are nevertheless taking on the majority of childcare and housework including the work of managing their children's online education. This stark inequality persists despite a doubling on average of the time fathers are spending on these activities, as compared to a similar survey conducted in 2014 and 2015. The paid working hours of mothers are not only far more likely to be interrupted while working from home, but almost half of mothers surveyed in 2020 were juggling childcare and other activities during those working hours, while less than a third of fathers were multitasking in this manner.[26] In their examination of gender and the quality of working life in the UK cultural industries, David Hesmondhalgh and Sarah Baker found that commonplace divisions of labor in industry reinforce similarly gendered expectations in forms of horizontal segregation between types of roles.[27] Their ethnographic interviews with professionals in music, publishing, and television production detailed the manner in which women were most expected to take on multitasking roles defined by sets of coordinating and caretaking-like practices. The gendered expectations as to who is most apt to take on roles defined by relational labor and the subsequent stratification of roles, then, also perpetuates a problematically exalted (and again often gendered) space for the maverick entrepreneur or demanding creative genius, who may shun such interpersonal responsibilities, devaluing what is perceived as "feminized" labor as disruptive to better uses of their time.

When I arrive at Augustine's townhouse for our second interview, it is clear that some reorganization is taking place. It is the first day of Augustine's maternity leave, but she still feels the need to be connected and managing the goings-on of her PR firm's teams. She walks me through the living and dining areas that have become her new home office because, as she explains, the stairs are going to be difficult in these last few weeks of her pregnancy. The computer is normally tucked into a small desk upstairs in what is slowly becoming the nursery. Augustine checks on multiple social media accounts from her phone but prefers to manage them from the desktop computer, now on the dining table. These accounts include her own profile, one for her PR company, and numerous others for clients and particular projects. While we are talking, she never misses a ping from her instant-messaging app. For Augustine, maintaining this comprehensive familiarity with the goings-on of her business means that multiple client databases, collaborative spreadsheets, and networked email accounts are open on the desktop computer screen beside client-specific binders and a few boxes of documents. These are shared files, networked with members of her team who are still in office or connected by mobile technology while meeting clients. As much as Augustine is checking the progress of particular projects, she is worried about not being physically present for her employees and has set herself up, despite her maternity leave, to be connected and available, shepherding her team of younger associates and interns through the day-to-day of the business despite her in-person absence.

Augustine is the contemporary manifestation of Britain's generation of early owner-entrepreneurs, additionally assuming a caretaking role to mentor and train her employees as the early owner-entrepreneurs would their own family members. Laying the groundwork for the industries within which they operated, these entrepreneurs were typically so involved in routine administration and day-to-day operations that they were the sole source of organizational and market knowledge as it pertained to their businesses and clients. For context, in Britain just prior to the pandemic, nearly 20 percent of the economy was composed of not just small businesses but also microbusinesses (with fewer than nine employees), while 76 percent of businesses (with no employees) represented the wide array of freelancers, self-employed contractors, or other owner-proprietors.[28] The accumulated practical knowledge of these workers is often left undocumented, a product of constant functional oversight accrued through daily interpersonal engagement with employees, industry contacts, and clients. Barring attempts to train others or codify this knowledge into sets of clear, routinized practices, this immaterial organizational knowledge becomes bound up with the identity of the entrepreneurs themselves and is often deemed to be intuitive, part managerial acumen and part interpersonal craft.

The flexibility and autonomy of entrepreneurs to work where, when, and how they see fit comes at a cost. This is the "autonomy paradox" of mobile and networked communications: the increased flexibility of one's working schedule afforded by mobile communication allows for an overall extension of work responsibilities and interactions beyond the time and spaces of work and is, in many ways, due to that flexibility.[29] In practice, mobile communication affords autonomy while also eroding it: managerial commitments are extended with the ability to monitor, approve, and coordinate the communication and workflow between staff and with clients while away from the office or otherwise occupied. The very technologies meant to free up a freelancer, entrepreneur, or executive to focus on ever-important relationship development with collaborators and clients are the same technologies that ensure they are always still available for the type of caretaking and supervision that their colleagues and employees may expect.

For many, the strictures of the nine-to-five office environment, including cultures of managerial surveillance and expected duration of what turns out to be very embodied, time-consuming work, are simply not conducive to meeting the needs posed by one's health or disability, child or elder care, or even the nature of competing work schedules across multiple contracts.[30] Whether working in a segregated back office or from home, there is a loss of opportunity to be in circulation among potential collaborators, clients, and employers, a loss of that shared space to learn to navigate the interpersonal space of work. These forms of segregation and isolation have been dubbed an "entrepreneurial ghetto" by the home-based freelancing mothers in interview with Carol Ekinsmyth.[31] This is qualitatively different from the "nomadic style of disconnection" from specific physically situated workplaces, idealized as the mode of work for the most aspirational and mobile class of knowledge workers, yet even they still risk the relational workplace isolation necessary to shift fields or develop new client and collaborator relationships.[32]

The sharp pivot to working from home during the COVID-19 pandemic demonstrated the fickle necessity of a working culture defined by these normative strictures of the physically situated copresent working life. In her examination of hiring practices following the Great Recession, Gershon points to the reality of managerial and organizational exclusion of certain opportunities for certain types of people; there are organizational structures that can be reformed, but amid the uncertainty of freelance contracts and movement between companies, for these individuals there is no longer a specific structure to target, adapt, or renegotiate for more equitable outcomes.[33] When voluntary or as a workplace accommodation, the ability to work remotely can contribute to inclusivity, as well as offer an alternative structuring of practice toward work-oriented productivity, caring responsibilities, and overall individual well-being, but during the pandemic remote working was enforced across sectors where it had previously been denied. Disability scholars and advocates alike argue that there is a "silver lining" to COVID-19: the reorganization of working life could very well improve the opportunities for and acceptance of working conditions better suited to self-employed people and employees with disabilities.[34]

Overcoming the Disconnections of Transnational Care

It is just before sunrise for Hanita. Her tutoring clients will be online momentarily, but this is the brief window when she and her parents can connect meaningfully, which, for them, adds up to being available for a video or voice call, whatever it takes to hear each other's voices, for a minute or two a day. "I wake up every day around 6:30 a.m. and automatically access my laptop to teach two hours of English via an online-platform . . . accessing the [teaching website]. . . . While I am listening to my parents WhatsApp voice messages, I am logging on. . . . [I] need to earn an income to sustain myself [but] the fact is that I miss my family."

Every morning Hanita accesses her client portal and gets ready for work but needs to make time for a flurry of WhatsApp notifications—all before class, at least on the weekdays. "My parents live overseas and the time change is approximately thirteen hours ahead (Bangladesh); thus, this is the most convenient time to wish them a good night." It's an expected daily distraction, but with family spread across such distances, it's worth it.

These are the transnational vicissitudes of maintaining connection, where presence is part of care, and coordination occurs across time zones and disparate schedules, to facilitate forms of communication those involved consider intimate. Key is understanding each other's lives and media practices, themselves facilitated by continual, repeated engagements. For parents and grandparents, or the adult children of aging parents, this involves vigilant forms of connection as care, particularly evident among the young adults studying in Toronto and away from their families for the first time.[35] These transnational families have explicitly scheduled check-ins, prioritizing more intimate, synchronous modes such as voice or video calls, bracketed by a diffuse continuity of asynchronous instant-message conversations throughout the day.

Enlai starts each day in the same manner. "The first thing after I woke up in the morning was to contact my mother by using WeChat. . . . Since I [began to] study abroad, my parents have always been concerned." Ruomei ends her day with a similar, habitual check-in with their family: "I watched a movie at night in bed and, as always, I FaceTimed with my grandparents," who are at home in China. These are moments of everyday transnational connection predicated on degrees of "friendly or careful surveillance," or rather care-full surveillance, between familial generations.[36] Others talk about setting aside Saturday and Sunday mornings for a weekly call to siblings in the Czech Republic or to aunts and uncles in India, while additionally having to coordinate across the schedules of parents who are still working, on top of challenges posed by differences across time zones. Even in text-based communication, playful and creative communication practices among family interlocutors, can deepen the experience of connection. From the functional to the emphatic, diverse paralinguistic visual features expand the ways to engage in and across platforms with others.

These moments of exchange—of connection—foster deeply intimate intergenerational moments when digital literacy is instilled through social practices. The more digitally savvy young adults engage the less media-immersed family members with emojis, emoticons, and other visual annotations to offer endearing adjuncts alongside the inbuilt platform affordances to add selfies, filters, screenshots, videos, and audio recordings to their messages.[37] Mirca Madianou's ethnographic work among UK-based service workers from the so-called Global South examines such care-oriented forms of connection by distant parents.[38] Those who have traveled abroad for work, in particular health-care workers and hired caregivers in private households, depend on a flexible range of media to ensure the continuity of their involvement in their children's lives back home. As I touched on earlier, Ticona's work with lower-wage service- and knowledge-industry workers in the US reveals similar feats of strategic time management: a stealing-away from prying managerial eyes and restrictive workplace rules to coordinate both habitual and unexpected family needs.[39] Studying the media habits of individuals across Australian, Chinese, and Japanese research sites, the ethnographer Larissa Hjorth and her collaborators found this type of care-oriented connection to be predicated on a connective continuity that crosses cities and generations as much as it does cultures, fostering a type of "digital kinship."[40] Such purposeful maintenance of social and familial bonds as media practices involves a mutual attentiveness to the form of those very practices, reflecting on and exploring their mediation—an expressive interpersonal field expanding what it means to be communicating through media, through practice itself.

The Flow of Mediated Play

It is an inescapable fact of contemporary life that mediated connection will influence our physically situated, face-to-face contexts. But our desire for engagement with others is not wholly defined by the assumption that in-person presence and face-to-face connection is the only form of authentic engagement in social life. There are numerous forms of mediated connection that require a particular atmosphere to be managed, and a type of engagement maintained, for the duration of the activity.

Phone calls, video chats, gaming, and other types of simultaneous or live media differ from the constant availability of email, text, and other forms of asynchronous communication by contributing to circuits of media use across multiple forms of online and offline engagements.[41] Cameron, who lives at home with his parents while he attends college, outlines how he is entertained in particular by game play when it is designed to be social: "After getting back from hanging out with my friends we decided to play some games from our respective houses. I was mainly focused on the games while we were playing and chatting over voice communications, deciding certain things we should do while playing. . . . Being able to play games from different locations and talk through the same platform simultaneously is something interesting."

Similarly, when the limited-time "ultra rapid fire" mode of the game *League of Legends* was reintroduced, Jason knew he was in trouble—not just because of the social commitment but of how that commitment is augmented by certain game features: "Today some of my gaming friends messaged me. . . . I had not played in a while. . . . I ended up playing with them until close to 3 a.m. and had [to] cancel all other plans like going to the gym and or doing school work. This is a team sport—making it hard to just leave." Like most entertainment media, game play is designed to be enthralling, and this involves cooperation with affordances for communication, so there are social pressures to maintain engagement and to be present and attentive.

Jia roundly states in their diary that online and networked games are not only environments where social interaction can take place but also that games are social spaces. With a block of their afternoon dedicated to game play, Jia and a friend are "trying to [play] but getting interrupted from social-media messages and calls, "so they keep their attention "on the TV and [Nintendo] Switch" and "ignore social-media messages for a while and keep playing. I want to play the game and not be interrupted." Immersed in the flow of a multiplayer *battle royale*–style game *PlayerUnknown's Battlegrounds* (PUBG), Jia points out that even when "playing the game on the phone with my friend in 'team-competitive' mode . . . , I was paying attention to the game [and] decided to play for a few hours"—in an attentive and all-consuming way that she also extends to describe the less competitive and more prosaic social simulation games like "playing *Animal Crossing* online with friends" using the console and TV.

The flow of media use in gaming has an emotional pull, whereby effort and strategy achieve in-game or diegetic goals.[42] Jia points out: "I decided to play for a few hours. . . . I enjoyed playing with friends because we won a lot." Yet the game play is itself social, especially when live game play is planned among friends rather than online strangers. This book opened with a quote from Lena ("Oh my god, there is a real person here"), when she realized that one of the gamers she was interacting with during their quest in the MMOG *World of Warcraft* was her age and someone with whom she could socialize. His in-game IM about needing a cigarette and her response that she'd take a break to refill her wine was enough for the two to connect as social peers and then play together for the rest of the afternoon. In this manner, the limits of our social world, of our opportunities to connect with others, are partially defined by our perceptions of media platforms as possibly being social rather than merely entertaining or informative.[43]

Many networked games provide modalities for player interaction, from user-oriented IM chat outside the world of the game to types of narrative interaction through actions taken by players' onscreen avatars. These are diegetic and nondiegetic layers of game play, drawing from the Greek notion of narrative; in-story game play and related interactions contrast the game settings, other menus, and player-to-player IM, all fundamentally outside the game-play narrative. There is, however, an expanding user-centric and agency-focused relationality to game play in contemporary game design, which relies on only a few traditional gaming elements so that play can be directly focused on interaction among users' avatars in a social rather than wholly goal-oriented gaming environment.[44]

Like social media, multiuser gaming environments are always available, but they differ in their need for synchronous or live game play (though not for all forms of interaction). This more rigid temporal backdrop is similar to those prized moments of watching TV with the family. There is a particular atmosphere that many prefer when gaming in a social way, and connecting with others through game play requires a more dedicated and monopolistic degree of attention, as well as a particular atmosphere for social connection.

Focusing on Distraction Together

To be immersed in the flow of media use can require durations of time that necessitate disengagement from other types of media, such as when digital play mitigates social-media use. Yet switching nimbly across modalities of interaction, within an app or across apps, can facilitate a different type of social atmosphere, refracted into different forms of engagement, where multiple types of presence mingle. When we manage multiple forms of presence across our communication environment, rather than restricting ourselves to one set of platform features, the immediacy of immersive engagement is replaced by a hypermediacy of multiple forms of networked presence simultaneously taking place across heterogeneous visual and temporal modalities.

While Suyin texts her three friends to arrange when they will play *League of Legends* together as a team that evening, switching between modes of communication to coordinate a time for game play, other users meander between one form of interaction to another, both offered within the multifaceted platform ecosystem. Xin describes just such an experience: "It is finally the weekend, time for some entertainment. My friend calls me on WeChat; she wants to team up with me for the game named PUBG. . . . We can pair up [as a] two or four people group and help each other to kill the enemies and survive until the end. I login with my WeChat account and match with her immediately because we are friends on WeChat. I talk to her during the game about the strategies and exchange information to help each other."

Like other dominant platform conglomerates, Tencent's WeChat entices third-party developers to its platform ecosystem with features that promote their accessibility to WeChat's enormous user base through streamlined user sign in, authentication, and connection with others in the existing WeChat network. Facebook and Google similarly promote their services as a developer's environment, a programmable interface for other platforms and apps.[45] It is not only the ease of game access but also the intensity of collective game play, including the temporal flow of inside- and outside-game social interactions, that keeps Xin coming back: "Even though we are killing lots of people, . . . we lose in the end. [But] the intensity and achievability [of game play] keeps calling me back to start a new round."

For other types of mediated entertainment, the convergence of accessibility and interoperability between apps, on mobile phones, allows one type of entertainment to quickly bleed into the next. Yuki, nineteen, was talking to her mom through the Line app owned by the Japanese Softbank Group, similar in many ways to WhatsApp for its diverse texting, IM, voice, and video-call features: "[Mom] was chatting with me about the new KPOP girl group, ITZY. We really had a great time because we discussed which members we had a crush on and how much love we have for their debut single. Unexpectedly, my mom asked me [if] I know how to do the choreography. I replied I knew a little. Then, as I hung the phone up, I immediately called one of my friends to record our dance cover. I did not know why my brain had told me to do this."

One video call turned to another. Chatting with her mother on one platform inspired Yuki's video chat with a friend through her device as a second platform to record a dance cover for a third platform, TikTok. Yuki is bemused by how quickly the inspiration struck her, but it is the flow of media use—facilitated by the ease of switching between calls, and then between video-call features, and finally to post the finished product on social media—that is of interest to us. There are scales of multimediality both within individual apps and across her device. She surmises that "it had been a long time since the last time I recorded a dance cover. Another reason is that I want to reward myself for finishing the midterm last night."

Seeking Dispersion and the Refraction of Presence

Multiple forms of presence mingle while degrees of engagement meander from one mode of communication to another. Managing those important moments of connecting with others is often bundled among the rhythms of other media practices. After completing her media diary, Margaret was shocked by her habitual media overload in the evenings. Watching British TV, she scans her work email account until the end of her division manager's day in New York, but she also cherishes this time to chat with her younger sister, who is time zones away but always online while she sits in university lectures in Canada. Above, Hanita's tutoring job relies on a gig-to-gig-style platform, drawing her into the transnational schedules of various user-clients worldwide, a schedule that becomes tangled up with daily check-ins from family in Bangladesh. Yuki's daily call with her mother inspired her and a friend to record a TikTok dance video, while Ruomei made an "unboxing video" of a new game console that had just been delivered, posting it to YouTube while killing time until her nightly video call from her grandparents. Different expectations of how we can and should be engaged are bundled together and overlaid among practices of maintaining presence for intimacy and care, for seeking work, and for entertainment.

Jack, twenty-four, has just left his job as a social-work assistant and is now working long nights in the service industry to save money and time for more creative artistic pursuits. He complains that a lot of people do not understand that sometimes hanging out online is just that—hanging out. Being present and fully engaged is not always the goal of connecting with others. Well before the widespread normalization of spending time over video chats under COVID-19 social-distancing restrictions, many users were already accustomed to casually whittling hours away on their devices with friends—mutually only somewhat engaged—in open video-to-video chat windows.

Disconnection mingles with the multiplicity of connection to allow the exploratory, haphazard plasticity of media use not predicated on productivity, intimacy, or an end-goal. An array of media scholars have defended these forms of engagement. Ben Highmore celebrates the "promiscuous absorption" of media-saturated life where engagement occurs through distraction, itself not a lack of concentration but a refracted, scattered, and therein disconnected concentration.[46] A more cynical and dystopian take on Michael Petit's "digital disaffect," cyberpunk sci-fi writer Bruce Sterling pointed to what he called the "dark euphoria" inherent in some types of internet use, a deeply ambivalent exploration of the mediations, glitches, and other more social *détournements* of connection: gleefully diving headlong into the depths of misaligned algorithmic recommendations or exploring the more antisocial and startling feeds of Reddit forums, Discord servers, or 4chan boards.[47] Outside these extremes, in our everyday life, Tim Markham asks us to value the "restless agility" of connection and embrace practices of "digital wayfaring," a way to better understand these difficult to identify but immediately understood digital experiences.[48]

If we can accept (or, indeed, celebrate) that these forms of digital connection hold value, then these meanderings across digital spaces can become social strolls, where just hanging out online can be disconnected from a given outcome yet meaningful in its own right; and that is a specifically social meaning. A decade ago, when Skype represented the dominant video-call platform in the West, Jack and his friends were already familiar with a wider variety of more niche-use, independent video-chat applications. Just as many people spend time together using their devices while face-to-face or physically copresent, they do so online as well. Jack explains that, when he is video chatting with someone for the first time, he needs to determine if they are "a talker or a typer" and that the talkers always expect his full attention: "it is completely different—pretty annoying." He compares those who expect full monopolistic engagement rather than the more casual "hanging out online" to what he refers to as the "phone people, who just don't get the message." By picking up the phone to make a call or speaking (rather than typing) over video chat, an individual signals not just a commencement of interaction but also an entire set of perceptions about both the relationship and the proper use of technologies.

Just as a prism separates and bends light into its constituent colors, our communication environment disperses the quality of fully engaged presence into discrete but overlapping opportunities for engaging with others and media platforms simultaneously. Managing presence in this way allows video platforms to provide an intimate window between the private spaces of users. Video can involve the situated and embodied presences of each user at their respective devices, but by separating this form of synchronous, mutual engagement from embodied audio (i.e., voice), then numerous other forms of near-synchronous and asynchronous engagement can occur—text-based instant message services, sharing links, files, posts, memes, and commentary across any number of platforms, while possibly dipping in and out of watching videos, game play, or online browsing. This separation of full presence into strands of embodied, synchronous communication allows for flexibility across more disembodied, asynchronous forms of digital communication and the different rhythms of engagement they require.

Practices for Organizing and Disorganizing Attention

Operating through the metamedia of our devices—between and below multiple platforms—the management of communication cannot be separated from its media. But humans do just that. With an increasing magnitude of interactions, and greater complexity in media repertoires, management practices begin to transcend the communication environment, which itself becomes the object to be managed. Our communication platforms are not just tools for organizing, storing, and retrieving communication; they are environments designed to organize our attention and availability, but through practices of disconnection, we regain degrees of agency in the flow and rhythm of asynchronous engagement and disengagement, of presence and absence, in real time.

Ethan, a thirty-year-old app developer, expresses what seems to be a simple communication-management goal: "I would love a better way to separate signal from noise." During our interview at a Spitalfields café in East London where he often works, Ethan dismisses several beeps from his mobile phone indicating that social-network messages had been received. He does glance at his laptop quickly to assess the new emails as they periodically appear in his inbox. A quick glance at a screen can tell users what needs engagement or immediate action and what can wait. "At a glance" was a phrase often used to market developments in classification and indexing, where tabs and other labels aided the user in locating particular files among others in their file-storage systems. "Mind, eye, and hand can soon be trained so that they automatically act together and do teamwork that is invaluable": this how-to-file guidebook echoes the types of disconnection inherent in communication management.[49] For Ethan, this echoes his sense of an idealized professional media literacy at the level of metamedia communication management. Speaking to the disconnected sociality it fosters, however, he then corrects himself: "In fact there is nothing that I would consider as interesting as direct SMS messages from mates." This desire for mutual engagement only grew amid the forced disconnection of the pandemic, where it was immersion in the latent possibility of unfocused engagement—that buzz of crowds and casual forms of copresence—that we craved.

For those unaccustomed to working alone from home until COVID-19, social-distancing restrictions and the switch to virtual work involved a variety of comparable, ongoing virtual hangouts defined in tandem by isolation. Mackenzie, twenty-five, points out that "for people who live alone, working from home has been brutal." In this context, some digital-service and knowledge workers have faced enforced managerial surveillance by video, alongside activity-logging and monitoring systems to track employee engagement on their computers or, rather, engagement with types of client- or productivity-management software. But Mackenzie is describing something different. "My workmate and I started video-conferencing in the afternoons, so that it is a little bit more like when we sat opposite each other in the office." Though primarily focused on their work, they can still chat, ask quick questions about shared documents, and even take coffee breaks together. They shift among different degrees of engagement, sometimes toggling the video or audio to attend to calls, but they are recreating that unfocused sense of being copresent—a compulsion for connection predicated on the prohibition of proximity.

Ambiguous Atmospheres

When the fear of missing out becomes fodder for our anxious scrolling, and workplace pressures find us refreshing email inboxes and persistently checking our mobile phones, a focus that is free from distraction can be difficult to achieve. The sociologist Christian Licoppe has studied how notifications from multiple types of apps or platforms interrupt our ability to do computer-based work; he calls this a "crisis of the summons."[50] To manage time means managing degrees of engagement and disengagement amid constant connection, managing one's active presence via one platform while purposefully maintaining a degree of networked absence from others, while only rarely ever actually fully disconnecting by turning devices off.

"It's like a back-and-forth journey between productivity and distraction." Many of us will recognize Hannah's frustration. "My phone is beside me as I do [this research], and it's definitely distracting. . . . If I don't take these little phone breaks, the task feels tedious [but] this usually ends up with me yelling at myself." She mentions that she "[picks] up [her] phone many times to answer texts or scroll through TikTok, Twitter, Snapchat, etc.," specifying that "I don't often even realize I've picked up my phone, and when I do tune into this, I'm like 'SERIOUSLY?!' " This is the temptation of constant connection that many seek to manage. Curtailing the automaticity of time-consuming and repetitive practices that allow us to maintain connection is a practice of communication management.

Samira describes an evening of her freelance work as a social-media director for a Toronto-based PR agency, "creating and uploading social-media content for clients." The task (or rather tasks) in front of her require a focused, productive duration of time to create "twenty pieces of content that aligns with their business brand within one to two hours." These posts need to be scheduled to coincide with a client's event, while the duration of work also needs to stay within her contracted hours. She frames this sensitive management of her digital work in terms of managing her communication environment: "[I'm] choosing between getting my work done within the timeframe or [being] distracted by my phone. I have a client's business on the line, so I couldn't risk being distracted." At thirty, Margaret works for a UK-based market-research company and similarly draws a bright line between durations of time for social communication and for work-oriented communication, though from a full-time employment context: "I just kind of compartmentalize my life so that during the workdays I'm just basically focused on my work. Say, for example, I go out for lunch; then I might pick up the phone to speak to my partner. But I don't really call my friends to have a chat, maybe send a text about any plans that we may have in the evening."

By disengaging from social media and personal communication via her phone and desktop computer during her workday, Margaret maintains productivity. She admits, however, that when lunch hits, "I find myself logging in [to Facebook] every day, which is a bit like—because I can. So it just becomes part of, like, a habit or a thing to do. . . . When twelve o'clock comes around . . ." Her sentence drifts off as she is clearly frustrated by this idea; then she adds that she is fine with this compartmentalization as a beneficial limit to her social-media use: "It's okay because I don't necessarily want to be on Facebook every day."

Communication management becomes a way to resegregate times and spaces for work and personal life, despite the opportunities to remain connected across so many different platforms, whether at work, at home, or on the move. Managing one's communication environment in durational blocks that separate work and personal life maintains strict limits on times and spaces not traditionally associated with work. In contrast to careers based on the right workplace "atmosphere" in tune with the lives of highly mobile knowledge workers, these are practices of disconnection that respond to the difficulty in maintaining the boundaries of working life, what Gregg calls the "presence bleed" of work-based connection intervening among the atmosphere and intimacy of personal life.[51] After a long day of work, Margaret describes her desire for wholesale communication absence and unavailability: "But then there's times when you're just like I want to cut the whole world off; you may put your phone somewhere else so you don't want to hear it or you may just go to voicemail. Or you just may, like, you know, just shut off for a little while and that's because that's the way you're kind of feeling at that moment."

Having said that, Margaret is still accessible on her landline telephone "... if my mum rings—many people don't have my home number ... we've restricted it to certain people ... whereas everyone else has our mobile number." She permits her parents to connect, even when she is "shut off" from the world, but admits that when the landline rings, she can then make the decision to answer or not, knowing that it is likely her mother.

Precarious Careers and Platform Dependence

Sometimes we just need to disconnect, but not everyone has that luxury. Despite the desire to limit distractions and focus on work, many early career adults increasingly find themselves without the opportunity for secure full-time employment that permits the management of one's day as if it were a traditional nine-to-five workday. Samira is a few years older than most of her classmates and returned to higher education as a mature student after moving to Canada from the Middle East. "In the middle of finishing an assignment for school, I am trying to stay off of my phone and ignore the notifications that pop up. With an important call that came through, I had to stop doing my assignment and take the call. ... While I lost time on my assignment, I did acquire time with a new client to help resolve some of their issues in their business."

The competing pressures for work and school make managing a productive and focused atmosphere challenging. Limiting one's availability while trying to finish work for a deadline could make the difference between a new contract or struggling to pay rent. Despite how reluctant Chris is to have his computer on at all times, in a short break during our interview he hopped up from the kitchen table and dashed into the bedroom to check his email. "I am waiting to hear back about a contract," he explains. He returned from the bedroom with his mobile phone in hand, to see if he had any missed calls or texts. "I don't leave [my computer] on until I go to bed and I don't constantly check it—but while it is on, I will go back to it quite regularly, and I quite like the fact that there might be something there that can give me a moment's distraction from whatever else I'm doing. So I would just leave it running in the background and I will look at it."

Outside of his evening shifts on a government contract, Chris juggles a handful of freelance-editing contracts at any given time alongside a steadier part-time role as a journal editor. His years working with the government have also been part-time and without job security. Often used in the service industry, zero-hour contracts (ZHC) like Chris's have become an increasingly common method for large employers to adjust their workforces in light of new client contracts or in response to business slowdowns or budget squeezes. Permissive labor legislation in the UK that allows ZHCs represents a precursor to the contractor (rather than employee) status central to the gig economy.[52] Both scenarios deny traditional employer obligations to this flexible workforce. Despite the utility of maintaining connection in the background while completing his editing work, Chris is sensitive to the counterproductive experience of having any device and its multiple communication platforms constantly at hand, with notifications, messages, or emails persistently streaming in and visible on the screen. Chris simply doesn't feel he has a choice: if he is still working (whatever the hour, given his nontraditional schedule), he will keep checking for correspondence related to contracts and pitches. Other nontraditional work contexts present similar challenges. This is part of what Julie Ticona calls the "digital hustle" of the precarious worker's continual search for work, opportunities, collaborators, and the like.[53]

Where constant connection is the norm, as if by default owing to social expectations and employment obligations, disengagement requires concerted effort. In that context, disconnection from work-oriented platforms translates into the "reward" of reconnection with other forms of more personal connection, earned only after patient diligence and productivity. Richard, thirty-nine, has a full-time job with a constantly changing rotation, just one of the reasons why he is looking for other work somewhere in London. He manages his day-off as if it is a traditional workday, applying a "stoic work ethic" to job hunting by limiting his engagement with social media. More specifically, he has dating sites open on his laptop with messages streaming in while he is job hunting: "They beep if I have a message, but I won't be checking them properly or actively seeing who's online until my work is done." He describes this as the trade-off, a "treat" to reward his commitment to filling out applications. This sort of disengagement is fairly common for Richard, who is not permitted to access social media at work nor to use his mobile phone. He explains that because of the demanding hours of his changing shifts, he often has to sleep through the day, "and I turn my mobile off a lot as well because I don't expect my friends to understand my rota[tion]. . . . So I just turn everything off, I unplug my phone. So I try to create as much radio silence as possible is what I'm trying to say." While others cannot disconnect because of their precarious positions, some types of work make constant connection undesirable and disruptive to simple necessities like sleep.

For precarious and early career workers across several sectors, success is not only about juggling pressures of constant connection and the need for productive concentration. Digital and platform literacy is central to finding work and progressing throughout one's career. Yuki is "searching for jobs on Indeed.com . . . because it is easy to apply and there are always a bunch of new job postings every time I enter a new application." But, she adds, bleakly, "Honestly, I have no idea what to do during my summer break because I am still not so sure what I plan to do for my vocation—for my career—my plan for the summer is to manage my YouTube channel. I want to be my own interviewer, though this seems unprofessional. For this summer, I just want to discover things that interest me, and try to somehow incorporate them into my future career."

Without clear options at the beginning of their careers, many turn to social media as a possible first step in developing vocational skills and crafting a professional identity.[54] Some turn to job-aggregator sites; others target potential employers. Either way, the amount of time it takes to craft an application weighs heavily. Filipa's nervousness captures this: "This afternoon I focused on sending an e-mail for a fashion internship at Vogue Brazil. The email was on draft for a very very long time." Similarly, Lian wakes up to messages from the CEO of an internship she is beginning in a month or so: "We messaged for a while, discussing what content I should add [to my first] article to improve it. I was extra careful about the messages that I sent[, which] were polite and show [the] right attitude when facing criticism. . . . There is a chance he might take back the internship offer. I do not want to lose my internship."

How we seek to control our mediated presence haunts early career and precariously employed adults, from the job-application stage throughout the uneasy years of entry-level positions. Following the mass layoffs and furloughs of the pandemic, competition for entry-level jobs will intensify. New graduates are finding themselves having to continue their fraught frontline service work as cashiers and clerks that sustained them as students. In the years that followed the Great Recession, a US-based study of metropolitan-area job ads found polarization of opportunity in response to the recession, where entry-level positions were more difficult to find as employers ratcheted up requirements for paid positions in order to attract more seasoned yet possibly underemployed candidates.[55] Via numerous interviews with entry-level cultural producers in the fashion, beauty, and retail sectors, Brooke Erin Duffy's account of such underpaid "aspirational" labor, taken in hopes of generating future work opportunities, is that it often reinforces inequities produced by socioeconomic privilege, favoring those with the time and often the familial resources to commit to such low-paid work.[56]

Internships represent white-collar roles created by employers as additional echelons of support staff to take on largely undervalued and routinized work. For the interns, these are purported opportunities to gain professional experience and interpersonal footholds in particular sectors, resulting in increasing competitiveness for the scarce and often still-precarious entry-level positions in paid employment. In their study of young women who have completed unpaid internships in Toronto and New York's creative sector, Leslie Regan Shade and Jenna Jacobson found that "inequality prevails" across gendered, racialized, and class-based lines where many believed these positions amounted to "paying their dues" by working full-time for little or no pay, while still managing expectations of extended availability in order to gain entry within an industry.[57] Unlike in the UK, unpaid internships and work placements are no longer legal in Canada but still persist, with young women being the substantial majority of unpaid interns in the arts, fashion, and creative media industries. In their qualitative textual analysis of one hundred entry-level job adverts and fifty internship ads across US job-search sites, Brooke Erin Duffy and Becca Schwartz focused on advertisements with "social media" as central to the role: a soft skill seen as sociable but also as creative and digital knowledge work.[58] Ironically, these positions involve the labor of creatively producing online visibility for organizations but are invisible within the political-economic hierarchies of these organizations. A demonstrable social-media presence is required to secure these un- or underpaid positions, which in turn diminish time for personal social-media work in favor of the organization or brand.

Disconnected Connection

Disconnection is not merely a turning away from connection; it is a turning toward something different, something outside of what any specific connection promises, but also something deeper that we might be able to forge in constant connection with each other. Often, we understand disconnection from a very utilitarian point of view, undergirding the very practice of selecting the optimal modes of connection relationally in a given context, a given time, or a given set of relationships.[59]

Our repertoire of communication possibilities is fundamentally intertwined with practiced degrees of disconnection to facilitate particular intensities of engagement and reciprocity. The pressures of maintaining constant connection and keeping up with multiple, overlapping modalities of communication can take a toll, not just in terms of the overwhelming pressures of connection but in the disconnection from those that we care about and from the full engagement with those experiences we value. We manage our communication environments by ordering opportunities for connection in several different ways and for different purposes. Concerted engagement is often deliberately temporal: durations of time committed to presence and mutual engagement or intermittent yet continuous forms of engagement. Managing and dividing our attention achieves a variety of ends: committing to time interacting with friends or family; the flow and immersion of entertainment, gaming, and other online forms of wayfaring; or creating particular atmospheres for productivity. Among a variety of other, often platform-specific techniques for managing disconnection, we manage connection by practicing disconnection, defined by different degrees of disengagement and managed absences.

For the platform industry, it is a commercial imperative to subsume practices of disconnection as features of connection. And so, platform designers have increasingly begun to incorporate features that allow for degrees of managing notifications, disengagement, and disconnection, which, counterintuitively, are achieved through further engagement with the platform. These disconnective affordances are interactive design features that seek to incorporate our prosocial everyday practice of disengaging from platforms within the data-producing affordances of their interfaces.[60] There are additional inventions by platform-based entertainment media, however, designed to fill those moments in between other activities—plugging those gaps that disconnection creates. Entire economic models of media production and social-media features—what Ethan Tussey defined as the "the procrastination economy"—have been engineered for these quick dips into the constant stream of social media, snack-sized streaming content, or game modules designed particularly to deepen and serialize those brief in-between moments of a workday, commute, or even lapses in attention while consuming other media.[61]

What if there is something lost without distraction, without the unexpected, without the contingency anticipated in boredom and definitional of interruption? What if there is value in a disconnection that is derived from endless connections and vicissitudes among our social media and connective platforms? Just as Couldry has pointed to the "writer-gatherer" intuitively or maybe only fortuitously ambling among online new sources, Tim Markham points to the types of productive, "improvised professional activity" that are not put off by intensity or interruption, where the unexpected is fuel for a "temporal momentum," which I would project onto what we may find in the jostling between connection and disconnection.[62] Digital wayfaring speaks more closely to the types of disconnection we find amid media use itself. Even early internet lingo carried this connotation; we did not search the internet—we surfed it—a World Wide Web of discovery rather than only uncertainty and anxiety.

The social legibility of our practices—of connection and disconnection—come to afford and constrain the social possibilities for interaction with others. Yet so much of how I have been speaking about disconnection has been a matter of individual agency, users in isolation seeking to better manage the intensities of constant connection, a disconnected sociality precluding mutual human engagement. We are more attuned to the reverberations and rhythms of social life in all of its contradictory multiplicity; we find balance through degrees of disconnection and connection, but if we do not recognize that we do so together, then a wholly individuated sociality emerges attuned to and idealized by the interventions of employment and platform imperatives in tandem. These interventions are concretized as social norms of practice that are then carried forward in time.

The more mundane, the more taken-for-granted, the more inconsequential we believe each degree of disconnection to be, the more indifferent we prove to be about the social—and in that sense moral and political—ramifications of how we connect and disconnect with others. What, then, would a more relational, social form of collective disconnection look like?[63] To answer this, I look to how we are brought together in connection and, for good or for ill, learn from each other in disconnection.

FOUR

Practicing Surveillance

Classifying and observing, searching for social cues while scrutinizing one's own digital footprints—our everyday lives are replete with social information. Our interactions and engagements with devices and platforms, and with each other through these devices and platforms, continually produce information—digital traces that offer clues to our everyday lives—both for consumption by other users and for automated collection by commercial-media platforms. Whether with strangers or acquaintances, coworkers or friends, romantic partners or family, when we interact, we glean insight from others' actions. When mediated by technology, the form of that information changes, as do the ways in which we act on it. Sharing is often heralded as the central pillar of the platform ecosystem.[1] Yet for the flow of information to function, there is another pillar, obscured from view because of its assumed passivity: observation and social surveillance predicated on, and productive of, disconnected sociality.

Participating in surveillance involves a reliance on typologies of use, a scouring of digital traces left by others, and a scrutinizing of the reception of one's own self-presentation across the platform ecosystem. Whether face-to-face communication, emails, text and instant messages, or social-media posts, engaging in communication allows us to build a picture of how others communicate and to gain a better understanding of the intervening mediations of the platform technologies that connect us. This information extends from subtle cues and personal details about one's communication preferences to wider assumptions about communication norms relevant to different contexts. These are found in the persistent digital footprints of past media actions, traces scattered across numerous social-media profiles, feeds in the interface-level archives we carry around with us: app notifications, SMS histories, email, and direct-message inboxes, alongside, of course, our own memory. Our persistent scrutiny of these diverse cues to how others communicate informs our own communicative actions online, yet this is accomplished through degrees of disconnection. Cognitively and emotionally, we cast others in the role of the individual receiver, imagining contexts for how they can and will be engaged, at times making assumptions by distinguishing between sets of people in our lives as informal audiences to our everyday actions online.

The loss of awareness about how best to connect with others offers a useful entry point for understanding how practices of surveillance facilitate interpersonal communication. Where everyday opportunities for accruing information about others are sparse or lacking, the shared awareness of how others communicate or would prefer to communicate dissolves, and this interferes with our routines of everyday communication decision-making. In such cases, an acknowledged lack of awareness contributes to forms of self-restraint and even to an anxious hesitation stemming from the inability to engage with others in the most efficacious and least disruptive manner.

Christina, twenty-seven, has a small core of close friends in London whom she sees in person at least two times or more every week. They share a constant stream of text messages as well as individual and group emails—mundane anecdotes from daily life and arrangements for meeting up in person. These close friends are aware of each other's schedules and everyday communication habits. One friend has recently moved out of the city and, without constant contact and the awareness flowing from such interaction, Christina struggles to connect with her: "I have got out of the habit [with my friend] of regular catch-ups so now every phone call takes more effort and time. . . . I was also oddly amused thinking that this was a bit of a Catch-22. . . . So today I sent her another email to ask her if she was available to chat on the phone over the weekend and, if so, what time would suit best."

Christina refrains from phoning this friend without advanced planning, as was once the norm, because she is no longer aware of her friend's day-to-day schedule. She elects to shift away from live modes of communication to an asynchronous email communication, to avoid any potential interruption or intrusion into her friend's day. She writes in her diary: "Now, my thoughts after sending that [email] were . . . sadness that I am no longer able to spontaneously ring my friends due to . . . not knowing what they are up to/commitments." Through more consistent contact with her other friends, Christina is aware of their communication habits and their availability as it changes throughout the day, and therefore knows when she would not be intruding, and could call them without having to ask permission first, via email.

"I'm surprised and bloody furious my mobile phone rang at 8.30 a.m. and woke me up," writes Richard about being the receiver of unwanted attempts to connect. "Because I've been doing this job for eighteen months now, it's settled into this thing where people presume that I'm available at funny times so the onus is on me because after the first three or four months they have stopped phoning me on an ad-hoc basis. . . . And I would have to say I was going to have to be at work at four in the morning or nine at night and why should your friends know your rota—it's ridiculous."

The antisocial hours of Richard's shifting rotation have meant that friends and family have nearly all become hesitant to get in touch. They lack the consistent patterns of interaction and crucial social cues on which to determine how best to connect. Both Christina and Richard are assessing how best to connect with others in the individualized terms of a *receiving self*: the other user or users whose reciprocal engagement is imagined with every attempt to connect interpersonally, including, at times, reflections on the physically situated and technological contexts from which they'd have to manage connection to others.

Lena rolls her eyes when considering how her friends' and family's lack of awareness affects her own communication decisions: "They don't actually know my schedule. . . . If they knew that I—actually I wasn't home Tuesday all day long for example—then they wouldn't SMS me asking me if I am home. They are just kind of, you know, poking and probing me." Working in fashion, both as an independent online retailer and model, Lena has been living in different cities across the EU over the last decade, with a short stint in the UEA before London. A number of her close friends and relatives live abroad or in England but outside of the London city center. Time zones matter as much as knowledge of everyday habits. Skype, the once dominant online video-calling program, is her primary mode of communication, what she deems her most "personal" platform. "So the Skype is always open. I'm always signed in [on my desktop and laptop]. . . . They'll ask me, are you [on] Skype—they'll send me an SMS asking. Then if I don't pick up the Skype call, they'll send me an SMS asking right away, 'Where are you? Are you home? What are you doing? Can you come on Skype?' . . . It's fine."

At first glance, sending an SMS by mobile phone before video calling on the computer seems to be about simple coordination, but it's as if Lena's friends first send an SMS to ask permission, give warning, or to otherwise initiate what would become the call. She clarifies how exactly she puts more effort into connecting with them: "Because you see [my best friend] . . . I know when not to [video call] her because she has a baby. I pretty much know a baby's schedule, so when the baby is asleep I wouldn't bother them. I make an effort to remember that, to remember [different] schedules. . . . I bother about these things, and they don't."

Practices of connection, timing, and production of knowledge about how best to communicate, in general and with certain individuals, mix with passive, partially disconnected forms of social surveillance, as well as more explicit attempts to seek information about how another communicates, based on the digital traces they leave online. Christina felt that she couldn't just phone because she didn't know her friend's daily routine. So, she emailed, although she was unaware of when the email would be addressed. By sending a text, Lena's friends and family have found a medium-based solution to Richard's and Christina's dilemmas. But Lena expects a higher degree of consideration so that she can time how best to contact them. The binary shift between synchronous and asynchronous communication represents a degree of disconnection from full, live connection—the most rudimentary choice among the highly idiosyncratic cognitive patterns that are now inherent in how we manage connections with each other. Undergirding these patterns of decision-making are practices of social surveillance.

Social Surveillance as Knowledge Production

The lofty promises of Big Data and the mythologized power of algorithmic content curation are accompanied by a wider struggle to find appropriate ways to talk about how exactly technology influences social life, particularly in relation to the imperatives of commercial platforms to collect and profit from data derived from how we communicate online.[2] The automated production of data is part of everyday interactions, whereby digital artifacts of our media practices produce traces of the types of connection occurring between users themselves and between users and media technology. Wendy Hui Kyong Chun argues that the public needs to reconsider devices and platforms as being "leaky": our private information is drawn across numerous, porous boundaries, among a variety of commercial and governmental actors.[3] Highlighting the industry's common reference to the data by-product of digital practices as "digital exhaust," Melissa Gregg draws our attention back to the human user, noting that "data sweat" might be a more appropriate term. If exhaust is the by-product of machinery, sweat is outcome of human effort.[4] In this case, the production of digital sweat is not the intention of our interpersonal communication. Rather, it is the by-product of those social lives acting in concert with devices, platforms, and network infrastructure. This echoes my own proposal that the perceived need or compulsion to maintain constant connection takes real, embodied, and time-consuming effort.[5] However, what if we were to look away from the commercial utility of this data production and to the production of knowledge and conventions about communication occurring between users themselves during their everyday interactions?

The practices of creating, disseminating, and visibly engaging with digital content cannot be fully disentangled from the less visible navigation, consumption, and passive engagement, by users, with digital content already circulating across their apps, platforms, and device interfaces. These are the dual aspects of online participatory practices, captured colloquially in the ways that we speak about online life, as well as by the ethos of how one ought to be connected, as extolled by platform marketing. Updating and sharing, friending and following, a visibility and vitality in our engagements with each other's actions online are championed among other intermediary types of interactions with digital content. These sets of observational and consumption-oriented practices have alternately been referred to as "lateral" or "social" surveillance, yet they recursively instruct us on how to connect, informing the "participatory surveillance" practices central to interpersonal digital life.[6]

This "little data" or, rather, local data of everyday life represent another entry point for understanding how the social world is partially constituted *through* interpersonal practices and *as* communication practices. This approach also provides an opportunity to assess how such everyday communication practices reinforce and contribute to the commercial imperative that underpins the platform and surveillance economies. In the next two chapters, I explore the practices through which users develop reflexive perspectives on communication practices for the purposes of negotiating and repairing their relationships with each other through their shared communication environment. In this chapter, I home in on practices of observation, and the development of user awareness of the pressures of the networked platform environment, as experienced through everyday work and social life.

Acts of surveillance—to survey, to watch over—are often conflated with clear institutionalized power differentials. State and security agencies watch over populations and platforms, whereas corporate entities surveil users of platforms to monetize their actions, preferences, and demographic differences for commercial profit.[7] Both forms of surveillance are thought to be unidirectional: those who surveil and those who are surveilled. Similar acts of observation and assessment occur, however, among the routines of our everyday social world. Some are the more conventional social hierarchies, still present when parents watch over children, teachers over students, or employers over employees. Yet other types of surveillance exist outside such explicit or formalized hierarchies of power. Power itself—or, rather, the ability of one's actions to influence the actions of another—is diffused, decentralized, and part of every social relationship, if not also any and every interaction.

Practices of social surveillance can also take on the prosocial role of providing an informative contextual basis, helping to facilitate interpersonal communication. In a matter-of-fact way, Andrew, thirty-three and on the job hunt in the environmental advocacy sector, explains that when you learn how another communicates, "You take that information and roll it into your own algorithm" about how to connect with others. Social surveillance refers to the sets of actions and practices that can provide for a degree of networked awareness about others' lives and about how they communicate, which is the central focus of this chapter. In the context of physically situated and face-to-face communication, we are familiar with the salaciousness of eavesdropping and gossip, as well as the more odious notions of lurking, stalking, and voyeurism. We draw terminology from these auditory, visual, and embodied forms of surveillance to project meaning onto our digital engagements.[8] In particular, the visual nature of digital media—interfaces, newsfeeds, profiles—tends to inform our reading of the more threatening aspects of passive online engagement.

Kate Crawford examines how these less-visible practices of user observation are more akin to listening.[9] In the same way that listening is necessary for conversations to succeed, auditory, not visual, metaphors imply the necessary and productive role of these practices.[10] In the context of mobile and online platforms, the role of viewing, reading, or otherwise taking in content is often overlooked because it is less visible, leaving few if any persistent digital traces for other users to know that their comment, post, photo, or video has been, or is being, viewed by another on the platform. Understanding social surveillance as a contributive practice on which networked and online communication depends prompts us to expand our definition of what sets of actions constitute a communication practice and to look beyond only those actions that leave observable digital outputs for other users.

Typologies of Use

Observation of how others communicate across spaces for social interaction represents functional practice within the wider gamut of interpersonal communication practices. Such forms of social surveillance provide a better understanding of the actions of others and the situated, everyday contexts that may influence their communication practices. This surveillance results in a sensitivity to communication decisions and becomes the basis for our own. Understanding these constituent dimensions of communication as sets of intertwined practices sheds light on the way shared knowledge of communication is constructed, negotiated, and expressed in the spaces of everyday social interaction.

Awareness of another person's everyday routines and the contexts that may influence their opportunities for communication combines with past communication experiences as the basis for communication decisions in the present. Social cues are often biographical in nature. Some may pertain to habitual patterns of media use, others to known and observed degrees of digital literacy. But there are also assumed communication conventions and commonly assumed typologies of use that individuals often relate more directly to mode of communication or platform, projecting these norms onto their presumed functionality, a sense of how best to use a technology often defined in relation to assumed best uses of other platforms. The early nineteenth-century social phenomenologist Alfred Schütz examined our reliance on shared assumptions of what "common sense" tells us about a given social situation, drawing from both observed or otherwise known actions of each other and any assumed biographical information. Common sense, he argues, is derived from the "interchangeability of standpoints" between individuals, where the contexts of everyday actions, and the determination of how biographical relevancies could map onto those contexts, are a space for informational exchange.[11] In the next chapter, we will explore just how incongruous assumptions about common sense can be and how these assumptions lead to forms of policing how we connect with each other—a normative assumption that our individual experiences are wholly applicable to the lives of others. First, however, this chapter will look at how we, as users, manage the fields of observable communication practices and digital traces of those practices in relation to our attempts to manage ongoing and future possibilities for connection with others.

Individuals make internalized assumptions about the physical location, environment, activity, and proximity to communication devices of those with whom they communicate or hope to communicate. Goffman points to the (re)construction of such otherwise "unapparent facts" as central to one's negotiation of any given social communication setting: "To uncover fully the factual nature of the situation, it would be necessary for the individual to know all the relevant social data about others. . . . Full information of this order is rarely available; in its absence the individual tends to employ substitutes—cues, tests, hints, expressive gestures, status symbols, etc.—as predictive devices."[12]

For this purpose, the notion of interchangeable "standpoints" takes on both literal meanings and more abstract, socially constructed meanings: one's knowledge and assumptions of the literal standpoints of another's physically situated environment are complemented by knowledge and assumptions regarding socially derived contexts of being free or busy, available or overwhelmed, occupied in interpersonal interaction or a pressing work duty.

Observable Interaction in the Offline World

I want to emphasize that such observable aspects of how we communicate are not restricted to the online world. The knowledge produced through practices of social surveillance is not derived solely from visible digital footprints of messages, posts, comments, and other cues that map out our online behavior. Observing how an individual communicates is as central to copresent, face-to-face interaction as it is to technologically mediated forms of interaction. Practices of social surveillance include the manner in which clear media preferences, degrees of difficulty and literacy in media use, and other aspects of everyday communication can be observed during face-to-face interaction, contributing further to shared awareness of what needs to be considered in the course of interpersonal communication.

Evelyn, a thirty-three-year-old mother of two young girls, provides an example of this when she refers to one of her close friends: "You know, she actually made her first eBay purchase last month and I did it for her. . . . And I literally had to walk it through . . . completely different in terms of our awareness of how to use a computer." With a short laugh, she describes this friend succinctly as "not a computer person" and knows not to email her without having to test that mode of communication first. She has observed enough through face-to-face interaction to be aware of this attribute. She continues, talking about her other friends, most of whom are mothers of children the same age as her own: "So we spend a lot of time [in] face-to-face communication but also because we're together you can also see what other forms [of communication] they use. When you're at their house, you know if the computer's on. You know if their landline never rings or if they get texts. You can kind of just infer what their lifestyle's like because you do spend time in their homes or with them while they're communicating with you or with others."

Face-to-face communication becomes, then, another modality through which communication habits can be observed. Lourdes, who is twenty-five and working in public relations, offers an example outside of the home and how it relates to her decision to contact a friend and colleague: "I'd probably call her. . . . I find specifically with her that she, it takes her a very long time to write emails. So I'm quite aware of the fact that it can eat into her day. So sometimes I think it's better just to kind of have a good, like, meaty conversation for fifteen minutes rather than her sit there, like, one-finger-typing for half an hour when I know she's got other stuff to do."

Lourdes draws a clear connection between her decision to phone rather than email and observable actions that are, again, not based on digital-platform activity or what is stored on devices but on physical co-presence. She continues, describing the motivation for acting on this awareness: "I've seen her do it before I guess. . . . I've noticed that she'll take a long time to reply to emails. Or even, simply, because I type quite quickly, I might reply to her and then it would take her a good half an hour to get back to me."

This last comment demonstrates conscientiousness for her interlocutor's efficiency and ease of communication, while also implying an awareness of how time-consuming digital communication practices can be for some. There is an implied sharing of the temporal cost here: the decision to adapt to the abilities of her interlocutor involves minimizing the effort to engage for the receiver and taking on the burden of connection as part of her decision-making. What is the easiest and best way to connect with someone based on their experience as the receiver of a message or interaction? Lourdes illustrates a willingness to adjust her communication methods to achieve mutual, beneficial forms of engagement. She and her interlocutor adjust to each other's perceived preferences to maintain the flow of communication.

To understand the communication environment of another is to understand situated, embodied, and contextual connection as it occurs in their everyday life. This involves an awareness of past opportunities for interaction within their schedule and physical environment, as well as biographical details, all of which contribute to a better sense of their type of communication environment, media preferences, and technological literacy levels. Not getting this right can delay or deflect mutual engagement, or even have it refused, owing to conflicting practices of managing engagement and disengagement across platforms. An individual's consistent reflection on the communicative preferences of others contributes to an awareness of the subtle manifestations of media preferences that are embedded within everyday interpersonal communication decisions.

Typologies and Timing

Surveillance need not always be nefarious. Social surveillance, in particular, is often for the purposes of connection. In the context of practical but affective forms of continual interpersonal engagement, shared knowledge about interpersonal communication habits acts as a temporally regulating and ordering force. Before examining the relevance(s) of user device, interface, and digital traces, it is important to consider that so much of human communication is already predicated on perception of the communication environment. In our temporally mediated, fragmented, and distributed engagement with asynchronous platforms, the continuity of perceiving, anticipating, and reflecting on mediated outcomes defers any certainty amid constant connection despite our best intentions.[13]

Evelyn, like Lourdes, constructs typologies of friends as part of her communication decisions: "I certainly have different categories of friends. And I might be just as close to them [or they may be] as close as some friends as others but *we've chosen a different way* of communicating." There are sets of communication practices for certain groups, but this is not necessarily determined by closeness or interactional experience. Evelyn alludes to an implicit process of mutual negotiation: "we've chosen" one pattern over another of how best to communicate.

Grouped sets of communication practices represent small-scale typologies with limited applicability to certain clusters of friends and other contacts. Evelyn understands these typologies in terms of the everyday contexts that affect the possibility and desire for interaction. She describes communication habits of the young mothers in her neighborhood: "we don't have time to go on email, check back and forth. . . . It'll often be a more face-to-face or texting type of relationship." Evelyn's communication decisions stem from an awareness of a typical mother's everyday possibilities for communication. Her broad assumptions about a young mother's schedule blend with a sense of how and when she wants to be contacted. This typology is based on Evelyn's practice of being unavailable or inaccessible at certain times, which are aligned with the young mothers she is close to. This awareness helps her define how to interact with others about whom she does not have enough biographical or past interpersonal experience to know hour-to-hour and day-to-day communication preferences. Evelyn's conflation of her own practices with those of the other young mothers—"we don't have time to go on email"—involves Schütz's "interchangeability of standpoints," the foundation for shared assumptions about others.[14] Such comparison contributes to an assumed common sense in communication practices, even when the limited and context-specific nature of those assumptions belies the very universality that often underpins assumptions about others. As Evelyn describes:

> Often because we want to arrange to see each other with the kids so I'll know—most children in my life tend to nap right after lunch. . . . However, I know some of my friends have very inconsistent children or aren't as strict mothers with schedule, and others are very rigid and I know that between one and three [in the afternoon], like, don't call and this, that and the other. And I know a couple of my other friends have morning naps.
>
> I find that especially with my mum friends, texting is very popular. We usually have a bunch of screaming kids; you can never have a proper conversation, and everyone's kids have a slightly different schedule. So someone might be trying to put their kid down for a nap, and they don't want their phone to ring, you know; you're going to catch them off time. . . . So for a very few of my friends I do actually pick up the phone now and call them.

Practices of social surveillance acknowledge the diversity of contexts and needs that would affect the communication habits of others, while also accepting that an individual cannot possibly keep track of the temporal pressures and everyday contingencies that define another's ability to manage their own communication environment. Evelyn generalizes her own practices of limiting engagement at certain times, such as during naps, and generalizes her inaccessibility on certain mediums, such as phone and email (until evening, once the kids are in bed): knowledge of her own practices informs her awareness of other people's practices. This is quite different from the typologies she constructs for other parts of her social network:

> My older friends by email and our—my friends my age by Facebook. . . . They've become big Facebook addicts. So I know that they're just sitting at work sneaking Facebook, so I'll just Facebook them—you know, send them a message there.

Whereas, with friends of mine from . . . in London or outside of London that live further, we know we have to pick up the phone because we won't see each other as often. And I think just a lot of my friends get slotted into different categories of how I interact with them.

Again the "relevances" about the individual's communication environment are conflated with an awareness about an individual's communication habits and the management of potential interaction. Evelyn knows that they will be checking Facebook at work or that for friends who are older than she it is best to email: they have not joined or do not check Facebook. She is not, however, referring to the individuals. She is referring to types of friends and categories designating how they communicate. She is effectively referring to the different ways individuals manage connection by limiting engagement at different times of the day. Such typologies are a conventional understanding of the differentiation and divergence of communication practices as they correspond to different daily routines and situational contexts.

Interfaces and Ordering

Communication decisions about how to connect with others follow and trace patterns of disconnective practices. With basic knowledge about home and work life, individuals are often aware of, or can make assumptions about, another's schedule and append to this knowledge an assumption of what communication interfaces they will be using at different points within that schedule. This involves an awareness or assumption of what interface and platform an individual will be using at certain points of the day and, thus, what channels may provide a greater chance for engagement, or less interruption. Among the many other biographical "relevances" (to use Schütz's term again), knowledge specific to another's use or access to particular interfaces contributes to wider sets of assumptions about communication practices, again organized into typologies of use related to biography. These typologies are partially disconnected from individualized contexts and are applied based on cues to group sets or types of communicators.

Zaina spends a lot of time traveling between the US, where she grew up, and London, where she and her husband live. At the time of our interview, in the wake of the Great Recession, a number of nuanced digital divides had emerged alongside the growing popularity of Apple's iPhone and the emerging availability of competing touchscreen phones using Google's Android operating system, both of which built on the popularity of now defunct email and IM-enabled Blackberry phones, common among knowledge workers at the outset of this research.[15] She explains the crux of her early technological literacy with an analogy: "I know—all my smartphone friends—all my friends, like close friends, I know who all of them with smartphones are, but I have to know these things for my job, right? So it's kind of like, if you're into fashion, you know which one of your friends have designer handbags. You just know it, right?"

As a technology reporter and thus as a professional early adopter of smart phones and social-media mobile platforms, Zaina's awareness of how others communicate is a digitally literate precursor to the social surveillance that has become commonplace among the constantly connected. This literacy involves navigating diverse and legible cues about the conditions that define the communication environments of others.

The availability of affordable data plans for mobile phones and the price barrier that accompanies each generation of internet-ready devices has been compounded by urban and rural infrastructure limitations. These socioeconomic and infrastructural divides cannot be wholly separated from opportunities for individuals to develop digital skills and literacy or from the degree to which connection is necessitated if not expected within their personal and professional lives. In the UK, at that time, and from past interactions, Zaina was aware of who among her close social network had an internet-connected or "smart" mobile phone, but she clarified that "I never make the assumption that other people have smartphones. Never. Because if I go back to New York, none of my friends even have [internet access on their phones], so I don't do emails on the weekends. Text, definitely." Zaina is aware that most of her friends are accessible throughout the entirety of the week by email because even if they do not have an internet-ready mobile phone, she assumes they are working in front of a computer, whether in New York or London. On the weekends, she assumes people are out of the office or otherwise away from computers; thus, she thinks of texting as a better option. Knowing about another's career allows for numerous assumptions about their work setting, the basic schedule of their workday, and this may include knowledge about the modes of communication they will be using during that workday.

In Zaina's banal statement, there is the assumption that a logical communication choice at any given moment not only involves a mix of biographical details but also interpersonal cultural realities specific to particular working lives and workplace settings. Margaret discusses the frequency of employers using Microsoft's popular desktop email software, MS Outlook or Outlook Express, and describes her awareness of how and when others will receive her interactions through that interface:

> So for people who I know aren't on [web-based] email very often—because of course you have to understand—there's always work emails which you can, well, you can use with your friends. So they'll always be on it because you know that their computers are on and they're looking at their emails. . . .
>
> So like if I send them an email and it comes into their [Microsoft Mailing Application] Outlook, because most people have Outlook in offices, they probably would get, like, just a pop-up that an email has come through and that I've emailed them. Or if I don't hear from them for a few hours then I'll follow that up maybe with a text.

Knowing that certain others are typically in front of workplace computers involves additional knowledge of exactly how the interaction will be received on a specific interface, if our assumptions and platform literacies hold true. Margaret's knowledge of the program features contributes to her awareness—for example, a notification popping up in the corner of a screen. Joanne, approximately the same age as Margaret, works for an international credit firm. She compares her awareness of interfaces, distinguishing two sets of friends based on biographical details: "Because I do sit in front of my email programme which happens to be open all day . . . I do find it slightly different depending on the type of industry that the person I'm making plans with is in so. . . . So friends that I work with, or friends that are in an office environment, it is always by email. Friends I know that don't sit in front of a computer all day, it is text."

Lourdes similarly describes why she chooses to email and not to phone particular sets of friends, specifically those with nine-to-five jobs: "I wouldn't necessarily call [my friends] . . . during working hours. I don't

want to interrupt their schedule, don't want to get them in shit for anything . . . for slacking off or anything." This assumption is more nuanced
than it first appears. Lourdes is forgoing the convenience of controlling
when to engage the interaction, which would be expedited by more synchronous modes of communication, such as a call, in an effort "not to
interrupt" the other individual's temporal control over their day. These
decisions are at least partially based on assumptions about the context
in which the receiver would find themselves, even taking into consideration the power relationships and possibility of managerial surveillance
in their working environments.

There are several types of knowledge produced during daily communication. Knowledge about communication practice extends from
assumed typologies of use across sets of individuals to more intimate
details of our sometimes obsessive and idiosyncratic communication-
management practices. Already-established patterns of interpersonal
connection and disconnection provide a stable background against
which specific media decisions become legible.[16] Where these forms of
second-order information are also expressive, decisions about how we
communicate that framing are interpreted, including the way particular communication occurs, from words and statements to body language
and platform-specific actions.[17] In combination, these forms of awareness
allow individuals to infer an ordering of how and when to connect with
others—an awareness of disconnection that cycles between and simultaneously draws on situational, biographical, technological, and individualized forms of awareness as a basis for metacommunication.

Understanding Digital Traces

Connection relies on an amalgam of biographical details, personal knowledge about how people prefer to communicate, and, importantly, what
can be learned about how they interact through traceable interactions.
How we speak about digital life—about the production of data and information concerning our media habits more generally—is consistently inflected by the rhetorics of computation. The impact of this understanding
is twofold. First, data is relegated to a realm that is unknowable, opaque,
and illegible to everyday users. Second, users overlook how much social
information they have access to and use during simple, everyday communication and media practices. We would do well to remember that the

notion of computing predates digital computers. The Latin etymology of *computer* includes *com*, meaning "together," and *putare*, meaning both "to think" and "to prune." This meaning can be understood by considering the pruning of natural elements, combined with a sense of "tidying, setting to rights, balancing an account, reckoning up."[18] Our everyday decision-making in relation to how we communicate involves balancing and pruning, thinking about and reckoning with the pervasive social cues of life.

When the word's two parts are brought together, *computare* suggests "to calculate," derivative of both "computer," originally denoting a person who conducts calculation, and "to count," as well as *compter* in French. These reflexive forms of rationalizing communication choices are amplified and reinforced by the traceability of digital practice, both in the visualized cues scattered across platforms and the quantifiable history of relational experience. In this manner, we decipher what counts, to calculate how best to connect, tidying and pruning the superfluous pressure that we place on others.

The layperson, myself included, has little sense of how to put to use the information from personal caches that platforms like Facebook or Google allow users to download. Digital advertising companies, wider consortiums of advertisers, platforms, and the data-brokerage firms atop the new digital-advertising-industry hierarchy all rely on the aggregation of user data that draws on much wider pools of both publicly accessible and commercially produced marketing data, disaggregated into numerous sets of highly targeted, purposeful, data-driven interventions in users' digital worlds. This extends from automated content curation across social-media platforms and targeted advertising among other forms of recommendations, to responsive environments of gaming and the algorithmic lure of other entertainment platforms adjusting to user patterns to fill those in-between, snack-like moments for mediated distraction.[19] The multitude of real-time, automated adjustments within our digital environment represents just a snapshot of database processes drawing from a myriad of shifting variables, collected from elements of demographic data to immediate contexts of recent web browsing, click-through rates, and scrolling actions, as well as particular flows of information produced and shared for particular commercial outcomes by apps, browser cookies, operating systems, and connected devices at any given moment. David Berry writes that as "an algorithmic totality," individual computational devices and networked databases are in a "constant state of exception," attending to all the diverse forms of input, such that the end point of any computational process is consistently deferred internally to the very process of decision-making.[20] To better understand how our actions produce data, we need to take a step back from what we assume we cannot know about those opaque processes to take stock of what we do know about the communication practices of others and how we come to know this as part of an ongoing negotiation of participatory surveillance, a consistently deferred set of inputs about the practices of others at the level of metacommunication.

Tania cites her full-time job as an assistant producer, and her young daughter, as some of the reasons why she is a somewhat passive user of social networks such as Twitter and Facebook, as well as LiveJournal, which connects her to her international friends, and Soundcloud, where she follows music producers and DJs: "I think it's just, I don't have much time to do communication. So that's why probably [my media diary] is a little bit boring. So I'm not active on social networks and . . . I mean, I'm more like *an observer*. . . . It feels like I want to gather some information for myself and for maybe future use."

Despite that sense of temporal scarcity in everyday life, our practices of near constant connection involve different degrees of social-surveillance practices. Users are constantly gleaning information about how specific others may prefer to communicate and how one ought to communicate more generally. This passive gathering of information becomes knowledge accrued for future use, disconnected from others but connected to the platform, for application in the wider gamut of understanding about how to connect and how to manage one's communication environment. This is not so much a matter of managing data—for instance, machine-to-machine or rather database-to-database processes managing platform content and digital advertising—as it is reckoning with the observable traces of user actions.

Traces offer a way to better ground promises of data's transformative power into something more tangible. Throughout the eighteenth century, the definition of *data* changed from indisputable facts—givens that exist prior to or outside of argument or analysis—to facts and evidence produced by an experiment or a set of observations. Data became the very product of the processes of discovery and argumentation rather than principles or bases for such processes.[21] Drawing from a number of

French contemporaries, the media theorist T. B. Reigeluth demonstrates how our contemporary definitions of data muddle the two, straying from material realities of information storage to the discursive premises of Big Data and machine learning correlation, prediction, and the weightings of preemptive intervention. This conflation points to a particular irony of the data-driven set of computational processes that govern many user opportunities across digital environments.[22] That computational promise of algorithmic intervention offers unprecedented possibilities for modeling user behavior in digital environments. Even in the shortest of sequential timeframes of user action, this modeling is predicated on the idea of cuing particular possibilities of future behavior, therein reducing or eliminating uncertainty based on measurements of probability and influence.[23] The black-boxed or closed nature of algorithms and machine learning obscures this process, save for the visible output, only a momentary, partial snapshot of continual processing.

Rather than being hidden from view, digital traces are always already "in-formation"; they are the mediating factors between what can be known about a given digital object or platform environment and what is legible to us. In this way, as Reigeluth argues, digital traces embody both of these processes within a digital environment: "a trace is both object and product of interventions and representations" while algorithms involve "a very specific temporal relationship aimed at reducing the relative indeterminacy of the future [or rather representation of the future] to a predictable and computational sequence of that which is to come."[24] Discussion of traces rather than data opens up avenues for exploring comparable forms of knowing that stem from our cognitive abilities and self-guided decision-making in relation to the legibility of an environment, despite being intertwined with concurrent computational processes of commercial control, influence, and recommendation.

The Gathering of Disconnective Cues

Our capacity to bring together and synthesize social information about how others communicate extends beyond the confines of any one given platform system, indeed beyond a variety of interfaces that represent the range of communication technologies we use. Rather, this capacity extends to the more amorphous field of our everyday communication environment: face-to-face, on-the-move, and determined by biographical details, degrees of digital literacy, and our migratory patterns from one platform to another. While traces of user action and the mediation of interpersonal communication by technology are legible within any single platform environment, we seek and gather cues from across numerous platforms to trace patterns of where and how others engage across the wider platform ecosystem.[25]

An offhand set of remarks by Tania teases apart the various types of digital traces necessary to understand the possibilities of connecting with others:

> Some [people] prefer texts. Some of them prefer calls. It depends on the people, I would say. . . . I just can count their calls and their texts. . . . But you know on Facebook you can see how [his] profile has been used. No profile picture, it's just like a couple of friends and never status updates, and stuff like that. So I do realize he doesn't use the Facebook. . . . And about everything else, I just know by experience. At first I called him and he was kind of busy, asked me to call him back at certain times, so I was thinking, assuming actually, it's easier to arrange meetings by text.

Social-surveillance practices involve these numerous temporalities and scales of past experience, observation over time, and explicit searching for traces of how others communicate online. David, thirty-three, who travels around the UK and EU about three days a week for work, explains that, among the numerous social and business contacts he makes, sometimes it is lack of recent experience that motivates a specific practice of searching for traces as to how others communicate:

> The reason Facebook won over email for the initial contact [with my friends from university] was because it had been a while since I'd spoken to her or had any kind of communication [with her husband] so if I were to email I was taking my chances that [it] was an email that they regularly checked, [if] it was still valid. At least if you can look on someone's Facebook [page] and decide whether or not they are relatively frequent or active users and so therefore you can be pretty sure, assuming they are active users that if you post or you send a message by Facebook or post messages, they are actually going to check it.

Our digital footprints online, in particular those produced by interpersonal communication, are observable in different ways depending on the architecture of platforms and the messaging affordances of a particular medium. Forms of individual and group address such as email, texts, IM, and voice or video calls leave traces and histories that remain largely observable only to those addressed. More publicly oriented platforms for address, with less determined sets of users, such as listservs, forums, and social-networking platforms, offer different types of user visibility.

George, thirty-five years old and Tania's partner, clarifies that his decision-making practices are most predicated on searching for social cues as to how others communicate: "It's not based on what people prefer; it's based on my knowledge [of] where people are staying the most [online]." George compares two of the more popular platforms for social networking and microblogging among his and Tania's sets of friends scattered across London, Moscow, and St. Petersburg:

> So if there are people who are using Facebook most, I will Facebook message them. If they're not that much into Facebook I choose email. . . . People who are Facebook "active" or LiveJournal "active," their page gets updated quite a bit. There's a lot of interaction on their page; there's a lot of self-publicizing going on [on] their page, so I know they're using it. . . . If they are kind of, you know, if they opened their account five years ago and still haven't bothered to upload a picture, I probably should write them an email.

Our uses of social-networking and microblogging platforms offer semipublic and wholly public focal points where traces of our platform-specific online interaction are available to others in multiple ways. Recent interactions are promoted and circulated based on various algorithmic content curation, to populate newsfeeds and notify other users in ways specific to platforms' determinations of how to prioritize fresh content and connection that encourages engagement by specific users.[26] Other forms of platform activity also persist as traces of latent and past activities: histories of interaction, observable across individual and group profile pages.

Everyday Affordances of Networked Awareness

Surveillance is written into our agility in responding to platform architecture and the diverse degrees of exposure we face when engaging with
others through more direct communication platforms such as texting,
IM, email, and across the various networks reached by a given social-
media platform. Peter is a network engineer often working on his own
entrepreneurial projects alongside six-to-eighteen-month contracts with
particular clients, slotted into relevant in-house teams and assigned to a
new office desk. He explained that his mother has now learned to read
the icons that demonstrate his online availability in the Gmail instant-
message chat window: "She knows when I'm in the office because it is
the regular green circle, but when I'm out and about with my laptop or
working from home, then the online indicator is a small green camera;
the video chat option automatically toggles on because there is a webcam
on my laptop but not the desktop at my client's office."

Lillian, a first-year university student, examines her "most intense
engagement with media content or people each day," Snapchat, which
she uses to post both photos and videos, alongside a stream of shared
and written messages to other users. She points out a particular element
of this platform compared to other social-media IM interfaces: "People
know if you read their messages and when you read it so everyone expects
some kind of reply, that is the main purpose of this app." As a feature
of particular messaging apps and platforms, the message-read indicator
once again drives users to imagine the experience of the receiving other.
How will a friend or acquaintance feel when they see we've read their
message, and what will be expected when they do so?

Expectations flow from connection, or at least from the observability
of connection. Xin is part of her campus rowing club and in the few
weeks prior to an annual competition in Toronto, she was exhausted
from continuous pressure and planning with teammates related to training. She explains that the team has a group chat on Facebook messenger—
"there is a notification from Messenger popping up at the top of my phone
screen"—but she chooses only to read the partial text summarized by the
notification that is visible on her phone's lock screen, "instead of opening
the Messenger itself." This tactic is, once again, motivated by knowledge
of how the platform promotes particular types of visibility: "My little
profile picture will jump to the bottom of the latest chat with all other

members who also review this message. That makes me feel awkward, so I choose not to open the application." By framing platform actions in terms of their visibility to others, users often make decisions about a *receiving self*—another user engaged with a platform interface—at the center of communication-management decisions. The degree to which we are reflexively sensitive to how others will observe our interface-level actions grows out of a similar entanglement with our communication decisions. We know that they will receive notifications that we and other users have followed one of the common social-media pathways for engagement: a click to share, favorite, or like, and possibly comment on, alongside the myriad of additional options to express love, care, hilarity, frustration, or grief, as the small icons of social-media "emoticon" reaction buttons indicate.[27]

These design features, which enhance visibility of our engagement with platform interfaces and messages of posts, center on the mutuality of observation and automaticity of being notified about these varying degrees of engagement. When privacy options allow for these features to be toggled on or off, again it is a matter of mutual visibility. Options of read receipts are available on many email platforms. There are message-read indicators for texting and comparable messaging apps, and there are features to see who has viewed or visited one's profile, post, or story. Such features are often predicated on the user symmetry or commercial asymmetry of social surveillance: you may have the option to access a greater range of traces produced by other users, though you are thereby consenting to the same degree of visibility or, on other platforms, gaining access to the sorts of user metrics that are paired with premium or business-analytics account features.[28]

Applications of Hypermediated Self-Scrutiny

The degree to which we are visible online is reflexively enrolled into our wider understanding of how to manage our communication environment, evident in how we explicitly negotiate visibility with others and how we purposefully engineer opportunities to assess and review our own presence online, beyond the metrics provided by each platform. Xin again outlines how users' sensitivity to platform features and the visibility they entail can prompt direct discussion about how comfortable we are with these forms of exposure: "When I check Snapchat in the afternoon, I see a note under my one friend's name: 'Screenshotted.' She tells me that my birthday filter is really pretty and she likes it so much; however, if I [am not] comfortable with it, she can delete [the screenshot of my post]. I think it is fine as long as I know this happened in the Snapchat system and get notified."

Following the notification that someone had taken a screenshot or screen grab in order to save Xin's recent birthday post as a digital image on their device, the two friends explicitly discuss whether or not this was OK. Xin explains that she appreciates these automatic notifications: "If it was from a friend that I am not close with, I'd feel a little bit defensive. This protection of individual's privacy is very good in my opinion." Much of Snapchat's early appeal to its users, notably younger than the average users of other platforms, stemmed from the impermanence of posts and messages, which expire after twenty-four hours, a feature that has been incorporated successfully and unsuccessfully by competitors such as Facebook, Instagram, and Twitter, alongside traditional options for posts that remain visible across users' profiles and activity feeds.[29] When another user takes a screenshot, thereby capturing the interface-level image displayed on their mobile or computer screen, the platform displays a notification informing the original poster that their otherwise ephemeral image has been saved locally on a friend or follower's device.

While many platforms add features to manage one's own visibility alongside the notification of others' actions, users often find ways to curate their own opportunities to assess and scrutinize how their presence online is received by others. This is a very unique form of self-tracking and, like so many other user tactics for managing connection, can be achieved through additional apps, plugins and features. Esther explains that, nearly every day, she reviews the breadth of her posts from the variously named user and client profiles that she manages: "Facebook? About every day. LinkedIn probably every day as well. Twitter every day. I am also on Four Square and Gowalla." She clarifies that she only reviews her output on the latter two location-based platforms on a project-to-project basis, when she is using them for strategic, event-specific client promotion. To manage her four different Twitter accounts, she relies on another app: "after that I go straight into my TweetDeck. I love my TweetDeck." Once an independent Twitter-client app, TweetDeck was purchased by Twitter and has since been incorporated into the rebranded platform as

"X-Pro" within an extended suite of subscription-based premium content-management features for multiple accounts. Esther explains:

> I have four different Twitter accounts. . . . So I have multiple columns on my TweetDeck. I actually have one, two, three, four, five, six, seven. I have seven columns running right now. . . . Three of those columns are for one account and the first one is all friends, one that lists "mentions" so I know when I am mentioned [by other accounts] and then other ones are direct messages.
>
> I then have another one for issues with the company. I have [another] company one because I am responsible for that account as well, and then I have a [keyword] search [column] for [company and brand specific keywords and mentions]. I also do specific columns of things that I am trending or the conferences I am attending to. So look here, I have one for the conference I was at last week.

For Esther, this platform-managed perspective that curates her ability to oversee her Twitter output across visible streams of multiple accounts, mentions, messages, and hashtag and keyword activity is still not enough: "I created another account . . . [and] the only friend I have on that one is myself. So I use it to read my own Tweets so that I can figure out my own [output]. I will go through it and read them all and I can start to understand where my mind was this week and I can see patterns in myself. So I use that for that."

Once again, to better understand the visible presence of our online interactions and media output, users assume the perspective of the other, the *receiving self*. In this case, Esther has created an account to assess any would-be user that may follow her Twitter profiles individually or in tandem, wholly disconnected from others in order to have a perspective of her own presence and visibility. This sort of systematic user-led self-scrutiny stands in contrast to the automaticity of notification and platform content that signals and prompts users toward ways of staying connected with each other or, rather, staying engaged by the platform while connected. During moments of interpersonal communication and overtime, these permanently connected early career adults, in particular given their interest in the communication-oriented professionalization of knowledge and creative sectors, derive their own common sense from the diffused streams of social cues and persistent digital traces published across numerous platforms.

Screenshots as the Triumph of Disconnected Sociality

Surveillance has curious effects on its subjects. It produces a knowledge particular to the setting of surveillance, a knowledge that internalizes, embraces, and at times transcends the programmed logic of platforms and conventions of use alike. Even in the early days of the everyday snapshot, photographers would bark at their subjects, "Don't look at the camera!"[30] Knowingly being surveilled contributes to a particular form of individual agency: we look to the camera; we worry about our professional reputation online; we scrutinize our social-media outputs; and some of us even seek to game the algorithm.[31] In the context of constant connection, there is an additional disconnective practice that both transcends and embraces the affordances of our devices and platforms through the many images that are not created through a camera lens of any sort but framed and saved on a screen.

The first mobile phone photo was sent by its inventor, Philip Kahn, in 1997, capturing and sharing an image of his newborn daughter. In his words, the ubiquity of the mobile-phone camera would mean that "every moment can be shared . . . from anywhere in the world."[32] But some users have long known that "anywhere" also includes the screen-based metamedia and platform ecosystems of our communication environments. The screenshot represents a vast and often overlooked set of surveillance practices that disconnect photography from its grounding in the real world. Today, the screenshot is being used to similarly disconnect our production of content for social-media platforms from sharing within that particular platform and through the default fields for content upload on the platform's programmed interface.

Ihra, twenty and living in Toronto with her parents, embraces the screenshot as a nimble and frictionless mode of engaging across most of the platforms on her mobile phone:

> 11AM—making and eating breakfast . . . shared a screenshot of tweet
> explaining that most women are afraid to walk down the street . . . it
> was relatable and humorous. I think it's important for men to know
> how their actions impact women and share these types of posts often.

4PM—commented on and shared picture of a letter on a bulletin board from an elderly couple complaining about their waitresses' [sic] nose and tongue ring and tattoos. My comment reminds people that we are not always obliged to listen to your opinions.

4PM—shared a screen shot of a Tumblr post describing a news report about a robber, it was funny and endearing. [Then toured through a gallery of photo memes in the evening choosing which to post, from Kermit the Frog to comedian Will Farrell [sic], SpongeBob SquarePants, and Rick and Morty.]

The visual capture of a digital environment is detached, to be shared or posted amid other contexts. This practice disrupts continuity of digital traces when sharing content through the default pathways within a given platform or between platforms afforded by the programmed syntax of the digital economy.[33] To share a screenshot is its own style, embracing the platform-specific aesthetic trends popularized on Instagram that result in homogeneous posting styles, what Leaver, Highfield, and Abidin call the repetitive "templatability" of visual social-media content.[34] For the screenshot, however, these template trends are embedded within the heterogeneous visual frame where one platform or app's content is posted on another platform. This represents a distinct digital practice that purposefully retains the aesthetic, technological, and historical references to platform-specific content captured.

Screenshots emerged prominently within gaming, game art, and photography to capture the outcomes of mediation and mediated practices.[35] Evolving from the little-known "PrtScn" (print screen) function of desktop computers, taking screengrabs is emerging as a common, hypermediated practice, intertwining mobile phones and social-networking platforms to save, post, and share digital images that frame the interface and software environments of mobile phones, tablets, and computer screens. Like other forms of hypermediation, the screenshot is a performative intervention that plays on a specifically heterogeneous visual space of digital multimedia, capturing the canvas of multiapplication device interfaces in a manner that constitutes something more than just representation:

11AM—shared a screenshot of text conversation discussing whether or not [my friend] would like pictures of a dog (they did!). Posted . . .

during another commercial . . . to make my friends laugh, and to suggest to [them] that I would also like to receive dog pictures!!

(AFTER catching up on group chat) 5:33pm received a private message from my friend while making dinner, she tells me some guy is messaging her. I laughed and said, "uh oh," and she sent me screenshots.

Adding the screenshot to other interpersonal practices—as emphasis, reminders, accusations, entertainment—entangles it with the very practices it represents. Amid everyday media use, individuals capture these indexical snapshots of interpersonal practices midflow, across a range of communication modes (video calls, status updates, texts, emails, and notes), alongside snapshots of their engagement with software and algorithmic outputs (game moments, program glitches, autocorrect mishaps, maps, search engines, and even humorous targeted adverts):

8:06PM—shared a screen shot of post saying "**** y'all (if I am distant) I'm trying to get my **** together." I shared this because I know a lot of my friends are on Facebook, and I'm not close with many of them anymore, and that's mainly due to life changes and too complicated to explain. Most understand but some don't. . . . This post was for them.

Uniquely, screenshotting as a practice expresses an awareness and reflection on the compounded mediations that users themselves introduce to social life, a hint at the deeper mediatization of everyday life, including the ambivalent and contradictory motivations behind posting about disconnection. Bolter and Grusin conceive of this as a hypermediated awareness centered on the "self that is doing the networking."[36] The form and flow of networked interactions are changing to include these visual, indexical, and trace elements of one's own engagement with media platforms and others' digital outputs. As we move into more automated and algorithmically driven environments, this reflexive act of the everyday user is crucial to understanding the decreasing spaces for control and voice we have in the data-digital world: a reflexive practice that deepens engagement with the multiplatform ecosystem through its connective and disconnective affordances.[37]

Disconnected Surveillance

When we consider everyday social-surveillance practices as sites of knowledge production, we do not merely learn about others and their personal media habits. We produce knowledge about both interpersonal life and the mediations of our communication environment. The practice of social surveillance also lends reflexivity to the metaprocesses of social change, in relation to how everyday life is subsumed within the domain of communication practices—what's called mediatization.[38] Reflexivity about practice, then, engenders a more participatory surveillance, where the development of relationships involves types of media-oriented negotiation between individuals, and across sets of individuals, that shape our sense of how one ought to communicate in any given social milieu, as well as how one can navigate social change in an era of constant connection.

We follow and trace the practices of other individuated users—perceived as other individual *receiving selves* like us—to facilitate mutual engagement. We follow others' patterns and preferences for time management, and their mitigation of connection allows us to share some of the temporal and cognitive pressures that contribute to their communication overload. Yet we also draw on biographical, situational, and digital-literacy cues for the typologies that we construct to aid us in our decisions among more loosely defined groups of interlocutors, introducing a degree of separation from the lived realities of particular individuals. This itself is a degree of social disconnection. It mirrors the "social sorting" of people, similar but different to the automatic tracking and processing of people as impersonal, aggregated blocks of demographic details and traces of user actions—central to platform-data production and the digital-advertising ecosystem.[39]

We accrue awareness about how others communicate not only from the frequent and ongoing interactions inevitable in any relationship (social, professional, or otherwise) but also from observations and direct engagement with the multiple degrees of presence and absence (engagement and disengagement, connection and disconnection) as they are managed by others. This intimate knowledge of each other's communication practices and everyday communication environments involves a form of communication that is below the level of explicit messaging content yet is chock-full of information at the level of metacommunication, through flow and patterns of practice, occurring between and beyond the scale of any one interaction.

This knowledge includes, but also extends beyond, simple technical literacy of a platform environment. It partially attunes users to algorithmic and commercially driven logic and thus to the wider platform ecosystem, contributing to literacy about default pathways for user actions or protocols: those technical sets of rules that format and display user actions into certain types of traces to which the platform responds.[40] Rather than a wholly technical knowledge, this is a social knowledge that includes our ability to see the legibility of others' media habits within the digital traces we find across the platform environment. From this, in the course of media use, we cobble together loose and fuzzy social protocols for the usability of the platform with the practice of others in mind, albeit toward our own individual and collective interpersonal ends to differing degrees.

Whereas platform advertising depends on creation of metadata unseen by the user, practices of social surveillance involve cues to digital practices, a social metadata, that users perceive and interpret in the observable actions of their peers. The knowledge we accrue through communication both incorporates and transcends the particular types of information designed to be observable on any particular platform. The scales of data sets necessary for widespread, targeted advertising, and the recombinatory aggregation of those data sets among the data-brokerage firms at the apex of the new digital-advertising food chain necessitates a common syntax of platform operations, promoting similar sets of interpersonal and social-media functions across a diversity of messaging, emailing, social media, and visual-content platforms. In her critique of the data-mining economy, Shoshana Zuboff argues that there is an "epistemological gap" between our knowledge of the communication environment and what platforms know about us; it is a permissive gap that allows these global infrastructures to direct and profit from mass behavioral modification.[41] There is, however, another critical knowledge gap that is often overlooked. Whereas the commercial imperatives of platforms shape our communication environment toward greater dataveillance by necessitating constant connection and participation within a surveillance economy, our social surveillance practices reveal something more than just participatory facilitation of connection or being users-turned-resources for the production of data-based commodities.

Practices of social surveillance produce new forms of wayfinding across our communication environment, both social and antisocial. According to surveillance-studies scholar Mark Andrejevic, as users we have always been "reflexively savvy." We locate ourselves within the digital-communication environment, domesticating opportunities to shape that environment, from the exploration of self-presentation and identity formation online to testing the very limitations of these surveillance-oriented digital enclosures.[42] These participatory practices and the social searching for information allow us to make connections with others.[43] But it is our embrace and appropriation of the sharing, surveillant, and disconnective affordances of social media platforms that shapes and communicates something about the nature of connection today.

Our propensity to domesticate not a particular media tool but the very practice of connecting has steadily migrated to the domain of everyday life, a new lay knowledge of constant connection drawing from traditions of technical experts, early adopters, and those committed to social change. Making and modifying the very ways we connect has long been central to the generative potential of digital communication: the early expert communities of open-source software communities who communicated politically in code; the gaming communities whose committed fandom involved modifying gaming products and steering industry output alike; and the activists and professional media practitioners who understand that changing the environment for media practices presents opportunities for social negotiation and collectively navigating shifting norms.[44]

An understanding of how we renegotiate the social yet technical contours of our communication environment is emerging from increased engagement with the industry-defined plasticity of that very communication environment. As we migrate between one modality of communication or another, disconnection is achieved, ironically, through practices of communication management that demand our wider reflection on, literacy in, and committed engagement to the communication environment as a whole. The everyday conventions that seem to necessitate constant connection involve practices that are increasingly defined by disconnecting from individuals—from real people—by following online traces to defer connection; engaging with loose, assumed typologies of users rather than particular individuals; and disconnecting from the ebb and flow of social engagement to both master and alleviate the pressures of overconnection.

The ideal type emerging from the neoliberal era of constant connection—the disconnected digital practitioner—manifests both a degree of control over their connection with others and a degree of sovereignty in use from the imperatives of particular platforms. This is accomplished through an excessive embrace of surveillance and a hyper-mediated engagement with the communication environment facilitated by intensifying and multiplying degrees of connection, including a dis-connected practice of self-scrutiny and disconnected surveillance of the environment itself.

Practicing surveillance is more than merely fulfilling commercial goals by following circuitous forms of interpersonal connection. It is also an often-overlooked skill set for those entering the knowledge-based workforce and managing the stages of a career today. Early career adults spanning the knowledge, digital, and cultural sectors carry a re-flexively engrained understanding of their visibility across shifting and connecting networked platforms. This knowledge flows from their own participation in environments where practices of social surveillance both facilitate communication and incrementally contribute to a sense of how one feels they and others ought to communicate. Practicing sur-veillance is a subjectivity-shaping experience that facilitates and shapes the limits of our social worlds.[45] The next two chapters will examine how disconnected digital practitioners begin to police the practices of others at the level of metacommunication, while also gleaning lessons from the normative force of such actions. The related coping strategies often accept the conventional expectations predicated on surveillance by finding both value and refuge through greater disconnection.

Amid constant connection, we are inculcated with a particular dis-connected ethos of surveillance. We are users connected to platforms, rather than everyday social beings forging connection; types of visibil-ity and connection better serve the digital-advertising industry than our desire to connect. When we lift our gaze and peer past our screens, beyond a given platform or interface, we may notice that this mentali-ty—an impulse toward surveillance—has a disciplining effect, passively but ubiquitously policing social norms and correcting behavior toward types of expected conduct on which very few of us would agree. If we are to find value in connection, and each other *in* connection, then the knowledge that we gain about real people using media may lead us in a better direction than simply following the definition of a given social setting dictated by the cues and prompts of platform interfaces.

FIVE

Practicing Authenticity

Something is lost when the mores of public and private selves translate into everyday contexts of constant connection. Practices of disclosing information are central to interpersonal life; sharing is the ethos of social media. Practices of publicity are implicit in crafting a professional reputation; such performances are idealized in industry. Both chip away at the conventional valuation of one's sense of self, replaced today by public displays predicated on sharing, networking, and reputation management. When these practices are mediated by workplace ideals and platform affordances alike, everyday performance of an authentic self may have less to do with one's identity and more to do with the normative forces that regulate, evaluate, and order public life.

At thirty-three, Scott has reached a point in his career where he is not only beginning to be seen as competent but is also the go-to consultant on issues of corporate social responsibility. With a confident air, he says he's "trying to be the same person in every situation, at work, in emails, out with my friends, or online. I haven't always felt like that was possible." A West Coast American of Irish descent, he mentions his sexual orientation in passing, as well as dating, but points more squarely to his sense that his private and professional selves do not have to be distinct. For others, this is a considerable privilege they may not enjoy. As Goffman admits, "the whole machinery of self-production is cumbersome," and, as I explore throughout this chapter, it "sometimes breaks down."[1] If we look to the pressures many experience across numerous online spaces, it is clear that "just being yourself" is not always possible, especially when the intersecting aspects contributing to one's identity do not align with assumed norms informing everyday communication negotiations.

Such complexities emerge when the opportunity to represent ourselves in different ways leads to conflict. Zaina has lived in New York and London for much of her life and is close with her extended family in both the US and the Middle East. She purposefully maintains at least two distinct online presences and accompanying sets of self-presentation practices:

> What I'm trying to do moving forward is post a little bit of my funnier videos [on Facebook]—I wouldn't put my boring interview with a CEO on there. Because nobody gives a shit. I have to remember that the people who are my Facebook friends are people who met me in my real life and don't give a shit about [my journalism] on the whole.
>
> Whereas those on Twitter follow me for a reason. . . . And they're waiting for me to give my opinion on certain devices and gadgets before it comes out to the public.

Zaina keeps one online persona for her social life and the other for her professional life, yet the overlaps between her social networks don't allow for a neat segregation of audiences. She complains about this complex, everyday challenge of managing self-presentation:

> Now I feel like everything is blurred. All the lines are blurred . . . the social lines . . . the boundaries . . . but you're almost creating a facade. You're creating a *social* identity. And if you don't realize that you're doing that, then you're in for a lot of trouble. Or you don't give a shit. [Italics added]

The emphasis on an online self as constructed and inherently social shifts identity from something intrinsic and essential to an externalized performance. With comic exhaustion, Zaina recounts receiving months of criticism from her mother after posting a party photo that her extended family felt was unbecoming:

Ohhhh and I changed my profile pic on Facebook and Twitter and LinkedIn [long sigh]. So, basically I'm sick of all that shit; sick of my mom hassling me—she got my aunts on it and they were all attacking me.

So I finally did it, changed it up. I did it in the evening and I changed it on [Facebook], Twitter, LinkedIn—changed it on all those things. In the morning I started to get "Really nice photo," "Oh sexy, love it." Then the guys were like "Photoshop—you don't look like that. That is not you." I was just like "Fuck you"—obviously pictures are a little more flattering than I look [in everyday life]; I ain't that nasty. . . .

Posting one picture infuriates Zaina's family; posting another to placate them draws criticism from her friends. Meanwhile, she only posts what she sees as neutral, professionally acceptable photos in places where industry colleagues may have access. Her frustration at being pulled in opposite directions is palpable during our interview. The expectation to police self-presentation seems to come from all directions, including distinct domains of her interpersonal life, and cannot be disentangled from her gender or, rather, from gendered norms dictating how she should conduct herself in public, reinforced by family and male friends through derisive, publicly visible posts.[2]

Gender intersects with different conventions of transnational familial milieus and other social spaces, themselves further circumscribed by the roles of ethnicity and social-economic status in public life. When these encounter workplace norms and career-based reputation management, the pressure to maintain a coherent presentation of self—meeting these divergent sets of expectations—is distributed inequitably. In her study of contemporary neoliberal emotional life, from the "cold intimacies" of the workplace to the rationalized economies of finding romance on dating apps, Eva Illouz outlines how, in the face of restrictive normative pressures, the diversity of our individual experiences, from social setting to social setting, contributes increasingly to an individualized reflexivity, "finely attuned to the constraints embedded" in any given situation.[3] Such forms of social knowledge, derived from individual situational experience, do not always translate easily into an explicit ability to name, elaborate on, or rationalize inequities, despite the degree to which they are felt and experienced.

Rather, practices of policing social life take on the much wider repertoire of publicly circulating tropes in everyday speech, informed by valorized media ideals and related types of conduct, professional or otherwise. When marshaled, these near-conventions often serve to close down the field for communicating individual and, indeed, interpersonal experiences. This, despite the current emphasis on embracing one's authentic self, both as part of the workplace and one's professional identity. When a sociality of constant connection touts particular forms of authenticity related to how we present and conduct ourselves interpersonally, it silences many voices, rationalizing the refusal of a subjective and intimately affirmed self in the name of something entirely different. We cope with the policing of our authentic selves through the well-managed disconnection of our sense of self from the prescribed expectations with which we define authenticity.

The Artifice of Authenticity

Public yet private; presentational yet genuine; interpersonal, intersectional, yet individualized—there is a pronounced ambiguity to how we've come to understand communication in general. When we speak of authenticity in the context of constant connection, it is often an implicit critique of everyday media use in general: something so banal and open to interpretation, a set of tropes about social life, that nevertheless represents an assumed "common sense"—an externalized, evaluative standard that informs our subjective sense of who we are and how we ought to conduct ourselves in a given situation.

In communications practice, we mutually define and coconstitute opportunities for connecting with and knowing one another. So many dimensions of our identity are repeatedly performed and reinforced through interactions with others. By locating ourselves within a social situation, our communication practices impose particular conditions, an iterative grounding, for the relational domain that has subsumed both work and home and that allows us to come to know ourselves and others.

Degrees of mutual engagement and reciprocity, or lack thereof, afford, mediate, or constrain the types of recursive processes inherent in mitigating connection and participatory surveillance, as I explored in the last two chapters. The degree of mutuality between individuals within these recursive processes is a practice-based site for social negotiation of how we connect, whereas a lack of mutual engagement reproduces and intensifies contradictions at the heart of a productivist sociality, leading to guarded degrees of disconnection. This chapter examines how the ambiguity of what we often call authenticity is used to valorize an increasingly impersonal and procedural sociality. This is done amid constant connection, in turn highlighting the need for disconnection, which ensures a degree of sanctity and separateness, where selfhood and social bonds can flourish.[4]

When we speak of ourselves—the self—we do so in terms of nouns rather than verbs, as if to speak of a tangible, coherent, essential, or inner self, when the ambiguities outlined above demonstrate that our contemporary fascination with identities is an ongoing, intrapersonal, and multidirectional process. In other words, our identities are not fixed. Social practices of self-identification and social classification keep them constantly in-practice. Practices of claiming one's own identity often occur despite, yet also in response to, pressures of external classificatory norms, undermining the very dichotomy of private and public, such that our sense of self is reduced to a resource for the construction of what are acceptable "authentic" public personas.

Associated with both legal and colloquial rationality in the Anglo-American West, the right to privacy is intertwined with a near sacrosanct defense of public expression as an individually empowering practice. The twin concepts evolved as extensions of economic freedom. The privacy to conduct one's affairs as one sees fit is circumscribed by the policing of norms and the conventions of public life, informed by the interests of countless others. Individual sovereignty extends only as far as a wider public and its demands on self-regulation. This pressure makes the individual increasingly responsible for managing risk and the unforeseen outcomes of public life. The policing of "normal" public conduct has a long history, predicated on forbidding particular sets of actions, in tandem with mandates for institutionalized confessions, whether religious or juridical, as to one's hidden motivations or desires. The authentic self is still performed and negotiated today through such arrays of communication practices.[5]

Over the past fifty years, mass media have celebrated the empowerment of making the private self visible to wider publics. Combative daytime talk shows of the 1990s exploited marginalized identities; at the same time, they promised access to broadcast audiences, thus self-definition in the context of public visibility—mundane individual experience, as seen on TV. In the early 2000s, reality television upheld competitive, individualist exceptionalism. Interpersonal conflict was depicted through ritualistic vilification and provocative, behind-the-scenes confessionals, which translated into "democratic" expulsions: voted off the island, out of the house, or from the creative-industry competition.[6] The imperatives of commercial media curtail the promises of individual and collective empowerment for marginalized identities. Public engagement comes at the cost of forceful, at times humiliating and violent, reinscription of normative moral and political hierarchies.[7] In his study of American daytime talk shows, Joshua Gamson calls this a "visibility trap," whereby identities thought not to conform to public mores of the general audience seek reparative engagement in a commercial setting—which is nonetheless based on producing entertainment and drama from deep social divisions and anxieties.[8] These TV formats stridently policed and punished falsehoods, at the same time allowing viewers to "[watch] non-actors in unreal situations that are part of a real life."[9]

The pairing of individual vulnerability with mediated, collective, and purportedly empowering exposure permeates all aspects of digital life. It underpins the prioritization and policing of authenticity in social and professional settings alike. Our media platforms have for decades programmatically ritualized public celebration of—and assaults on—forms of staged authenticity. The commercial and economic inflection of public participation now embraces a contradictory hybridity of authenticity and artifice.

Programmed Affordances and the Cult of the Entrepreneurial Individual

Increasingly part of confessional genres predicated on public scrutiny, selfhood has a mediated authenticity, as an asset to be employed in public life. Long before the gig economy's enrollment of personal assets (homes, cars, skills, and time), commodity-oriented notions of labor permitted individuals to "rent" part of themselves for wages, with a remaining, inalienable sense of self—that is, personhood—not wholly defined by that economic relationship.[10] This classic version of labor assumed self-as-property: time and bodies are rented out in relation to market realities. This transaction upheld the division between individual sovereignty and public forms of economic engagement.[11] Contemporary neoliberalism does away with such distinctions, so that one's whole subjectivity—sense of self, as well as actions and reactions that constitute the presentation of self—contributes to the "self-as-business."[12] Individuals are flexible collections of skills deployed through a public identity and through an individual autonomy that ideally combines authentic digital engagement with economic sociality.

In the era of constant connection, crafting that public self is predicated on connection with others yet fostered by degrees of difference and separateness amplified by the idealization of individuality, and as such, it is fortified by practices of disconnection. Mediated by the design of commercial platforms and wider, algorithmically curated environments, authentic self-presentation reframes the self as a commodity for public consumption, even within contexts of unwaged media use. The pressure to maintain a coherent and accepted self across the everyday communication environment is so ubiquitous that it is a quotidian stressor that nevertheless speaks to a publicly oriented identity.

Hannah airs her personal frustrations with her appearance alongside assignment-deadline woes, commiserating with her best friend over social media: "We then Snapchatted each other photos of our faces before putting on makeup and discussed our acne and how it affected our self-esteem. My attention while doing all of this was on my own personal problems such as my inability to do my assignments, my skin, my anger at the world, etc."

Social media represents a space where public expression of expectations, derision, and shaming take place. Yet it also offers communication modes for interpersonal support and for thinking through some of these experiences with trusted others. Private IM connection offers a more intimate backstage à la Goffman's dramaturgical approach to the presentation of self. Frustrations can be discussed and commiserated over, disconnected from the more public front stage of status updates, pictures, and videos.[13] Practices that reflect on personal concerns in that privileged space of mediated public life have historically been denigrated as lacking in seriousness and value to the wider public: the topics of morning and daytime news and talk shows were dismissed for attending to the overly "domestic" concerns of their female audiences; reality television and adjacent genres have been dismissed as low-brow entertainment because of the mundane, hyperbolic interpersonal drama involved; each wave of successive social-media platforms trigger alarmist and intergenerational criticism that users are failing to regulate their consumption of such apparently meaningless "narcissistic" content."[14] This policing of private lives in public offers a detailed map of the contours of power, inequity, and everyday prejudices embedded within everyday communication conventions.

To better understand everyday life, Erving Goffman studied the "encompassing tendencies" that limit and redirect interpersonal communication within extremes of mental-health institutions. If we can set the stigma of mental health and the taboo of incarcerated identities aside, then there are valuable lessons to be gleaned from these extreme examples, where barriers between work, play, and homelife are purposefully broken down so that all aspects of life are conducted in full view of a totalizing, mediating institutional authority. Our contemporary mediations of the self across digital platforms, whether for dating, job searches, or interpersonal communication, all involve a similar degree of "role dispossession," a "trimming" of contextual personal information from our "real life" to better facilitate administrative processes central to the institution or platform's internal logic.[15]

In *Asylums*, Goffman finds that the programmatic organization of individual identity and social life allow for their collective management through segmented blocks of particular population types rather than leaving space for individual and interpersonal negotiations of subjectivity. Within the platform economy, there is also a trimming of identity and a constraining of communication formats, which ensures the frictionless, circulatory efficacy of networked engagement. Individuals and individual practices are in connection as social-media content, alongside the production of verifiable demographic details, as well as insights gleaned from the patterns of our digital footprints—individuals as targeted consumers and individual practices, disaggregated from the individual, as data-mining commodities. Where authenticity norms and their policing prove to be restrictive and disempowering, a variety of coping mechanisms emerge. These include intransient practices of public confrontation, self-protective withdrawal, and wholesale adaption of norms that reinforce and reproduce hierarchies of exclusion and inequity.[16]

After finishing her hour tutoring high school students online, Hanita logs into a fitness app and pulls up a few favorited YouTube workout channels. She states a number of motivations—"to obtain a good summer body . . . to feel good and transition to a healthier life"—before homing in on a franker explanation: that she is a varsity volleyball player. Hanita celebrates social media as a trusted informational resource that "can aid in techniques, technology, and especially . . . give you amazing tips on fitness." But social media is also a space where lifestyle-marketing and brand-identity logic mingle in the self-presentation of online content creators, or "influencers."[17] In their diaries, Frankie and Xin demonstrate how intertwined these commercialized sources of information are with everyday life, both online and off:

> I posted a pic of my cat and watched makeup tutorial videos. I posted that picture because he is so adorable and everybody needs to see it and I need to attend a special event so I need to put on makeup and since I had the time I might just want to keep myself more educated about the makeup [that] I'm putting on my face. (Frankie)

> At night, I do not have anything to do so I decide to watch some cosmetic tutorials on YouTube. I search up one of my favorite YouTuber's names and all her videos come out for me to pick. I can view how many people like a certain video and choose a popular one to start with. As the video is playing a sponsored advertisement, I scroll down to see other users' comments on this video. (Xin)

Diverse motivations for using social media—interpersonal, entertaining, informational, commercial—are increasingly obscured and blended. A platform for posting pet pictures could simultaneously be a space to search for or be algorithmically served recommendations for branded makeup tutorials from promoted and professional users. In relation to wider celebrity culture, the anthropologist Eric Rothenbuhler examines media as a system for "recruitment, training, expulsion, status distinctions," amounting to what he calls "the church of the cult of the individual."[18] The quotidian rules of self-presentation are both exaggerated and reduced to hyperritualized iconographic representations of those who gain social recognition, attendant on self-promotion and degrees of synergy between traditional media and digital platforms.[19] These function as mediated promotion for particular templates of self-presentation that orient and instruct as "representative examples of how to be a representative example."[20]

On visually oriented platforms like Instagram, Snapchat, and TikTok, entertainment mingles with culturally informative takes on health, fashion, and sexuality that nevertheless engage with influencers' strong opinions on topics including #MeToo, Black Lives Matter, LGBTQ+ rights, climate change, and mental health.[21] The algorithmic amplification of system recommendations means, however, that circulating typologies framing debate also frame how to conduct oneself and are reduced and pushed toward the extremes. Savannah explains the challenges of navigating online spaces as a young woman: "I put up a video on my one Instagram acct I use for my art about how I always put on lipstick and then immediately want to take it off. One guy I barely know sent me the story with just the message 'lol' in almost a passive aggressive way. . . . It was a weird experience because I'm not sure if he actually thought the video was funny or not. I still haven't replied and I kind of avoided Instagram for a bit because I don't know what he actually meant."

For Savannah, Instagram is only an outlet for sharing her creative output. While she is eager to build an audience for this art-oriented account, she feels the need to keep the account private because she does not want to attract unwanted attention or harassment from strangers. Even ambiguous messages leave her feeling uneasy and avoiding the platform for a few days, afraid that her lack of response would provoke a negative reaction.

In his sociological analysis of emotional (yet sanctioned) abuse of patients by institutional staff, Goffman points out that those who seek to police the conduct of others often instigate a situation that produces "a defensive response," which then becomes collapsed into the situation as an additional failure to meet the prescribed norms: a looping effect of personal mortification, whereby any face-saving tactic or coping mechanism becomes grounds for further ostracization or punishment, often publicly highlighted to instigate further collective punishment.[22] The affordances of connective media that promote the exploring and building of identities alongside and through a sense of networked community also represent opportunities for exploitation by antagonistic users who seek to undermine and attack personal identity to stoke discord.[23] Whatever her commenter's motives, the fear of potential ridicule or harassment contributes to yet another looping effect that severs the normal relationship between people and their communication acts—a mortification of the self—that

stuns and silences, driving many to self-censorship and degrees of disconnection from public engagement.

The realities of such aspirational careers, supported by a robust social-
media presence and the crafting of a public persona, often coincide with
employment precarity: no clear promise of reputational or financial
reward, despite the extensive emotional labor of mingling personal with
interactive forms of public consumption. Duffy and Wissinger's research
on the experience of young creative content creators—bloggers, vloggers,
Instagram influencers—shows a consistent practice of mythologizing
online forms of creative success as fun, authentic, and entrepreneurial.[24]
From YouTube to Instagram and TikTok, platforms predicated on amateur media production have become more formalized in their circulation
of templates of successful self-presentation, alongside entrepreneurial
avenues for monetizing or professionalizing use. In her book *(Not) Getting Paid to Do What You Love*, Duffy outlines further how gender and
class are written into the uncritical idealization of individualized self-
expression and the aspirational labor of managing what will be perceived
as an authentic online self, where the private is rearticulated for public
consumption, predicated on an elusive promise of economic stability that
rarely materializes.[25]

When gender and race intersect with these valorized practices of display and confession, affective forms of peer-to-peer engagement contribute to an ameliorative and reparative production of knowledge: a valued,
enjoyable interpersonal engagement that nevertheless reproduces wider
forms of social regulation. In their study of social-media blogs published
by young Muslim American women, Shenila Khoja-Moolji and Alyssa D.
Niccolini examine how empowering practices are motivated by a sense
of individual responsibility to attend to the vulnerabilities of their racialized identities and to advocate for other young Muslims in the West by
attending to post-9/11 prejudices.[26] These practices, however, are coupled
with self-surveillance and degrees of self-censorship in anticipation of
criticism and possibly harassment from both Muslims and non-Muslims
alike. The authenticity of these practices may contribute to a sense of
ameliorative empowerment, but its template is a particularly Western
neoliberal self: flexible and entrepreneurial, yet individually responsible
for reshaping prejudicial public norms, despite the vulnerability and harassment this may invite. There is an uncritical valorization of exposure

that obscures both the risks and the transformative potential accompanying direct public confrontation with normative forces.

From early YouTube vloggers to everyday users and aspirational influencers on Instagram, Snapchat, and TikTok, staging authenticity often involves offering a window into one's personal life by remaking one's private self for public consumption.[27] These social-media spaces are fundamentally different from the text-based affordances of early virtual communication via desktop computers—staging a visual representation of the embodied self that cannot wholly be disentangled from private life. Here, cognitive-evaluative shortcuts are prioritized, in particular the visual valuation or devaluation of others. While scanning social-media streams, users engage in rapid binary judgments that depend on existing tropes of media representation: yes or no, "hot or not," appropriate or inappropriate, normative or deviant.[28] Where so much of our everyday interpersonal communication and media content are heavily influenced by commercially propagated norms—often gendered, sexualized, racialized, socioeconomic, or ableist—connective platforms and other social media offer the opportunity to reflect on and challenge those norms. This, however, is also a domain where such norms are reproduced—intensified, even—when others correct, cajole, and police behavior that strays from what is deemed acceptable. In the face of a challenge to one's authenticity, a number of coping strategies emerge in the management of exposure. Yet these strategies are more acute when one is performing an acceptable, authentic self in the workplace, where engaging normative convention is a matter of economic security.

The Emotional Labor of Self-Censorship

The work of regulating one's behavior can itself be a burden, managed situation-to-situation, moment-to-moment. In the early 1980s, the sociologist Arlie Hochschild introduced the concept of emotional labor: the cost of sustaining and managing the expected veneer particular to working contexts through the management of one's own emotions.[29] Yet this self-regulation attempts to avoid the subsequent emotional work of having to manage the inappropriate responses of others who assume the practical, commonsense, or unassailable value of biased interpersonal conventions. Among the numerous, near-ritualized reminders that digressions from the norm invite, at best, scrutiny, everyday interpersonal interactions contain subtler forms of invalidation that afford and constrain our behavior.

Practices of strategic withdrawal emerge through segregating domains of activity: crafting divisions between communication modes that can also provide a form of information and audience control for presentations of the self.[30] As Margaret discusses:

> Facebook was just created for friends, that's my impression of it. . . . When I decided not to include my family [on Facebook] I did it more for my own security—my own, like, data protection I guess, because I didn't want anything to be divulged that may . . . maybe look really bad or . . .
>
> Workmates: the same. I didn't want to be caught out in case I was sick one day, you know, in comments. . . . Also there's a bit of image control as well at work where you don't necessarily want people to know what you've been getting up to and who your friends may be or what your external life [outside of work] is all about.
>
> And then [ex-boyfriends], simply just because I think it's a bit creepy for them to know what I'm doing.

Margaret outlines numerous, distinct social sets she wishes to exclude within the more personable domain she hopes to craft on a particular social network: family, colleagues, and exes. This segregation allows her to craft a separate image of herself that her use of social networks may contradict, segregating domains for a performative form of digital code-switching when and where necessary. In professional, interpersonal settings, code-switching and other forms of self-censorship seek to mediate the inequity of normative power, a shield from systematic inequalities that stem from racism, chauvinism, and other prejudices.[31]

The navigation of routine working tasks and nonwork-related banter can be replete with microaggressions, often unconscious and unnoticed by others.[32] Sometimes the immediate objective of needing to cope with such situations does not produce authentic engagement but facilitates the ease of interpersonal connection by mobilizing others toward commonly shared purposes in order to mitigate potential conflict despite the individual costs and labor involved.[33] Yet this still amounts to a deployment of one's communicative resources and emotional self-regulation toward a relational status quo—an avoidance of the demarcation of difference, without a public consideration or challenging of commonplace prejudicial rationales.

The multimodality of contemporary communication platforms permits, however, a proliferation of Goffman's front and back stages in both professional and personal lives. Between individual repertoires of media literacy and practice, and across connective media platforms, there is a great deal of slippage and inconsistency. Alice Marwick and danah boyd outline how the networked affordances of social media collapse contexts that may otherwise be assumed, understood, and demarcated by and for different groups of interlocutors.[34] Yet for many Black, racialized, or other marginalized workers, the disruption and forced disconnection of social distancing during COVID-19 actually offered respite from microaggressions and the emotional labor of managing interpersonal workplace politics. Sociologist Winfield Washington and Organization Studies scholar Audrey Murrell point to how remote work, segregated from real-life professional contexts, offers a sanctioned degree of situational withdrawal: most evident in asynchronous communication, with even video calls allowing cameras to be turned off and microphones to be muted to avoid confrontation and the labor of managing one's visible frustration.[35] These shifts reveal the complex contradiction between the commercial- and labor-oriented imperative toward sharing and authenticity, whether online or at work, and the responsibilization of user or employee to navigate a terrain where the invisible labor of protective coping mechanisms can be cast as antisocial or, worse, inauthentic. But the malleability of connective platforms allows such norms to be undermined, as individuals adapt their own media use toward the opportunities for disconnection that a given platform affords.

Self-censorship is not always immediately accessible to those who may rely on such practices. Managing the disclosure and presentation of self is so often couched in shared, normative assumptions and internalized as "common sense." In Mikaela Pitcan, Alice E. Marwick, and danah boyd's study of young, upwardly mobile New Yorkers, practices of self-censorship, notably performing a received idea of respectability, were common among those eager to shed any trace of a lower socioeconomic status.[36] Online self-presentation in the study strategically catered to assumed norms not of peers but of imagined employers and other potential high-status viewers. Where these practices involved avoiding contacts and content thought to be "lower class," they internalized and reinforced racist and gendered assumptions, while celebrating economic strategies for self-improvement. To say that these are assumptions is not to imply that they are incorrect: online performances of one's gender, in particular for women and more so for women of color, were consistently oversexualized and therein evaluated as lacking in respectability: a contextless set of assumptions that, in turn, also justify online shaming and other forms of harassment.

As Margaret and I continued our interview, it became clear that her approach to personal social-media posts was not only about separating the personal from the public but also about managing the misunderstanding and risk that accompany exposure online. "It is not my job to explain it to them," exclaims Margaret, hesitating momentarily as if to assess my own social literacy and openness to this idea. She outlines how most of her marketing colleagues, in particular the managers, are men, and there are several common gendered experiences to which they have simply never showed understanding or sensitivity. Indeed, gendered biases constrain as much as they afford, in a stratifying fashion. Hadiya Roderique's research into the corporate and financial sectors of Toronto reveals just such an asymmetry: expecting fathers enjoyed the benefits of increased social support—through a new commonality with their male superiors—whereas many expecting mothers in the same demanding fields experienced a withdrawal of support and expressed a need to segregate their professional identities and interactions from the realities of pregnancy and parenting.[37]

Margaret elaborates on the effort that it would take to manage her coworkers' potential biases and misunderstandings about her social-media presence. Regarding taking a sick day, she explains: "Yes, I might be posting online, in fact I might be out getting groceries or coffee. It could be a mental health day or something else . . . like, you know . . . [pauses] How I use my sick days, well, I don't expect them to understand." "Disclosure disconnect" describes the risks of presenting different sides of ourselves online: the disconnect is between what we disclose to different audiences who have divergent windows into our lives.[38] Impressions, personal or professional, matter to those who may not have the cultural literacy, open-mindedness, or desire to view hardship or difference without judgment or, worse, with accusations of dishonesty.

With such forms of informational control so present in everyday life, we often turn to more anonymous, disconnected digital spaces for support. Digital platforms have long fostered more discrete spaces for re-claiming agency related to health, for example. Users narrate and frame private experiences in more public, interpersonal ways, yet the opportu-nity to do so often comes at a cost. In Shani Orgad's study of early text-based women's-health forums, users translated the silence surrounding breast cancer to a form of interpersonal recognition and understanding not available to them offline.[39] Such validation and control were empow-ering and rare, facilitated at times by the anonymity of disembodied text-based forums and in other instances by the shared cultural biases among linguistic and diasporic communities coming together online. In contrast, Mikayla Gordon Wexler and Christopher Dole's more recent study about mothers caring for children with chronic illness shows how Instagram brings a literal visibility to otherwise invisible struggles.[40] The platform offers a visualized, embodied conduit to representing realities of care: a worldmaking space to foster intersubjective validation of oth-erwise hidden emotional labor and practical experience.[41] Ironically, this public exposure often comes with a flood of messages and comments, which translate into a burdensome relentless sense of responsibility for the affective and relational care of others online. There are always limits to the types of self-representation that digital platforms afford, particu-larly because they open private lives to the vagaries of networked public expectations.

Over the last decade, platforms have responded to this desire for infor-mation control. "I make heavy use of the limited profile," explains Ethan with his hands raised. These are the "warm" social-media affordances that offer management of privacy and disclosure through habitual, rou-tine practices and contrast with the opacity of "cold" affordances, which constrain and preclude user intervention.[42] Such affordances speak to Chun's assertion that social media brings about unanticipated crises that disrupt habitual practices and prompt reconsideration of how best to engage with a platform.[43] Across these shifting affordances, users prac-tice a "privacy calculus," which includes assessing discrete situations, attending to the wider cultural and political standpoints that differen-tiate between individually focused and collectively focused cost-benefit analyses, and perceiving uncertainty in outcomes of personal informa-tion disclosure.[44]

The Platformization of Countersurveillance Strategies

In a grave, matter-of-fact tone, Esther explains that freelance consultants should assume their emails could "get read by everyone in the company," adding, with a nod, "I am very distrustful." Indeed, one of this book's younger, UK-based participants phoned me in a panic just before their final research interview: they had been put on disciplinary probation just hours after mentioning their employer by name in a Facebook post complaining about their struggle to stretch their meager contract earnings until the end of the month. It was not until 2017 that a European Court of Human Rights ruling stipulated that employers were obliged to give more explicit warning to staff if they intended to monitor workplace communication and internet use.[45] The court sided with the Romanian plaintiff, who had been fired after personal details of conversations with his fiancée from a professional Yahoo instant-message account were read by managers. While the ruling did not forbid forms of managerial surveillance such as automated monitoring and keyword searches for employees' public statements about employers, it targeted the monitoring of private social communication at work and other persistent online traces of media use and digital interaction.

Esther was thirty-three when I interviewed her outside a tech conference in London. With a longer history of web use than some of the younger research participants in this book, she prizes spaces for anonymity online, alongside careful curation of multiple professional online presences. She works as a digital-platform and network-sales consultant, living in London but managing relationships between US and UK venture capitalists among her tech-entrepreneur colleagues across Scandinavia. She is wary of the competition that exists among her collaborators, which necessitates a professional vigilance to ensure the privacy of conversations with CEOs and investors. These relationships are on a project-to-project basis, often using company- and project-specific email accounts, in contrast with her use of her own professional email account for managing ongoing relationships with other freelancers and contractors. With thirteen active email accounts at the time of our interview, Esther admitted the functionality of many contemporary, cloud-based email services afforded the ability to work from a single "master" email account, though she appreciates and excels at managing multiple accounts and has a clear sense of what motivates her to do so. The utility of multiple and distinct accounts involves their management across separate platforms, to keep like with like and to ensure segregation among her interlocutors as she shifts among roles, project-specific personae, and the various "hats" that contemporary life necessitates.

Options to post publicly or privately, to secretly demote the content of "friends" or followers without blocking or unfollowing them, or to limit posts to particular predefined groups of followers are accompanied by increased granularity for managing degrees of privacy. These effectively mimic the ways users were already managing privacy through, for example, pseudonymous accounts designed to coexist with eponymous accounts. The internet has often provided spaces for discovering via identity play that goes beyond simple masking. The text-based internet relay chats and forums of the 1990s and the generally impenetrable "social steganography" of their syntax and references were a way of hiding in plain sight and were the precursors to the fake Instagram accounts, or "finstas," of young adults today, where more exploration is possible than on real-name accounts, which invite parental and other forms of surveillance.[46]

A single gay man in his early thirties, Ethan outlines his personal and professional frustrations with online exposure: "You cannot hide your 'likes' . . . which I hate because sometimes you like things that, you know, others might not approve of and you don't want people knowing. And then also you can't hide events you say you're attending. . . . If I only have a business relationship with someone then definitely limited profile, yes. I don't want them knowing I'm going to some crazy after-hours party that goes till two in the afternoon the next day."

With a smirk Ethan dryly adds: "My mother wouldn't approve of that either." But then he explains clearly that there are tactics for managing not just personal boundaries but also the misunderstandings of others, alongside the risk that potential biases and outright prejudice could pose to his professional life. Ethan goes quiet for the first time in our hour-and-a-half interview. "So that makes me really mad actually."

Across many media sectors, employers increasingly infringe on the privacy of early career job applicants, arguing that the public-facing dimension of media justifies the scrutiny of social-media activity, if not for the sake of the employee's reputation, then as an assessment of prospective candidates' prowess in presenting and branding themselves.

Midway through the hiring process for a coveted summer internship in China, Grace is clear on just how important her online presence is, even for these unpaid entry-level positions:

> During the preinterview, the human resources managers would often add my WeChat. . . . Though we do not know each other, we can still see each other's life through posts. . . .
>
> Before sleeping, sat on my bed, I opened WeChat to add [the HR manager's] WeChat and I usually check Douyin to follow up on Chinese [short video] trends though I do not like this app at all. I've found that if I do not know the trends—especially the trends in Douyin—it is hard for me to get accepted [for work].

Where precarity is increasingly a feature of creative- and knowledge-sector employment, the professional aspects of one's online reputation complicate attempts to manage segregated domains. The pressure to grant prospective employers personal access to one's social-media presence—in this case WeChat's interpersonal messaging, as well as "moments" microblogging photo or video posts—is perceived as a necessary surrender of privacy. Tellingly, the need for reputation management is conflated with the need to keep abreast of the latest social media trends circulating on platforms that have captured the coveted youth market. Douyin, mentioned above, is ByteDance's social-media platform for short user videos, popular among domestic Chinese users, with TikTok being the parent company's mirror platform for users beyond mainland China. While we craft, manage, and guard the exposure and circulation of digital practices, paying close attention to how reputation capital is accrued through self-presentation, there are other forms of social capital that must be fostered and on-display.

How norms of practice depend on digital-infrastructure affordances is not dissimilar to how particular rigidities of thinking—the presumed common sense of shared economic rationales—are baked into situated interpersonal settings, both in the workplace and across numerous commercialized media platforms. But when such social settings constrain how we feel we ought to be able to communicate, rather than accommodate an authentic sense of self, they speak to contextual social norms and become a generative resource.[47] Emphasis on social rather than technical knowledge contributes recursively to strategies for attending to one's own authenticity, alongside the typification of authenticity, prescribed by particular group settings.

The Asymmetries of Professional Authenticity

The invisibility of norms is essential to their functioning. Common knowledge, perceptions, beliefs, conventionalized interpersonal practices, and customs of behavior within an interacting group, whether shared or not, can be consistently referred to and employed as external or objective facts informing future action.[48] Berger and Luckmann write that actions that are taboo and policed are largely those for which no circulating normative typification exists.[49] Whether social cliques, working teams, or professionalized identities within a particular industry, such groups maintain an ethos based on practices that define, limit, and protect boundaries of appropriate conduct. Over time, there is an incorporation and, implicitly, a validation of individual identity where it aligns with that conduct. Additional, reactive practices emerge to police conduct within that frame of reference, reinforcing what is and is not acceptable to the group by dwelling on any incidences of individual action that stray from the assumed norms of expected and undifferentiated conduct.

In today's workplace, normative ideals of professional conduct mask forms of exclusion, alongside a managerial promotion of employee authenticity. Across knowledge and creative sectors, this professional imperative involves embracing an entrepreneurial identity that enlists one's whole self in service of work. Susanne Ekman's ethnographic exploration of a large media-and-publishing company demonstrates how the idealization of authenticity is central not only to one's professional identity but also to managerial control.[50] In the face of casualization and flexible contracts, knowledge-based and creative work is increasingly framed in terms of a self-directed, self-realized professional identity that aligns with one's emotional well-being and fulfillment.[51] This managerial and industry-specific expectation precludes the strategies of situational withdrawal that Bourdieu and his collaborators found in his 1990s study of disenfranchised, precarious workers in France. Eyes down and headphones on, workers reduced their interpersonal interaction with colleagues to whatever minimum was necessary to successfully compete jobs, disconnected from others to avoid the politicized personal conflicts between those in privileged positions of economic security.[52]

The disparities of socioeconomic insecurity often mask and compound other inequities inherent in contemporary managerial surveillance. Surveillance studies scholar Simone Browne asks us to reconsider such inequities as speaking to the longer histories of Black and gendered bodies being precluded from white, Euro-American definitions of productive students, workers, citizens, and even media users.[53] She points to bell hooks's analysis of historical political violence and the coping practices that emerged in response: enslaved peoples developed a deep literacy of the violent surveillance they were subjected to, fomenting a constitutive and collective desire to resist the exclusionary matrices of white-settler colonial power, while nevertheless necessitating protective practices of self-censorship in everyday life.[54] To avoid indiscriminate violence by obscuring one's gaze and avoiding conversational styles that could be misconstrued as "talking back," these performative practices of disconnection are accompanied by other hidden layers of communication—feats of resilience that stand in relation to asymmetries of power. Today, the communication of authenticity is similarly attuned to the neoliberal structural inequities that otherwise flatten and obscure individual identities in the name of economic security.

Imperatives toward professional norms are not simply organizing structures in the knowledge economy; they are deeply personal concerns, specifically in light of competitive pressure to prove one's value as an employee time and time again. The result is a performative and competitive culture of "peak efficiency" that in and of itself becomes an anxiety-ridden set of interpersonal performance practices: new employees seek to justify their hiring, the time and investment that is their training, and possible advancement with each and every workplace action and interaction.[55] This contributes to a responsibilization of the individual for the conditions of their employment, which is internalized as patterns of blame for success and failure. Stratification can inure those who have profited from hierarchy to the stifled mobility of those below, while fostering a sense of self-blame in those who have not. Richard Sennett argues that when such "complacency is married to individualism, cooperation withers."[56] The sociological outcome of these economic arrangements fosters individual rather than collective, organizational, or systemic forms of responsibility, thereby breeding indifference to the circumstances of others, reducing social life in the workplace to an asociality among individuals who are each managing their own personalized sets of successes and uncertainties. Gregg's research into the forms of efficiency thinking that underpin rationalization in economic life and the stratified division of labor "normalizes asociality and asymmetry in the guise of professional conduct."[57] In this context, the sense of how our successes and uncertainties are intertwined, and how they are reproduced through an uncritical acceptance of conventional workplace practices, is lost to many.

Modern management has appropriated authenticity to instrumentalize entrepreneurism, creative innovation, and employee satisfaction. This pressure occurs alongside and despite the growing prevalence of project-to-project reporting, the standardization of technological knowhow, and the reputational pressures that focus on compatibility and commitment to group identities and standards. Orgad and Gill examine the celebration of "confidence culture" in corporate discourse, a translation of entrepreneurialism that disproportionally contributes to gendered distinctions between what is professional and what is not, celebrating traits that many would disavow as antisocial or even "toxic." Contemplation is denigrated as doubt, consideration as prevarication, and interpersonal negotiation among colleagues as lack of individual confidence.[58] Illouz similarly highlights how a managerial tendency to evaluate recasts self-censorship in the face of conflict or inequity as "emotional intelligence," which actually devalues subjective, affective experiences. Writing about gendered, racialized, and queer experiences, Sara Ahmed observes that frustration and dissonance produced by conflict and unequal power in the workplace is too often cast as an individual's professional or personal failing, shifting blame from the situation that stokes discontent onto the aggrieved individual.[59] These loose codifications lock the experience of others into a particular definition of professional conduct, where emotions are observed, rationalized, and therein made manageable for self-regulation. Conduct is policed, voices are silenced, and inequity persists.[60]

Professional authenticity serves as an evaluative standard—often without clear, objective codification in policy or guidelines—to assess commitment to working life as an inherent aspect of self. What professionalism should look and act like becomes a malleable assemblage: productive, authentic, confident, and emotionally regulated; however, what is "taboo" or unprofessional is just as malleable: these are differences that have not yet found a home in one of the many circulating tropes of what it means to be professional.[61] This ambiguity has utility. It obscures how normative power is asserted through heightened scrutiny of difference and nonconformity. Online and in-person, this pressure to conform is obscured by socially constructed, policed notions of correct conduct in interpersonal life. Self-censorship and managed disclosure represent conduct informed both by conventions and knowledge of inequity—a powerful resource to call on when required.

Chasing the Authenticity of Third Places

Our sense of self is inherently social, yet it is also challenged by expectations of and interactions with others. For this reason, we commit to interpersonal practices, personal routines, and community spaces where we believe that our sense of self can be fostered. COVID-19 destabilized the equilibrium between authenticity and expectation by forcing many to stay home, a disconnection from public life that was accompanied by being perpetually online.[62]

Kaitlyn finds both intimate and public engagement with what in many situations would be racialized aspects of her identity. She does so through reparative and pleasurable social actions that challenge otherwise prevalent institutionalized inequities. Whereas the university setting represents a blurring of personal and career-oriented domains, students have increasingly called for accountability and institutional reckoning with historic, systemic, and implicit biases concerning gender and race.[63] In this institutionalized context—both problematic and empowering—Kaitlyn messages with friends about tickets to a campus theater production about Blackness, discrimination, and power. But with news of COVID-19 class cancellations and social-distancing rules spreading on social media, she whittles the night away "listening to Africana music with friends and painting," adding a postfact note to that diary entry: "the last night we hung out." Social and intimate situations like these affirm authenticity, when internal self-identification and external classification seem less at odds.

In addition to restrictions on casual and intimate face-to-face encounters at home, COVID-19 restrictions meant the shuttering of public cultural and entertainment venues that offered a similarly affirming domain for diverse identities to thrive. Christoph Bagger and Stine Lomborg examined how the shuttering of "third places"—libraries, bars, restaurants, and cafes—exacerbated the already difficult boundary management of working from home amid social-distancing restrictions. The closures also led to a "forced disconnection" from collective social spaces often sought out to foster and possibly explore one's sense of self.[64]

We seek these contexts for connection that stand in contrast to disconnected practices of self-censorship, self-monitoring, and self-restraint but that are often necessary to sidestep the potential emotional work of contestation and conflict. They are not, however, devoid of policing authenticity. Third places may offer something different from work and home, but they are still circumscribed by normative, conventionalized expectations of conduct, with hierarchies of their own. In popular media, white, socioeconomically mobile, cis-gender, and able-bodied gay men are often a normalized representation of queerness, which marginalizes other LGBTQI+ identities through divisive, limiting, and policed manifestations of "homonormativity" to which many queer settings are responding in tandem with the additional external pressures of "heteronormativity."[65] Helen Kim's research into the youth cultures of the South Asian diaspora in London uncovered a clear, similar policing of linguistic, dress, and communicative styles in venues and nightclubs that catered to the Desi community. Policing "how Desi is Desi" was reinforced through definitions of class-based and gendered authenticity that performatively shed normative cues associated with nondiasporic life, such as aspirational early careers in the UK capital.[66] The inclusiveness of these social spaces, unfortunately, is still indirectly inscribed within the hierarchies of wider socioeconomic exclusions.

Different corners of Ginika's life—distinct relational domains that are digitally mediated and transnationally distributed—affirm different aspects of her identity. At twenty, she is often responsible for her school-age sister while attending college in Canada. She takes her sister to a doctor's appointment while planning the surprise family video chat for Dad's birthday several time zones away via WhatsApp, texting friends to make plans while on the bus and fitting in moments of contemplation and prayer through her daily Bible-reading app, which she has chosen for its lack of social-networking affordances. This private backstage that grounds her sense of self as part of the East African Christian diaspora, and of her church more generally, contrasts, but does not necessarily conflict, with her everyday life with friends and classmates, and vice versa.

The myriad self-presentations that everyday situations mediate, affirm, and police contribute to how we know and understand what our authentic self is and could be. The refraction of one's sense of self through the constant management of self-presentation—across platforms, modal contexts, and physically situated domains of social interaction—radically challenges binaries of private and public, backstage and front stage.[67] Degrees of disconnection in how we communicate may not afford a sharp, impermeable boundary between private and public selves, but there is a degree of separateness that is key to orienting and locating ourselves among shifting social milieus.

Echolocation as the Authenticity of Online Spaces

Our identity is something that we do, and it is something that we do together.[68] Hierarchical pressures—be they institutional, media-based, or professional—may frame how and who we ought to be, but they do not determine lived realities and social experiences, which provide a sense of self in everyday life. Institutional classification of normal or idealized types does not occur in a vacuum, and it is not passively accepted, nor is it unaltered. Rather, it is negotiated through practice or internalized through prescriptive rationalizations of social conduct.[69]

Our social lives extend across an entire landscape of possible practices, iteratively navigated through social performances that orient and defend the self against the pressures of externally imposed frameworks for how we ought to communicate. The rupture and discontinuity between these processes of identification is destabilizing and distressing, challenging our ability to locate and understand ourselves in relation to the wider social world.[70]

Constant connection provides continuous and highly routine communication practices that become feedback loops, demarcating the boundary between an intimate self and its more public definition. Annette Markham examines how this is the "outcome of continuous accomplishments" derived, in particular, from relational practices of "echo-location," and how we recursively make "micro-adjustments" based on the numerous pings, echoes, signals, and responses we receive amid communication.[71] Over time, these adjustments and their reciprocation renegotiate a new way of communicating with others—a relational ethos of how we connect and why.

Kohji woke up and began checking emails in bed to make sure his client was not late for their Japanese tutoring session that Saturday morning. He regularly turns to Twitter and Facebook for his Japanese and North American news, but that day—March 11—tweets from friends and others that had gone viral dominated his feed: "I found thousands of tweets about the Great East Japan Earthquake six years ago." Facebook's "Memories" features also served the posts on Kohji's profile wall on March 12, so many years after the 2011 Tōhoku earthquake and tsunami, prompting him to search YouTube for videos of the tsunami, then to chat with friends over Facebook Messenger and his mother via the LINE app: "All this media content pulled on my heartstrings—every year around this season, all over Japanese [language] posts and media." His English-speaking classmates in Toronto were largely oblivious to the anniversary.

There is a certain vortex-like quality both to our attention to and our participation in crises, captured in breaking news and media-oriented monumentalization of tragedies across digital platforms, iteratively recalled and reinstated in memory. The monopolistic nature of such global media events prompts emotional engagement that, in turn, contributes to degrees of solidarity and social cohesion however fractured and multiple: even in opposition, derision, or horror, our mediated engagement represents a type of participation in historic events, cultural phenomena, conflict, and crises.[72] The algorithmic curation of social-media newsfeeds and timelines contributes to this. The temporality of recent, popular posts responds to users' networked proximity, based on previous interactions, and all but ensuring an increasing degree of collective engagement. The affective dimension of platform-mediated publicness stems from our projection of collectivity onto streams of social-media content; no matter how ephemeral they are, we can still perceive them as meaningful.[73]

Like the "push" notifications that highlight photos or social-media posts on their anniversary, these individuated, interpersonal, yet public collective memories have little sense of the positive or negative nature of that experience. These programmed social media affordances prompt memories that differ qualitatively from our own practices of producing media traces for the purposes of remembering. By strategically curating a "media accounting" of our lives online, serving a similar purpose as diaries, scrapbooks, or photo albums, we are undertaking what Lee Humphreys calls "remembrancing"—a social and communicative practice.[74] This is different from the quantitative accounting of posts for their likes and shares and from the performance of more public-facing identities.

Trace by trace, we continually affirm our sense of self throughout everyday mediated interactions, owing in part to the insularity and separation from unlimited public scrutiny that we craft through media but also through the ongoing nature of interpersonal life. There are contours and fault lines to these relational domains that serve to segregate the personal from work, friends from family, the intimacy of separateness from the vagaries of shared public life. While we rely on platform affordances to effect these divisions, there are particular transnational and linguistic divides that build on those modal distinctions. These should not be dismissed as so-called social-media echo chambers that have dominated alarmist (and debunked) popular discourse and news headlines; rather, they represent numerous degrees and scales of shifting networked publics at any given point on any given platform.[75]

Miguel, who recently moved to Canada from Mexico, emphasized the distinction between his Spanish- and English-language group chats on WhatsApp—the former catering to his interests in politics through the numerous news stories shared among friends throughout the Americas, the latter a morass of everyday microcoordination and memes among work and university friends locally in Toronto. Filipe, originally from Italy but based in Toronto for studies, similarly outlined the unique value of a personal network of university-age friends in different regions of the world. Together, they shared stories of misinformation among their local peers, the everyday challenges that different phases of the COVID-19 pandemic brought, and the different levels of policy lockdown restrictions from their respective universities across three continents: a valuable set of perspectives that nevertheless carries the weight of social responsibility to inform others in their local communities.

Constant connection means that we often find ourselves acting as a bridge between social milieus. This carries significant value, a type of social rather than economic capital offering greater reciprocity and depth to existing relationships, as well as opportunities for new connections. In his early, predigital-network analysis of social relations in everyday life, Mark Granovetter examined the integrating strength of individuals who represented the "weak ties" between more coherent social groups, despite alarmist accounts of social disintegration or mass individual alienation.[76] On closer inspection of group dynamics, an individual who spans the gaps between more closed networks, communities, or groups is best placed to diffuse innovative practices and points of view between social settings, facilitating integrating bridges among adjacent social groups even when the group identity or ethos may otherwise seem incompatible.[77] While tech companies and workplace management both evangelize the facility of networking and connection, the complexity of knowledge production amid such interpersonal networks depends on degrees of distance, difference, and separation.

At the individual level, autonomy and knowledge grow from that disconnection between social situations and groups—contradictions that produce a certain type of social capital. Luke is nineteen and commutes into the expanding suburban periphery of Toronto from a largely white, agricultural, and manufacturing working-class county north of the city. He consciously skips past the recommended, trending videos served to him by YouTube algorithms, confident in his well-curated subscription list on that and other platforms, itself a reminder of his diligence in crafting a balanced and informative approach to media consumption. He is equally explicit about the personal and interpersonal values this effort produces. Following marches for International Women's Day, Luke scours nested, politicized forums or "subreddits" on the Reddit platform for reactions from the more extreme corners of the internet from which GamerGate and other attacks on women in games and media emerged. Rather than promoting chauvinism, Luke was set on informing his Discord messaging community on the wildly diverse interpretations of equal-rights news coverage. It is this type of work—the free labor of users—that ensures the functioning not just of single platforms like YouTube, Reddit, or Discord but of the wider ecosystem of connective media as a whole.[78] Luke messages his friends on the voice, video, and multimedia instant-messaging platform Discord, with the fruits of his research labor.

Luke's use of Discord speaks to its history. It's a platform that, for the experienced user, seamlessly and passively fits into the fluid management of the wider browser, platform, and gaming ecosystem. The Discord app was released in 2015 as an alternative to the Voice over IP (VoIP) feature embedded in popular multiplayer games and other instant messaging and group chats for use during game play, before emerging as a flexible digital-communication platform beyond just gaming. Rather than spanning the chasm between distant locales and transnational knowledge bases, media practices like Luke's bridge the gaps between flows of information across particular platform settings and types: a source of social capital emerging from digital and informational literacy rather than more traditionally understood cultural literacies or industry-specific know-how.

Luke's information-seeking practice is a type of "relational labor":[79] one not (yet) connected to a profession but nevertheless relying on the well-developed management of a communication environment in order to contribute something of value that fosters interpersonal connection. For this aspiring journalist, it is a playful and participatory social experience that informs how and why he is connected with others: "Each piece of significant information that I consume throughout the day is passed through instant messaging to peers, friends, and family." Luke understands his behavior as mutually beneficial, a networked community where "the same peers and friends interact with each other and myself in order to fill in holes in comprehension with regards to any given article or video." Luke's attraction to the functional architecture of Discord centers on its "personal server" community feature: a repository of interpersonal messages and shared media "so that it can be looked back on for all time." Like the reciprocity of mutual engagement, reviewing this archive is also a social and technological practice, a remembrancing that provides a sense of value to the practices of managing both interpersonal relationships and his communication environment in tandem.

Practice and identity alike shape the contours of these habitual spaces, their relational ethos determined by the perceived value of how individuals come together through communication. When Bourdieu looked at how what he called "social capital" is valued and accrued, he argued that a completely diffused, utterly discontinuous interchangeability of social actors would diminish social coherence to the "mechanical equilibria" of the social setting, in this case the programmed affordances of platforms and the algorithmic management of content flows.[80] There is a separateness that sustains social connection, iteratively performed and negotiated through the flow of mutual engagement. The result is a relational ethos fostered in connection with specific others that translates into types of social capital that help orient us beyond any one engagement or setting.

Ping and response: we locate our social worlds within ourselves and find their value through intimate and prosocial spaces of inclusion. But when a platform provides for a seamless ping of likes and shares, while also algorithmically assembling viral-post responses and each user's past media use, how and where exactly do we find ourselves, without the mutual engagement of others?

Distinction and the Pruning of Social Opportunities

Abandoning whole modes of communication and, at the same time, appreciating the connective possibilities they afford are telling at levels of both personal and social change. Often, we manage engagement with online platforms when interpersonal contacts and platform-specific knowledge are related to a specific project or set of goals. Other spaces come and go, waxing and waning along with the social value we place on them but also with our sense of what different types of media practices say about us or, rather, how our performative refusal to use particular platforms distinguishes us from others.[81]

Despite the industry contacts and followers developed over the period of a year, Elisabeth explains how excited she was to delete Twitter after completing a particularly lengthy string of client-specific intellectual-property projects, exclaiming, "It's just, like, who cares? Who are these people? . . . It is not relevant to my life, and I just don't have the time." These social connections are utilitarian: work-based, project-to-project, or specific to a career transition. This opportunistic disconnection is defined by the abandonment of individual professional goals for establishing connection in favor of recouping the time such interactions take.[82] These are not only utilitarian practices. There is a particular cultural cachet to being overconnected and overly busy. There is also performative social capital in disconnection.

Personal life is now subject to practices of pruning, often easily facilitated by a singular platform. Like many of us, Henry has threatened to delete Facebook and balked: "I think I wanted to distance myself from the continual chatter of Facebook. . . . So if there's someone that I care about or feel close to I decided that I wanted to send an email to them." Whereas this set of decisions involves transferring intimate, valued personal contacts to a different platform, there is still a frustrated ambivalence to a wider network of acquaintances on social media: "Facebook feels like a kind of fun, like, indulgence rather than, like, replying to texts and emails, which is just kind of, like, part of the essential ebb and flow of day-to-day life for me. So I think I'm kind of, like, 'You really think I have the time to be on Facebook.' But, like, usually I do."

As with Elisabeth's shift away from Twitter, Henry could be acting out what Bourdieu calls a "strategy of distinction," publicly presenting his nonuse of Facebook as an identity shaped by resisting its banality, thereby seeking social capital through disconnection from a particular mode of communication.[83] But is his decision to use Facebook itself only a matter of taste and of how others perceive him? "I think I feel affronted that they think I will just be on Facebook." Henry admits to being mildly taken aback. Gaining time is a motivation for abandoning the platform, even though Henry admits he does, in fact, have the time for it but does not want to be known as someone who has the time for it. Understanding the pressures to prune and constrain interpersonal communication means looking at our sensitivities about how particular media practices reflect the well-crafted sociality of our public self-presentation.

Faced with a similar conundrum, Richard, thirty-nine, makes a different decision. After their new relationship became more serious, his boyfriend became frustrated with Richard's reluctance to delete Grindr, a location-based sex-and-dating app for gay men. After a long and vexed exhale, Richard explained that, while at first, the app was definitely for hookups and dating, it had become a conduit for meaningful social interaction that he wasn't sure how to otherwise recreate or sustain. The app had become a third place among other queer and gay men, where Richard could develop a longer-standing rapport through instant messaging, mixing those who were already his good friends with acquaintances proximate to workplaces and different neighborhoods, whom he sometimes even recognized and greeted in person.[84] In short, Richard had fostered a networked community. And he only knew how to maintain it through the public social-media platform that had made it possible in the first place.

Disconnected Authenticity

In the era of constant connection, we should be wary of any appeals to authenticity, in particular those that police what it means for others. To proffer an objective standard to evaluate how others present themselves—as an authentic or inauthentic performance—is to overlook the performativity necessitated by particular social situations, and the inherently subjective nature of selfhood amid the plurality of private, public, and professional lives. Where the platform mediations of our digital selves offer modalities for interpersonal engagement, authenticity becomes the status quo, reinscribing normative power differences in online and workplace settings alike.[85]

The policing of authenticity completes the metaphorical circuit of our surveillance culture. Where constant connection translates into persistent exposure, surveillance, and scrutiny, contexts between social situations and diverse domains of everyday life collapse.[86] Social media's affordances and commercial imperatives idealize an entrepreneurial practitioner, entirely committed to the all-encompassing reputational framing of self-as-business. Restraining the divergence and experimentation of self-expression fostered by online spaces or embracing the proscribed expectations of professional authenticity serves to disconnect us from meaningful social interaction, reinforcing the boundaries and exclusions that disconnect us from others.

There is a self-affirming practicality that permits the cognitive, affective, and relational shortcuts at the heart of so many of our communication decisions. These are based on the self-perpetuating evidence of conventions, observable through the participatory practices of social surveillance and self-scrutiny, alongside reputational and managerial scrutiny. What we often accept as common sense draws on how actions are more validated the more common a consensus about norms seems within a given situation. As Bourdieu quips, "what is essential goes without saying because it comes without saying."[87] Ahmed critically examines these social facts in terms of how "a norm is something that can be inhabited" and when it is easily inhabited, when it "fits well," it does so without the discomfort of going against assumed or expected courses of action within a given situation.[88] The ease and comfort of inhabiting a norm or practice can often go overlooked, written off rather than examined in relation to diverse possible interpretations.[89] Others may find that such expectations do not fit well. Where one's identity is itself being policed, then normative conventions preemptively question any difference in terms of expectations, stifling subjectively experienced realities and the exploratory possibilities for one's identity.

Constraining the ways in which we can present ourselves and interact with one another serves to delimit the opportunities we have to know and become individuals in connection with others.[90] This chapter has examined the coping strategies of those who find their communication practices policed by the undifferentiated and suffocating application of normative conventions, their difference devalued in interpersonal practices, in terms of technological, moral, and political standardization of self-presentation.

When our actions do not conform, they are exposed and marked as different. Where our subjective sense of self does not align with public expectations, our agency is reduced from locating one's self—vis-à-vis others, a social situation, or even a career—to continually being positioned and repositioned by others. Given that knowledge, creative, and digital-sector careers are increasingly precarious and follow a project-to-project basis, the reputation-based economy that governs the working world equates to a perceived necessity. The emotional labor of avoiding interpersonal misgivings involves longer-term social-economic security, given the real possibility of depending on one's reputation among managers, peers, and entry-level colleagues alike for future contracts.[91] The toll of self-censorship is only matched by the desire not to be wholly colonized by normative expectations that run contrary to who we understand ourselves to be and how we hope to live our lives. Expectations about how we ought to communicate and be perceived professionally are often manifest as impositions on group conduct, limiting possibilities for self-expression and personhood based on insidious, pre- and proscriptive group identities that masquerade as universal or agreed-upon ideals of interpersonal or professional conduct.[92] Whereas these impositions of normative authority are not apparent to some, they are jarring and ubiquitous to others.

The disconnected practitioner serves as a template for regulating and reproducing normative forms of authenticity, albeit in different ways for different reasons. The workplace idealization of entrepreneurial prowess in tandem with a wholesale commitment of the self to work celebrates a potentially antisocial, but productive, manifestation of individuality, nominally unmarked by the gendered and racialized marginalization that difference often entails. Where difference is construed as a private deviation projected onto professional expectations, there is homogenizing and deindividualizing tension, which denies opportunities for authentically diverse selves to be expressed and to flourish. Zygmunt Bauman remarks that identity has been transformed from an "ascription into an achievement," no longer the anchoring and immutable sense of self to carry into one's career and life projects but rather an individual responsibility, something to be curated and managed, which today is a highly mediated set of ongoing everyday tasks.[93]

The ability of a group to decode conduct and interpret identity is a kind of social literacy, one heavily skewed by the power dynamics of a given social situation, despite the plurality of perspectives involved. It is crucial to remember that the stigma of difference is not about an individual's body, appearance, speech, identity, or actions. Difference is the outcome of social processes, where interpersonal communication and accepted norms are projected onto a social situation, with uncritical acceptance an assumed and inherently majoritarian bias. Stigma only emerges indirectly from the social information individuals convey about themselves; its main source is the definitional expectations of others about social setting and conduct.[94] Ian Hacking observes that whereas processes of identification, both self-directed and socially acknowledged, can be understood as "making up people" by offering spaces of possibility for identity and action, stigmatizing practices and the forced obscuring of one's sense of self from public exposure is more akin to "unmaking a person."[95] When the policing of authenticity emerges socially among media practices, mediated rituals serve to demarcate what can and cannot be spoken about or seen in public: who gets to speak or, rather, speak for themselves.

There are many manifestations of disconnection, from the situational withdrawal that attends only to the immediacy of necessary interaction, to the encompassing tendencies of enforced proscriptions of conduct. The internalization of these standards occurs through the aspirational hallmarks of neoliberal selfhood, which contributes to an acutely immediate and chronically compounding depersonalization of one's communication environment. Everyday interpersonal life is defined by performativity and censorship rather than voice and exploration through connection with others. Where accounting for obstacles and potential conflict becomes inherent to practices of self-censorship, conventional ways of interacting are locked in a pattern, scuttling any promise of social change.[96] The plurality and intersectionality of identity complicate such accounting but also provide powerful foundations for what Susan Leigh Star calls the "refusing translation" of difference. Instead of norms, one finds a steadiness in the open possibilities of whatever is not always immediately comfortable.[97]

Faced with the policing of identities, in tandem with communicative proscriptions, we refuse translation in a number of ways. These tactics of coping, self-censorship, and contesting are often woven together as strategies of the disconnected practitioner faced with the tensions of constant connection. Normative correction toward an uncritically accepted

ideal can be experienced as disaffection, a censoring or, rather, an enforced disconnection from one's own experience. Beyond merely managing boundaries between one's private and professional lives, there are
practices of self-surveillance, self-restraint, emotional discipline—and
the toll this emotional labor takes. The word *dissidence*, drawn etymologically from the Latin *dis* and *sedere*, means literally "to sit apart."[98]
This is altogether different from those practices demarcating a highly
sought-after "distinction" from others, often in terms of, for example,
socioeconomic status or other forms of social capital.[99] In terms of institutionalized settings that define and police communication practices,
Goffman notes that any "sustained rejection . . . often requires sustained
orientation to [institutional] organization, and hence, paradoxically, a
deep kind of involvement in the establishment," which itself is echoed in
Ahmed's observation that critical diversity work in professional settings
"generate[s] knowledge not only of what institutions are like but of how
they can reproduce themselves."[100] This social experience affords invaluable perspectives, although it is an additional labor to continually be the
lesson for others.

The policing of authenticity is a lever by which opportunities for
voice, not just agency, are limited. Practices of disconnected sociality
emerge in place of a discursive expression of the self in relation to others.
Individual agency and the experience accrued in interpersonal life
become isolated from others, and we cope through greater engagement
in managing the communication environment. Lost are opportunities
to foster greater intrapersonal understanding: the reinforced idealization of staging authenticity is reproduced, while also necessitating the
laborious management of interpersonal boundaries and self-censorship.
With economic uncertainty and the security of working life hanging in
the balance, degrees of individual choice to participate or not in social
media and other connective platforms—that final vestige of consumer
sovereignty—no longer apply.

Where opportunities for voice, to express oneself and one's definition
of a situation, are diminished, and no choice or exit is possible, the digital life of constant connection increasingly disconnects us from each
other in everyday life.[101] We desperately need to identify, encourage, and
expand the field for reflecting on how we forge a better connection. When
everyday interpersonal practice is itself understood as discourse about
social change, then metacommunication may offer that opportunity for

repair. These may be disruptive practices or unsettling interventions, but they may provide spaces for others to speak. Intransigence, refusal, frustration, and even outrage challenge the passive acceptance and reproduction of normative violence. Intersectional and transfeminist scholars have long advocated that the messenger must risk being mislabeled as the problem: by taking on the mantle of the "killjoy" we offer prosocial contributions to social change through communication practices.[102] Instead of individualized, disconnected coping mechanisms, we must seek a mutual sense of what authenticity could mean in connection with others.

SIX

Practicing Metacommunication

Attention shifts to *patterns of connection* when practices of managing everyday communication environments draw from experiences of constant connection—and from awareness of such shared experiences. These patterns of connection themselves become meaningful as negotiated sets of practices that structure everyday life. They represent a vehicle by which we develop and understand interpersonal relationships. Despite the seamlessness with which conventional everyday life hangs together, with its status quo cohering around norms of communication, there are continuous performative expectations, as well as acts of acquiescence and power, inherent in how we connect. The conditions for communication are in abundance. Yet we can scarcely manage the persistent contingency of interruptions and the constant, task-based flow of communication. To a degree, we disengage, at a particular scale. We manage communication and its environments at the level of changing practice, or metacommunication. Communication overload and increasing economic insecurity exacerbate our unwieldy expectations of others and our internalized senses of responsibility. These pressures come to define our day-to-day existences, sapping our time and attention by translating so many interpersonal desires for connection into practices of communication management, predicated on a relationship to technology, as opposed to a relationship with others *through* technology. How we adjust to, manage, avoid, and reproduce such pressures is a communication practice itself: an intelligible, expressive, and communicative set of interpersonal practices.

Such practices constitute the language of metacommunication, which is encoded and decoded by our shifting perceptions of technologies and the situational opportunities for mutual engagement particular to a setting, a relationship, or a set of relationships. As engagement between individuals and groups modulates across numerous modes of communication (even face-to-face copresence), many vital aspects of everyday life are being negotiated. This *reflexive* management of communication practices mutually constitutes *relational* opportunities for how people are connecting. Where we can maintain meaning and legibility at the level of metacommunication, partially disconnected from the inundation of signals at the content level, we can engage in *recursive* interpersonal negotiation of how we ought to communicate, through practice itself.

Dominica, twenty, spent an evening stewing over a particular communication conundrum, knowing that platforms and irresponsible content-creators profit, at least in terms of increased circulation, from misinformation and hate speech:

> People often misuse Snapchat when they go on their feed to watch a Snapchat show. These shows are consecutive thirty-second clips [with] a wide range of topics—from short stories about news in the world, to quick and easy three-minute recipes, to celebrity gossip.
>
> Not to say that these organizations aren't credible, but they do profit more [from] what are attention grabbers and allow people to be the mediators instead of following strict journalistic principles.

Platforms and their designs mediate opportunities for connection, but they increasingly envelop our very sense of what it means to connect. Our inherent understanding of communication is sublimated into technological and commercial ideals: how platforms—email, social media, or mobile apps—are meant to function. There is something similar about our reliance on assumed conventions of connecting with others, on communication practices, and on ways of managing our communication environments. All often go unnoticed until they fail.

The frustration in Dominica's diary entries is palpable. She is concerned that members of her social circle and extended family are not only consuming misinformation about a deadly virus but also spreading it:

> Even in terms of getting news from each other—friends and family on the platform—a lot of people were spreading propaganda, especially about the recent COVID-19 pandemic. For example, many news organizations were talking about the outbreak of COVID-19 in South Africa but mentioning that foreigners, not native Africans, were contracting the virus exclusively.
>
> And since education on social platforms go more or less unchecked and are rapidly spread because of the socialization aspect, I saw a lot of Snapchat stories saying Black people cannot get the virus (which is totally false).

This issue struck a personal chord with Dominica. Vaccine hesitancy has been high among Black people, Indigenous people, and people of color (BIPOC) in Canada, the UK, and the United States alike, owing in part to a history of trust-violation by medical and governmental institutions. Dominica decided not to weigh in publicly on the platform, instead contacting her few friends individually to discuss the implications of this false information. She disconnects from the socially expected interface default of seamless, continuous, and public engagement with content, switching instead to more concerted, private, mutual engagement with specific people. These communication choices are purposeful and interpretable by others, legible as the *practice of practice*, as metacommunication.

Corrections come in many forms. Unlike the prosocial example above, corrections often serve to enforce the status quo of communication practices, thereby reproducing normative structures, even when the individual is seeking refuge from them. The ubiquity of these pressures and framing of norms in terms of perceived technological functions often involves the internalized framing of assumed conventions, whereby individual users restrain and manage their own communication decisions in terms of what they believe are the individual and collective expectations of others. Reflecting on a taxi ride between tech-industry events, Zaina gives her marked opinion about how a certain technology should and should not be used: "I hate when people call. Worst is voicemail, right?

Voicemail has just got to be the most disruptive thing ever. I mean, it's so archaic. . . . Couldn't they just text it to me? Or email? Email, I'll get it right away. I have a smartphone."

Zaina has clear views on technology hierarchies. It's a matter of perception: her determination of the "correct" choice comes from how she discerns efficacy. But when Zaina emphasizes her ownership of an internet-ready mobile phone, a technological reality, she makes her viewpoint seem objective. If she has access to this technology, others should understand that it is the more appropriate option:

> I have a friend and she calls me a lot—she's the one I talk to a lot on the phone and stuff. She always leaves me voice messages, and I understand why it is; she's running from meeting to meeting so the only time she can really talk is when she's leaving meetings. . . . I actually told her "Can you stop leaving me voice messages," which should really belong in a *Seinfeld* skit. She was like, "What do you mean," and I'm like, "Stop sending me voice messages. I don't want to check them, just text me."
>
> Then she sent me a long message. It was a whole diatribe, "I'm so sorry you feel like that, but I'm not going to change the way I leave messages for you. Can't you adapt the way you get the messages from me? . . . Does it really take that much time for you to listen to my voice messages?"
>
> I said, "Does it really take a lot for you to not leave a voice message, and I'll call you back?" But she's like, "But I'll be in meetings all day." I don't want to listen to a two-minute message, even with virtual voicemail. I don't want to. . . . She got mad at me; she was really yelling at me.

A tech journalist, Zaina assesses her interpersonal communication as skewing to the function of tools, rather than the interpersonal impact of practices. Even while considering the pressures of her professional and personal lives against those of her interlocutors, she prioritizes a singular view of technology use. Throughout her interviews, she is quite critical of people who "aren't thinking" or just "don't get it." For Zaina, how to communicate should not be a question of others' personal circumstances and preferences, an opinion that causes immensely frustrating conflicts between her, her friends, and her family.

We often have incongruent perceptions of how best to communicate, cycling through habitual social and technological descriptions to rationalize our own idiosyncratic practices of managing the communication environment. We appeal to why and how tools are used—the types of interactions they permit or afford—as well as the personal knowledge we have about each other to justify often-inconsistent rationalizations. Our lived and enacted knowledges of communication inform our decisions about how one ought to connect.

Metacommunication has not failed to transmit the situational context in the above scenario: Zaina is aware of her friend's communication practice (she is running between meetings). Rather, metacommunication fails to resolve conflict in these friends' incongruent perceptions of technology. This conflict now spills over into explicit content-level communication, with flow of communication stymied in a less-than-ideal détente: "So her [sic] and I have had a really weird relationship, where now she leaves me voice messages, still as long if not longer, and I don't leave any voice messages." Their frustration with each other continues at the level of metacommunication. Neither is willing to forgo her individual control of the communication environment for the sake of mutual engagement and connection that suits each person involved. This conflict derives from individualized rationalizations that prioritize the costs of connecting with others, amounting to barriers to sociality and connection that heighten interpersonal tension.

How we communicate and negotiate connection involves a constellation of practices that also go unnoticed until they fail. Such failures may, indeed, offer the best vantage point for understanding each other. The philosopher Emmanuel Levinas has written that "the failure of communication is the failure of knowledge."[1] Mutual engagement provides the basis for any interpersonal communication. Over time, this engagement becomes the basis for our perception of each other and the relationships we form. *Metacommunication* is a concept proposed and developed throughout this book to capture the attempts of individuals to communicate at the level of that practice-based machinery, both to mediate the potential for breakdowns in interpersonal communication, on the one hand, and facilitate increased tension toward individuated senses of expediency, expectation, or efficiency that particular degrees of disconnected sociality provide, on the other hand. These are metacommunication practices, and they contribute to an ongoing, everyday discourse—practice *as* discourse; a discourse *through* the shifting form of communication practices—about how interpersonal communication can and should be conducted.

Reproducing Disconnection through Metacommunication

Given work's increasing management of our temporal sovereignty, personal management of mutual engagement is a matter of connection and disconnection. The dispersed, complicated matrices of networked presence and absence are facilitated by participatory surveillance practices yet are policed, and often asymmetrically negotiated, at the level of metacommunication.

Metacommunication occurs at different scales, depending on an individual's attendant engagement with the communication environment. Much like communication management practices and the development of interpersonal relationships, metacommunication belongs to a scale that subsumes, but nevertheless inflects, decisions on an interaction-to-interaction scale, without precluding people's awareness of their participation in something that is expressive and communicative. When it is a reflexive practice for managing one's communication environment in relation to others, metacommunication becomes an intrapersonal negotiation, a form of intervention on media practices that is itself a productive, communicative practice, seeking a degree of social negotiation to connect beyond conventions.

Recent scholarship from numerous social, political, and professional settings has demonstrated a similarly concerted "acting on media" for the purpose of changing how we communicate with each other. As I mentioned in chapter 1, Zuboff's early labor research at the close of the 1990s sought to differentiate the productively social practices and technological know-how of "acting with" others through technology from "acting on" technology, which couples a deskilling of labor through fragmentation of work processes into circumscribed technologically mediated task sets. These distinctions effectively segmented socially oriented knowledge work from socially isolated digital labor, a mirroring of white-collar and blue-collar work for the knowledge economy.[2] By the early 2010s, a clear schema of digital work was emerging among labor scholars, delineating the cognitive and creative work of producing digital outputs as distinct from the use of digital tools to facilitate interpersonal connections. These were then also distinguished from the types of cooperative digital work that sought to establish opportunities for connecting with others, shaping both the environment of media practices and how that environment is perceived and understood.[3] In the knowledge economy today, however, the qualification of labor as "digital" is largely tautological, an empty signifier in the era of mediatization.[4]

Metacommunication is cooperative digital labor that seeks an interpersonal or collective rearticulation of the very opportunities for coming together touted by digital media. Over the last decade, this collective dimension of "acting on" media has emerged as an explicitly prosocial and political set of practices for change.[5] Sebastian Kubitschko's fieldwork with Germany's highly literate digital activist circles traces a proliferation of political interventions that go beyond the interface affordances of platforms, recasting practices of "acting on" media technologies and infrastructures as discursive and opportunistic sites for social change through, for example, the development of privacy tools and other interventions that promote greater data literacy in the public.[6] Among media-production professionals, in particular Canadian public-service digital archivists, we are similarly seeing such purposeful reflexive practices contributing to what Asen Ivanov has called "evaluative repertoires," schemas of media-centric knowledge produced amid the cognitive and situational handling of digital objects to better understand, while also purposefully communicating, the many and often overlooked decisions we make while handling and transforming digital objects.[7] Hilde Stephansen suggests that research needs to actively examine how such interventions are similarly occurring within the reflexive repertoire of communication practices among everyday citizens, a layperson's "acting on" the media that engages how and what kinds of knowledge about communication are produced and what practices serve to mobilize change through that knowledge.[8]

The Mediations of Correct Usage

Self-correcting how we connect with others often carries with it an assumed, though oversimplified, binary—right and wrong—regarding the perceived utility of an app or platform. This correction also sidesteps mutual negotiation of communication by rationalizing connection in terms of the commercially guided affordances of platforms, on the one hand, and communication practices defined by terms of media, on the other. The psychologist and sociologist Sherry Turkle suggests that social media can be a "transference object."[9] In early childhood psychology, a blanket or stuffed animal serves as just such a mediator between the self and the outside world, stepping in to represent both the self and others at different times and in different ways. Engagement with one's social world is transferred toward—projected onto and displaced by—engagement with the technology in both practical and emotional terms: in this instance, "acting on" technology serves to limit and disconnect from opportunities to "act with" others.[10]

In negotiating how we can and ought to connect with specific people or simply others in general, there is a lot more at stake than the simple choice between one mode of communication over another; it is the negotiation of the engagements and relationships that constitute everyday life. At the scale of metacommunication, conventionalized media practices are ideologies amid negotiation.[11] Media practices are both manifestations of political economy and mutually constitutive performances that reproduce and embed matrices of power and individuated neoliberal responsibilization with the practice of everyday life. These are rarely explicitly ideological positions or conscious activist interventions into everyday communication, yet when the political potential of metacommunication is overlooked, the persuasiveness and allure of our disconnected sociality spreads passively.

George describes the dual pressure to connect and restrain himself from connecting in a particular way: "I don't like troubling people for no reason. So what, some people consider, you know, social grace, calling people, asking them how they are. I don't mind when people do it to me. I don't feel that I'm within my rights to actually trouble people if I don't have anything to say to them in particular."

George recasts the pressures of communication in terms of rights, implying another category of responsibility to those with whom he engages. For some, this may seem like a provocative and exaggerated appeal to the moral, legal, and political language of rights, but if one accepts that interpersonal interaction is foundational to the makeup of society at large, then connection becomes a matter not just of the social world but also of wider politics. Esther speaks in more concrete terms about the rights of her colleagues: "I don't text work colleagues, ever. Because I consider it a friendly thing and it is invasive and for work-related stuff I think it is. I would find it very invasive, so I wouldn't. I don't consider it a professional medium. So that's how I think about it."

Tensions of constant connection—availability, temporal pressure, contingency, interruption, and the blurring of domains—become levers for negotiating a better way to communicate. How we communicate becomes an active discourse about the shape of social change, the role of technology, and the political-economic pressures that we must navigate through communication practices. This is the space for performing and negotiating the social and political implications of how we connect. Rather than subscribing to the commercially ascribed mediations of platform design, or the neoliberal inequities that have come to define the professional working environment, metacommunication is a space for negotiating media ideologies among individuals hoping to connect in a better way. Today, the language of disconnected sociality stands in for the moral and political realities of our communication practices.

In addition to his day job in network and software sales, Peter runs an events-and-clubbing photo blog and its supplementary social-media profiles. This keeps him quite active and social in the evenings after work, and out all weekend, every week. He discusses how his perception of social-networking platforms has recently changed:

> I use Twitter for self-promotion, shameless self-promotion only. I think it has absolutely no value other than that. I use it to promote my website. . . . I have Twitter followers and sometimes they say things to me and I actually ignore them. I've got Twitter with fifteen hundred people or whatever, so I think Twitter for me has replaced the mailing list.
>
> When I first got on Facebook I kept it personal for maybe like two or three months and then I had all these friend requests and I just thought "Oh fuck it," and so I accept them all. I just make it all a promotional tool.

The way Peter gives up on fostering personal connections through Twitter and Facebook is telling. At first, he tried to create multiple Facebook accounts, one for close friends and another for promotional networking with loose acquaintances, though he was spending too much time and energy engaging with the platform itself and not enough with other individuals in a way he deemed meaningful. In the end, it is his perception of the platform—what he deems its correct usage—that changes, justifying a set of communication-management practices that preclude opportunities for more personal connection. He now sees the platforms simply as tools for self-promotion; they have no other social value as a connective platform. He does not stop using the platform but simply stops using it for any form of mutual engagement.

Dominica is frustrated by the way others use Snapchat. Her frustration has less to do with the correct use of the platform than with the corrosive quality of practices that the platform promotes:

> I don't use [Snapchat Streaks] in the conventional way that most people use streaks. Streaks are essentially a way to increase your Snapchat score and be more connected on the platform. When you consecutively send videos to someone, you get an emoji of a flame next to their name indicating they talk with you every day. It seems like a good way to stay interconnected but in reality, it's very impersonal.
>
> People often send mass messages to people to keep streaks in the name of their Snapchat score [for] popularity and nothing else. Thus, I have a system of when I get a streak message (often signifies with an S on the picture/video), I reply with a comment instead to start a real conversation that they can't use a mass message to reply to.

The correction Dominica seeks through her unconventional use of Snapchat is derived from a deep literacy of the platform's affordances, and a prosocial desire for a degree of mutual engagement, despite its programmed tendency toward a disconnected sociality through gamification and the promotion of engagement with algorithmic recommendation streams and feeds—content over users. At the level of metacommunication, Dominica is negotiating connection with others rather than with the platform itself.

Rationalizing how and why platforms should be used in particular ways is itself a social practice, serving to limit and shape the contours of social opportunities. The manner in which these practices anchor and therein mediate how we connect with others is legible to others in a manner that may transcend the use of single technology in isolation and speak more to perceptions of technologies in relation to one another across the wider communication environment. Bourdieu points to systems of classification amid practice that reproduce their own logics, such that ways of doing things are not considered arbitrary or idiosyncratic but are taken as self-evident. There is a degree of misrecognition here. An assumption that reproduces the normative force of conventions—even near and inconsistent conventions—when they are taken for granted, unmarked by difference from a norm, will often go unnoticed. His study of practice relies on the conceptualization of "doxa," which implies a degree of reflexivity in our strategic responses to norms and rules through an "awareness and recognition of the possibility of different or antagonistic beliefs."[12] Yet these rationalizations represent an assumption of a purposeful rule-bound set of comparisons that are assumed to be superior for their apparent intellectual rigor rather than their social or emotional grounding in situational contexts. While such rationalizations seem to defuse the orthodox strictures of formally policed communication rules through reflexive reconsideration of practice, they can serve to prioritize personal individualized preferences in the management of otherwise social settings. Often, this individuated approach limits an otherwise heterodox openness to change, replacing the plasticity of everyday social life with the corrections of normative force.

Changing Relationships, Changing Connections

How we interact and connect with each other is not just a practical decision, nor is it based only on the popularity of one medium over another. It is conflated with, and experienced as, the substance of a relationship. Whether spending time together each week in person or through social media, chatting on the phone, texting or instant messaging in the evenings, patterns of communication can act as reference points for negotiation of stasis and change in a relationship. Such negotiation does not take place in relation to a single action but through a wider gamut of cues, signals, and realignments relating to how we connect and disconnect, changing the relationship itself. Metacommunication has consequences.

Andrew describes how he would "wean" old friends and former romantic partners off different modes of communication to signal a change in the relationship, specifically platforms that he believes connote lesser degrees of intimacy through degrees of more closely managed availability. He understands, however, that such strategies are commonplace: a woman he was seeing had stopped replying to his emails and was ignoring his texts, yet he sees "her act of requesting this 'friendship' [on

Facebook] as an indication that she doesn't want to break things off completely." Where one mode of communication was expressly closed, another was opened.

Drawing on his engineering background, Andrew seems to view the "rules" of how best to communicate as more universally shared, based on the technical affordances of one platform compared to another. "I can gauge how close I am to a person by how many potential means of communication I have available to me to contact that person and/or how many lines are actively being used." Despite this, Andrew is sensitive to the signaling in certain relationships as renegotiations of how best to communicate. He not only monitors the changing patterns of communication to consider shifting the degree of intimacy in his relationship, but he also expresses and reacts to changes in relationships in a similar way.

In a comparable fashion, Christina decided to "relax the . . . embargo" after quarreling with a close friend. Though she continued to ignore the friend's calls, texts, and emails, she sent a social-networking message to show that she does not want a "permanent rift." Against the relational backdrop defined by previous interactions, Andrew and Christina assume that shifts in connection are expressive and can even indicate a change in the relationship. Maintaining connection, but in a different mode, is understood as the desire not to forgo the relationship altogether.

Signaling the way communication needs to change when the nature of relationships change is integral to professional relationships as well. Eugene describes a comparable situation but with a friend who has just been promoted ahead of him at their firm. Though a different relational ethos than that of peers, the shift in this manager and team-member relationship is still renegotiated at the level of metacommunication. Eugene is still adjusting: "I think he's trying to send me a message like this is the proper way and what you were doing before was very unprofessional. I sent him an email, not bitchy in any way . . . and he didn't respond to that. Before, he would have been willing to engage in a [email] conversation but he just didn't respond. The next day, if he wanted to know something . . . he would come to see me in person or call me. . . . He does everything in person now."

Now his superior, Eugene's friend attempts to recast their relationship in part by shifting how the two communicate. Though indicative of workplace surveillance and managerial accountability, the friend's refusal to continue their previous pattern of casual banter through continuous email communication is a signal demarcated by a shift between modes of communication. Like the renegotiation of the relationships above, these shifting forms and patterns of engagement are neither conveyed explicitly in the content of any interaction nor clearly expressed by a single interaction but are only understood through the shift in engagement becoming a lasting change.

Metacommunication is often used to effect a new relational ethos, to rearticulate connection where previous ways of communicating are no longer appropriate or desirable. None of these shifts involved any explicit negotiation on how to communicate at the content level; the shifts were communicated relationally through modes of engagement at the level of metacommunication rather than through spoken words or text-based messages. This renegotiation is made explicit through changes to communication practice itself.

In the context of previous mutual engagement, which is understood effectively as the context of their relationship, the refusal for connection across certain modes of communication is expressing that the personal relationship has diminished. Such decisions are also affirmations of what modes of communication are appropriate for the new form of relationship. Thus, metacommunication occurs in two ways: first, to express a change in the relationship and, second, to communicate how those involved should engage from that point forward.

Rule Breaking as Normative Corrections

Intentional practices reveal communication conventions when they defy interpersonal expectations. In communication, this is all the more apparent when communication decisions include a rationalized dismissal of what others expect, how they will react, or a departure from an implicitly negotiated relational ethos—that is, a way of understanding how to connect that is developed through past interactions among particular others or in relation to a particular setting.

Predicated on the normative assumptions of what one ought to do, or should have done, norms are not the same as conventions. Norms are instead predicated on expected conformity to assumed regularities of action and reaction, of interaction and expectation. The distinction comes from the recursive way in which we respond to actions of others and incorporate past experiences into future interactions. How we conventionally connect with each other involves what Berger and Luckmann call a "reciprocity of typification" as we begin to play expected roles vis-à-vis one another.[13]

The habituation of how we interact with particular others can afford or constrain opportunities for how we connect, contributing to what I have been calling a *relational ethos*, determined and negotiated by communication decisions amid interaction. In her study of women's magazines and self-help books over four decades, Eva Illouz explores the changing frameworks for policing how we interact with one another, especially how a particular sociality of rationalizing emotional experience has become an idealized type of social capital: "emotional literacy" points to a specific type of reflexivity and self-regulation, but the normative expectations and corrections that deploy this term tend to refute individual experiences. Where personal experience of a given situation is subject to externalized objective scrutiny, in particular in hierarchical and consequential settings like the workplace, the assumed conventions to facilitate particular types of interpersonal transactions are prioritized and policed, despite the costs to oneself.[14] We are practicing a type of violence when such rationalizations are imposed on others, effacing their experiences, preferences, and emotional responses, all of which are otherwise justifiable.

Lourdes and Sydney live together in a cramped, affordable apartment in East London. They've been in a relationship for four years, all of their early twenties. Sydney manages the programming and marketing at a large, live-music venue; Lourdes has been supporting herself, working the odd shift, until she landed a temporary but full-time administrative role for a large online retailer. As they both mention in their interviews, they spend mornings together, and if they do not arrive home at the same time in the evening, then whoever arrives first will invariably phone the other to check in and coordinate dinner or evening plans. During the day, they have developed different communication patterns, defined in part by their awareness of each other's habits and by the physically situated social contexts from within which they connect. Yet there is a disconnect regarding the appropriate way to communicate that transcends technological assessments of a particular platform or app. Their negotiation, or lack thereof, of how best to communicate speaks to the normative force of conventions, the gendered aspects of romantic relationships and workplace settings, and the unequal discretions and indiscretions those norms permit.

Lourdes spends a considerable amount of time doing freelance writing and consulting for small creative companies. Sometimes she is paid; sometimes she is not. Nevertheless, her days working in-office and in-person are valuable opportunities to prove herself as professional, to learn and develop new contacts toward securing additional contracts or a role on a permanent basis. Sydney is perfectly aware of how Lourdes prefers to manage her availability while in this professional setting: "Well I guess the fact that she, because I've questioned many times why she decides to have her phone on silent when she is at work and she always gives the same answer: 'I don't like my phone ringing all the time.' What I have found is the girl that she works with, if I ring her mobile, then my girlfriend will answer it and that is the way I can talk to her. So that is what I have learnt to do now."

Sydney's experience of Lourdes's constant unavailability directs a lot of their communication to email. Sydney knows the social and physical setting that leads her to practice this type of disconnection, though he overlooks her reasoning for this when it suits him: he can likely still reach her by telephone, just not on her own telephone, by interrupting both her coworker's day and her own. This represents a breach of professional etiquette possibly more egregious and embarrassing for Lourdes than her own phone ringing, but for Sydney, it is simply a matter of whether or not his action will succeed on a whim. In settings of communication scarcity, where connecting is technologically difficult, we engage in what Rich Ling and Jonathan Donner refer to as "approxi-calling," a strategic set of practices whereby personal addressability, afforded by mobile phones, extends through an awareness of both practices, with their everyday contexts, schedules, and face-to-face social or work settings.[15] Yet in this context of communication abundance and managed practices of disconnection, this is opportunistic violation of known equilibria—one individual rationalizing the benefit of acting against expected and explicit conventions of the social situation.[16] From this standpoint, the individualized "correct" navigation of interpersonal connection extends to whatever opportunities to connect the communication environment affords, regardless of what others may prefer.

Lourdes has developed a similar awareness of her boyfriend's personal communication preferences in tandem with the physical situation and perceived social pressures of his workday. Despite the infrastructural reality of connection and her situational knowledge to do otherwise, she consistently respects the patterns of disconnection that define his communication preferences. Both interviews reflect this discrepancy:

> He actually doesn't like to talk on the [phone]. . . . I think because of his environment, he works in the office. . . . Like they can pretty [much] get away with what they want there, but I think it is that kind of thing where in the office [with] the other men, you don't really want to be on the phone to your girlfriend that much. (Lourdes)

> She might ring me or I might ring her. Generally if she rings me I will always answer. . . . I think she knows [I'll answer] because I tend to. I work in a very relaxed office where we are incredibly free, and if I want to go out for two hours in the middle of the day no one is going to question that. (Sydney)

> So it is a very relaxed [environment], and so I will sit at my desk and talk to my girlfriend. I am not going to sit there and go "Oh I love you, you are so beautiful." But I will sit there and have a general personal conversation with her without having to think I have got to go to the other room or I have got to go outside or anything like that. (Sydney)

Lourdes's awareness of Sydney's context, that he may be embarrassed to be on the phone with her in front of his colleagues, has become part of her communication decision-making. Their final preference for communicating favors email and text, which allow both to communicate and coordinate their days without disturbing Sydney's office environment, marked by expressive gestures of connection Sydney feels uncomfortable with over the phone. Lourdes chooses to compromise between her and her boyfriend's preferences, given the particulars of their social situation. His decisions are justified by what is technically possible—not by a particular platform's affordances but across the myriad opportunities for connection across the wider everyday communication environment.

Unwritten rules and implicit negotiations on how best to communicate are metacommunication at work. Yet the assertion of individual control over a situation also expresses how one believes the communication environment should work, demonstrated by appeals to an objective framing of technically correct uses, based on platform design. Andrew explains his own closely managed control over how and when others can connect with him: "In chat windows, I'm constantly invisible. . . . I think I was happy to see that. . . . I am somewhat manipulative about trying to control *when and how* I'm contacted and by whom, whether I'm being *vulnerable* to a chat—and I sometimes don't like to be put on the spot with a *live thing*.

Despite the admitted moral ambiguity of his communication decisions, this is not a courtesy that he would extend to others.

> So the example [in my diary] where I [blocked my number] myself before I called my ex—*that was me acting aggressive*—I was fully aware of what I was doing, I'm not stupid—and I did not feel like being considerate to her. I was trying to catch her off guard.
>
> So when people don't go along with *it*, I'll either be offended, and that's when I assume that someone understands *the rule* and is just being rude or inconsiderate, or I just recognize that they're just being somewhat aggressive.

By telephoning his ex at work, Andrew purposefully shifts from an established pattern of interaction, both during and after the relationship. This is a temporal boundary to her work domain, maintained through managed degrees of disconnection, patterns that those close to her are expected not to transgress. Andrew explains that this was "an emotionally charged issue that required a conversation." But what is the "the rule" he was referring to? Patterns of how best to communicate had already been negotiated between them, representing what I have referred to elsewhere as a *relational ethos*. This negotiated ethos, the "it" with which he normally goes along and which would offend him if transgressed, was the product of numerous sets of interactions between particular sets of individuals over time: a habitual pattern of how best to communicate, developed and negotiated at the level of metacommunication. Purposefully deviating from this, while technically and practically successful, would be considered aggressive. Andrew is perfectly aware of this. He assumes that his ex, too, will interpret his phone call in this way.

Karina is quite close with her employees. Her brother even works for her. It is therefore impossible to untangle her work and social worlds.

She is quite aware that the power dynamic between employer and employee makes it different from other social interactions—here, she *can*
single-handedly inflect the relational ethos. Whereas this is an unbal-
anced negotiation within a workplace dynamic, it is a salient example
of attempting to maintain a relational ethos that overlaps with the management of the domains of work and social life through communication
practices:

> I am careful about contacting them outside of work hours. I would
> never call them outside of work hours—I get texts from one girl outside
> of work hours, but I probably don't text her back in those instances.
>   . . . I may be working, but I want my staff to *not* take the way that
> I work as an example of how I want them to work. I feel I am the one
> who has to put the boundaries there. I do email at ridiculous hours at
> times, one or two in the morning, but I always start by saying, "Ignore
> the time."
>   I explain myself usually. . . . I just don't want them to feel that I will
> be impressed outside of work hours.

Karina is concerned that any one of her communication choices will
be understood as an attempt to insist on engagement outside of work
hours. By choosing not to respond to her employee who sends text messages outside of work hours, Karina is ensuring that she is not expressing any expectations for engagement during this time. Similarly, when
Karina herself sends emails in the middle of the night, she understands
that it is necessary to be explicit that she is not signaling a need for employees to reciprocate her communication choices. Platforms have responded to these tendencies and offered scheduling features for emailing
and social media alike, the latter algorithmically managed for greatest
opportunity of engagement with followers. This power dynamic, though
quite different from the social setting and specific to employers, provides
an insight into how single actions, in contrast to the habitual ways of
communicating, can muddle the state of a relationship or otherwise express a shift in the context of interaction.

These are rule-breaking corrections. They demonstrate how we can
assert power in situations because others have chosen not to or are not
in a position to do so. Where individuals seek prosocial negotiation in
terms of what may be best for others, sometimes metacommunication

needs to be complemented by explicit consideration and deliberation of mutual solutions. Where individuals see opportunities provided by the failure of others to exploit the situation to their individual benefit, what is technically possible is sometimes recast as a matter of social or digital literacy, overlooking the power imbalances introduced or asserted when one party is attempting to mutually negotiate a better way to connect, while the other is not.

Conventions mask socially enforced norms. They are expectations of conformity. In his philosophical examination of conventional decision-making, David Lewis theorized that what lurks within our normative appeal for particular behaviors is an individualized rationality that has less to do with moral or social values than with a cost-benefit analysis of maintaining equilibria among interactions while calculating the cost benefit of violating expectations. Norms only become accepted social facts when "they are—under some description—uniform."[17] The assertion of power amid social interaction is an affectation of one's own description. It is an individualized rationale that sees uniformity from the vantage point of personal actions, not of others' interpretations and expectations of similar experiences.

Conflict by Design

Increasing user engagement or connecting the world are just a few of the over-simplified commercial imperatives that govern platforms. These lead to unanticipated social outcomes, what economists call externalities to the rationalized calculable aspect of risk in market innovations and interventions. These are the consequences, whether positive or negative, within an assessment of economic exchange, external to the conditions of the exchange.[18] In the case of platforms, the rudimentary versatility of a platform's affordances provides for the widest possible types of engagement within the programmed fields for user interaction. Whether that engagement is pleasurable or upsetting, or contributing to social cohesion or conflict, is external to the commercial calculations behind the platform design. Some celebrate and profit from these unexpected outcomes; others are hurt by them. Yet the platform imperative of increasing engagement is blind to these differences.

In the wake of anti-Asian racism that accompanied the spread of COVID-19—a xenophobic trend of harassment and violence stoked by populist Western politicians and misinformation about the pandemic—several participants in this study felt a sense of responsibility to ameliorate the situation as best they could, given their nationality, Chinese ethnicity, or East Asian heritage. Suyin, a nineteen-year-old Hong Kong Canadian, outlines just such a situation: "Today, when I was playing League of Legends, there was a player who was racist in the game. He had been using a lot of bad words to insult other players. I think playing games should focus on cooperation with teammates. I decided to report the player to the game company at the end of the game."

This type of digital citizenship is informed by perceived circuits of normative media use. A user may understand "correct," meritocratic media use, derived, for example, from the goals afforded by a game's design and requisite skills to succeed—despite interpersonal settings characterized by racist or chauvinist breaches of social norms among gamers.[19] Outside the gaming environment, however, what are the programmed opportunities informing a sense of appropriate conduct and an individual's feeling of responsibility to check the actions of other users?

Social-media platforms and their algorithmic management allow for the curation and differential display of content, hashtags, groups, or pages—a very different procedural environment from the often clearly defined pathways for cooperation, competition, or success of many gaming environments. The Shanghai-based, Chinese-language HUPU platform is an online sports community focused on basketball, international football (soccer), and e-sports, with forum-like user groups and live-broadcast commenting functionality. Park, who goes by Parker in majority English-language settings, is an avid user: "Checking HUPU, I noticed people commenting that we should not show mercy to people who are infected [with COVID-19] in the USA, especially those people who did not do well in self-quarantine. I argued with their comments: Every life matters, so I will not say anybody deserves to get infected. I still hope these infected people recover soon, and I think sending [hate-filled] comments is very immature. I am frustrated about these mean comments."

HUPU is sports-oriented, but like many other social platforms, its underlying programmed-functionality goal is to increase engagement with the platform, and between users, where possible. Park is attempting to do the right thing by engaging with other users—a normative correction of their antisocial behavior—yet taking on this social responsibility disrupts the conventional equilibria and invites potential online abuse into a setting for social practices that would otherwise be considered enter-tainment. While catching up on the latest COVID-19 restrictions across several YouTube channels, Park found a different set of problematic reac-tions to the situation, feeling similarly obliged to intervene: "Some people still do not pay attention to this [dire] situation and keep throwing parties all night long. I decided to comment about their not-so-bright behavior, suggesting [that they] stay home." He equivocates momentarily: "People from different countries deal with this virus differently, but some of their solutions are wrong to me so I need to say something about it."

Kai feels a similar responsibility to be a good digital citizen, aug-mented by his experience across diverse platforms and the contrasting messages circulating among different transnational communities and their respective Chinese and North American user bases.

> Today is Sunday and I have nothing to do. I am flipping through things on Weibo for entertainment. The familiar Mandarin messages about what has happened in China recently [give] me [a] sense of tightened connection to my home country—a fantasy that I am still in China.
>
> I checked Twitter to see people's view on the coronavirus, and it is shocking that a huge number of people are blaming the Chinese, and even calling the coronavirus the "China Virus." I started arguing with those with hate messages, [pointing out] that the virus has no nationality, and what they are doing is practicing racial discrimina-tion. It feels meaningful.

Ruha Benjamin, a sociologist of race and media studies, examines the troubling consequences of how we are made as users to perform "correctly" in certain ways and on certain platforms when faced with antisocial and discriminatory behavior.[20] First, the laissez-faire modera-tion of conflict online places the responsibility and burden of managing antisocial and racist behavior on individual users themselves, who are often racialized or otherwise marginalized by the very behavior they feel obliged to correct. Second, the algorithmic curation mechanisms of many social-media platforms are programmed to encourage user-to-user interaction—the more intense the better—thereby automatically promot-ing material that garners attention and interaction, even if users were seeking to criticize such behavior to begin with.[21] Benjamin outlines how this represents the "gamification of hate," where racist and other discriminatory online behavior cajoles others into engagement, which is then rewarded algorithmically by greater exposure.

If we follow this programmed logic of gamification and social conflict through to the interpersonal logics of video-game play experience itself, we see a valuation of platform- or game-oriented affordances over mutual engagement. Permitting, and indeed promoting, participation despite the harassment that forces others to police interpersonal norms is a particular sociality of disconnection, encouraging an "acting on" the media despite the deleterious effects from "acting with" others. Lisa Nakamura demonstrates that even when racism, sexism, transphobia, homophobia, or ablism are evident in game design and the interpersonal dimensions of game play between users, the technological underpinning of the game itself becomes understood as the basis for a "procedural meritocracy": a diligent commitment to the labor of game play, the demonstration of technological prowess, and skill acquisition, all of which ostensibly offer a mask for players who are in other respects marginalized. Thus, freedom from harassment is often perceived as skills-based success, a full colonization of in-game cognitive and communicative labor toward the strictures of implied and user-policed community norms. Corrections in relation to the utility of gaming options and game-play interactivity represent an apparent, meritocratic path to self-improvement, despite both explicit user biases and systemic game biases. In the preceding chapter, I noted that these types of personal dispossession are required to avoid confrontation among other users, representing another degree of disconnected sociality policed through the expressive forms of acceptable game play. At the level of metacommunication, conventionalized media practices are more clearly ideological when users internalize the same evaluative repertoires necessary for inclusion and to avoid harassment.

The legibility and literacy of platform design contribute to the social expectations that mediate and foreclose opportunities to connect. The way we engage with the forms of sociality afforded and promoted by platform programming has lessons for the organization of both personal life and workplace or career-related communication norms. Expected reactions of others, and the possibilities for future interactions, reproduce the status quo, normalizing both an individual's responsibility for publicly attending to their marginalization by others and the imagined outcomes of conflict, mortification, and shaming made possible by the networked, circulatory affordances of connection itself.

Overcoming the Forced Disconnection of a Global Pandemic

COVID-19 social-distancing and lockdown measures precipitated a sudden, mass disconnection from both casual and intimate face-to-face encounters, creating a seismic recalibration of communication practices that shattered habits and conventions alike. The forced social disconnection of safety mandates led to forced digital connection.[22] The shock came from having to reassess how best to manage a communication environment that was changing not in terms of affordances but in terms of how best to connect, disconnect, and express preferences related to what is acceptable and necessary.

Faced with unprecedented stress and confusion in the early weeks of the COVID-19 pandemic in Canada, Aaliyah felt the need to reassess how she communicated with classmates and instructors alike in an attempt to consider the pressure and stress of the term being thrown into disarray, with classes going online for the first time:

> I am choosing to engage with my classmates about the next steps regarding our final assignments. I recommend that it is best to give the professor at least until the weekend until one of us emails him hounding him about how the semester is going to unfold.
>
> I came to the decision because I wanted to be empathetic toward everyone as well. The COVID-19 virus has been stressful for everyone, but some people feel the weight of it a little more than others. Making the suggestion to wait meant that we were respecting that everyone has to work with ambiguity, and it is important to give space.

Aaliyah is changing the way she communicates in response to the pressures she is sure others are facing. She explicitly asks her classmates to do the same, even though their patience in waiting for clear guidance may not always be recognized or even legible (as the instructor was likely still attending to a barrage of emails amid the rush to adjust lesson plans for virtual teaching).

When travel restrictions, lockdowns, and working from home were implemented in response to the pandemic in 2020, expressive shifts in connection became an important prosocial tool at the level of metacommunication. Zeynab points out that "most of the time, my friends and I do not even call each other because we prefer texting" but that under social-

distancing restrictions in Toronto, "not having a face-to-face communication for a while caused us to choose calling. It felt like we were closer
when talking on the phone rather than texting." Park similarly assessed
and reassessed the types of connection WeChat affords and how shifts
between them could be an expressive practice that reassures and cares
for those close to him who are in distress:

> Checking WeChat, I saw moments posted by my friends complain-
> ing about [how] their flights got cancelled, so they are not able to go
> home. I called one of them and showed my sympathy. Why? It hurts
> someone if he/she cannot go back home due to the current situation.
> So I need to make them feel better.
>
> Using WeChat when my brother sent me a video chat invitation, I
> accepted the invitation and started to tell them what is going on in To-
> ronto right now and ask them not to worry too much about me. I know
> my family is worried about me; the COVID-19 situation in Canada is
> not as difficult as it is in the USA. So, I hope to make them less worried
> through this video chat.

The numerous forms of interaction across the WeChat platform offer
an expressive landscape for choosing how to connect. Park does not
follow up on the short-term video posts—or moments—of his friends with
a comment or reply; he chooses to call. Knowing his family is concerned,
he makes sure to take the time to answer his video-chat invitation from
his brother. Of course, this affective signaling of a shift from regular patterns of communication can go both ways. A few days later, stuck in his
apartment, Park was using WeChat again when "I saw a message from my
close friend in China, so I sent a video chat request to him and talked to
him about how bad I am feeling during the quarantine. My friends care
about me, so I need to communicate with them and share my experience
with them."

The affective bonds that connection facilitates contribute to our understanding of when, how, and through which modes of communication
we can express support, and share in joy, grief, or frustration. This literacy emerges from the complexity of our constant connection, where
communicative choices themselves can sometimes be expressions of
care. Though not technically communication negotiations, these single
communication decisions shift away from regular patterns and are thus

indicative of an already negotiated relational ethos between individuals, upended and renegotiated in the context of COVID-19.

A momentary communication choice expresses itself against a value-laden and contextually nuanced backdrop of the shared patterns of how we seek, find, and connect with each other. A careful, or rather care-full, navigation of connection and disconnection became purposeful intervention to change how we communicate, seeking an affective legibility to media decisions and collective sharing of communicative pressures in the face of unprecedented social isolation. Unfortunately, these moments of actively engaging intrapersonal negotiation are often outweighed by the atomizing force of a conventionalized disconnected sociality.

The Pressure and Self-Policing of the Disconnected Status Quo

The space of metacommunication carries both expressiveness and legibility, extending beyond just the recognition and negotiation of how we ought to communicate. The normative force of how we assume we must communicate involves the internalization of expected corrections, such that we no longer need to be policed by others. We police our actions ourselves, often despite our motivations and desires.

Eugene and many other interviewees allude to a supposedly natural division and ordering of how people are expected to and do interact in orientation to different relationships and different opportunities to connect: "They're different groups of people, in that I never Facebook my work friends. . . . You add them as a friend and *they won't [message] you or you won't [message] them*—they're just there. . . . The people who I talk to and whose walls I post on, it's generally *quite a set group* of people. There's some sort of second-tier friends who once in a while will get something." There are unwritten rules that stymie opportunities for connection, yet how these norms of disconnected sociality are shared, communicated, and negotiated often occurs below the level of communication.

Peter, who, earlier in this chapter, explained how he has given up trying to connect in a meaningful way with others over social media, compares the management of personal space in public to the expected norms of social-media use:

> So they sent you a friend request, you accepted it, but because they
> don't know [you well], they wouldn't be able to say hello to you or

wouldn't be able to send you a message or wouldn't be able to write on your wall and it would seem too awkward.

So it kind of polices itself. So people keep their distance. Within your Facebook profile there's a core, right, and then there's a bunch of people at the edges. It's self-policing. So if you're in a public space, typically in London, people don't go up to each other and start talking to each other. You'd think the person was a nutcase and you'd probably be right. So Facebook is the same thing, right. It just takes care of itself. People don't cross that boundary.

Where norms of communication are "self-policing," what is it that is being policed? Despite a lack of clear conventions, the desire and value of connecting with others is curtailed, routed, and mediated among expectations of how our communication environment should be managed. To avoid facing these real and imagined social consequences of trying to connect with others, the assumed norms that others follow are internalized through practices of self-restraint in communication: "people don't cross that boundary."

Farzan, the thirty-two-year-old editor we met in my preface, describes himself as a social butterfly, yet he laments the pressure to conform to particular ways of connecting:

> But I find that the circle [of close friends with whom I use the phone] is still incredibly hard to break out of. . . . Like people are shocked if you step the relationship off from social networking [sites] to, you know, [calling or texting] because it implies a huge amount of commitment.
>
> Yes, it can be people that would happily spend hours with you, but they're shocked if you want to kind of move it on to a phone or try to arrange [to meet] . . . because it's very stressful.

Straying from the expected pattern of interaction is "stressful" and "hard to break out of" because of the implications of how communication practices are ordered in relation to each another, an assumed common sense that pertains to how modes of communication and the practiced distinctions between them come to represent types of relationships and degrees of commitment or intimacy. Farzan assumes that a shift in communication modes would "shock" his acquaintances by potentially crossing such a boundary. These distinctions between mediums and the roles for each platform are exaggerated because of the fear that a shift in mediums could be miscommunicated at the level of metacommunication.

This pressure to adhere to the assumed ordering of how best to communicate, and with whom, is internalized. In this manner, practices of self-restraint contribute to the ongoing reproduction and reinforcing of interpersonal conventions. Yet Farzan sees this as somewhat unrelated to the actual wishes of acquaintances, who "would happily spend hours with me." The pressure is perceived as external to his and their desires, for it is reified as a correct manner to communicate through ongoing metacommunication, where assumed procedural norms of a disconnected sociality are both expressed and interpreted amid practice.

The pressure to act according to the appropriate modes of communication is so great that Farzan chooses to subvert normative conventions to avoid any imagined individual or collective reaction: "In the evening, I texted a group of friends saying, "Who wants to go for dinner?" Which feels like a very old-fashioned, weird way of doing it . . . so I texted lots of friends, probably leading them all to believe they were the only one that got texted. But I just thought they could all go together if . . . but only one person got back to me, so we went for dinner and actually I was home by ten."

Decisions to subvert norms are complex. Rather than practices policing norms or breaking implicitly negotiated rules of how best to communicate, subversion rests on what others will read into our decisions at the level of metacommunication. This practice relies on shared perceptions of mobile-phone and SMS affordances, in relation to other modes of communication; it relies on the assumption that the receiver of an individually addressed SMS will interpret this as personalized attention, with a concomitant possibility for more engagement, though there is an underlying motivation to limit negative social outcomes and the vulnerability of one's breach of conventions being publicly exposed: "Like if you do it as a [post or] status update, there's two problems: One, nobody will get back to you. And two, everybody will think that you're depressed or something. . . . Because [posting that as a status update] seems full-on. It seems like there's nobody that you can actually communicate with."

A breach of assumed norms not only precludes anyone from accepting Farzan's invitation but would also draw the shock or judgment of others. This pressure is strong enough that he strategically manipulates reactions to appear to be acting within set conventional patterns of communication for fear of straying from them. Paradoxically, Farzan is limiting the possibilities of connection with those in his social network to avoid the outsider status specific to the context of constant connection: somebody who has no one with whom they can communicate.

From Disconnection to Metacommunication

To conclude this chapter, I ask readers to take their participation in crafting a better way to communicate seriously and to do this through a purposeful, expressive, and intelligible practice of metacommunication. In tandem, constant connection and the everyday uncertainties of mediated and economic contingencies insist on hypermediated management of our communication environments. There is a softly coercive expectation of participation.[23] This fosters a degree of vigilant awareness of communication overload, which continually colonizes our attention, reordering and mediating everyday life. Together, these produce a particular way of connecting, a disconnected sociality. Taking metacommunication seriously extends the horizons of such decision-making. It is a more socially minded rearticulation of media practices in the face of the persistent technological and productivist reengineering of norms and expectations in digital life.

Metacommunication is an expressive set of practices that renegotiates our relationship to the communication environment and interpersonal communication practices themselves. At the level of metacommunication, everyday interpersonal practices become a site for rearticulating opportunities for connecting with others through technologies. Put in the parlance of recent scholarship I have explored throughout this chapter, practicing metacommunication has the prosocial potential for "acting on" those small-scale, localized near-conventions of interpersonal life to afford new ways of "acting with" those others in response to the pressures of constant connection. But there are other antisocial media practices that are so well-attuned to contemporary digital life that they promote self-serving forms of disconnection among individualized, isolated users who are continually rewarded for contributing to the pressures of connection that we all face.

The expressivity and intelligibility of our media practices at the level of metacommunication effect a space for establishing or renegotiating the plasticity of how we connect with others. Small-scale, local, and interpersonal—when we cobble together the how and why of connection in particular ways for given relationships, we do so in terms of collective relational ethos rather than individualistic desire. Metacommunication is reflexive, relational, and recursive. It is reflexive in a cognitive manner, evaluating both the affordances and practices that mutually constitute a given situation. It is relational in its constitutive shifts in mutual engagement with others. And it is recursive as a vehicle for expressing and negotiating new ways of connecting with others.

The normative dynamics of conformity amid social change are already tipped in favor of reproducing existing pressures by integrating difference toward what is assumed to be conventionalized sets of practice.[24] When a personal sense of agency and difference among domains of everyday life collapse within an opaque automated system that has displaced user commitment to convention with environmental platform governance of communication, social actors employ a diversity of critiques and coping mechanisms to challenge that loss of agency. Amid practice, various media ideologies are enacted and expressed, with moral, technological, and political implications that are not always consistent or reconcilable. These are more than just strategies for survival; they are critiques in action and are performed through the practice of everyday communication.

Communication-management practices involve expressive interpersonal negotiations in response to a lack of communication conventions, which can still variably assert normative corrections or justifications of conventionally expected forms of practice. Or they may represent coping mechanisms, tests, critiques, and subversions in relationship to practice-based norms.[25] This can take many forms and is intelligible and communicative. At the level of metacommunication, negotiated reordering of everyday practices can communicate a rejection, ambivalence to, or embrace of diverse dimensions of the status quo, enacting notions of mutual rights and responsibility or individualistic assertions of self-interest. Where practices seek to ameliorate the anxieties and tensions that characterize the everyday communication environment, metacommunication offers opportunities to foster a collective ethos of care, when practices express a desire to repair what is lost in the new sociality of constant connection. Time and connection, surveillance and authenticity each represent sites of practice through which everyday forms of power are negotiated—*as* and *through* communication practices.

How we connect with others is a social and, therein, moral set of decisions. When understood in terms of contributing to or stifling social
change, everyday connection becomes a set of politically laden practices.
Whether we recognize this or not, our media practices rationalize, project, and reproduce particular media ideologies that serve to define any
given social situation. Our proclivities toward controlling the communication environment have ramifications for interpersonal relations, when
"acting on" the media serves to disconnect use from "acting with" others.
Seeking to control the environment despite its impact on others, to uni-
laterally tip the balance of control by breaking established patterns of
communication for one's own benefit, is an ethical—possibly unethical—
decision, not only a matter of technological literacy.

Disconnected sociality comes at the cost of connection with others,
in both the immediate sense and in the trajectory of longer-term social
change. When we lever disconnected practices toward our own individualistic ends, we express and reinforce this particular form of hypercon-
nected yet disengaged sociality in everyday life. These actions emerge
in tandem with commercial-platform imperatives designed to promote
constant intensity of digital engagement and the manner of economic insecurity that draws us toward a monopolizing commitment to managing
our communication environment. These modalities of individualistic,
disconnected behavior reinforce and reproduce one another, such that
disconnecting is seemingly impossible but also existentially necessary
in the face of constant connection.[26] The contradiction arises from the
alignment of connective-platform affordances that facilitate antisocial
behavior with the affordances that we rely on to practice disconnection.[27]
The resulting ethos of disconnection skews toward the technologically
and productivity mediated imperatives of the digital economy rather
than toward a relational ethos characterized by mutual attunement with
and understanding of how we hope to connect with each other.

As atomized users, we are encouraged to uncritically embrace compounding mediations on social life, which expect us each to be responsible for the programmed facility of platforms, despite the unexpected
crises and confrontations that networked life can produce. The affordances of connective platforms facilitate individual rule-breaking at
odds with mutually negotiated patterns of engagement while amplifying
our exposure to antisocial behavior. The efficacy of these disconnected
media ideologies rests with our internalization of the contradictions and

tensions they produce. The resulting invisibility of disconnection's moral and political dimensions relies on the neoliberal tendency to blame individual decision-making and practices for not overcoming shared societal tensions. The wholesale responsibilization of the individual extends cycles between perceived failure in social literacy and perceived failures in technological literacy. The myriad of tactics of the disconnected practitioner, then, offer an ideal type for navigating the sorts of social ills that masquerade as individual failures. Disconnection then serves to reinforce and reproduce the individualized responsibilization of managing constant connection—managing one's own communication environment. The costs of constant connection are individually taxing, despite the role of platform infrastructural design and normative embrace as homogenizing and policing professional expectations.

The limits of constant connection are unmistakably clear. As users and workers alike, we have adapted the levers of commercial and managerial power through practices of disconnection to ameliorate the burdens of communication overload. Yet these very practices serve to entrench the individualization, segmentation, and stratification of what seem to be dwindling opportunities for navigating meaningful social connection, while attending to expectations and pressures of working life amid constant connection.

The disconnected practitioner often yearns for something more meaningful in connection but with a clear sense of the social consequences of connecting beyond the status quo of conventions: self-serving but isolated, attuned to the technological efficacy of what is afforded by platforms but at the cost of what is relationally—and, in the longer term, societally—possible. In contrast to this are those grasping, searching for a better way to connect. They may not see themselves as the model for a new type of digital citizenship, but their prosocial interventions at the level of metacommunication represent an emerging form of discourse about how we could find each other in connection, to forge a new way of being connected to each other. Metacommunication is about understanding the efficacy of our media practice as a discourse about media practice, an interpersonal discourse that offers a space for participating in a trajectory of mediation, mediatization, and the wider changes to everyday life.[28]

Our communication environment is a shifting set of tools, a manifold site of interpersonal negotiations of everyday mediated life through which we participate, reproduce, and negotiate particular forms of everyday interpersonal life. Media scholars have long called for research to move beyond the study of media practices as individual and nonpolitical in ways that programmers, media producers, and activists have always understood.[29] Amid the tensions of constant connection, increasing individual responsibilization, and deepening economic insecurity, what matters today is that every individual must take communication seriously, but we must do so together, not as platform users or employees but as everyday practitioners who seek to act on media for the sake of connecting with others.

Taking metacommunication seriously asks us to embrace what is social, and human, about constant connection. We seek to connect with each other correctly, or as best we can, though we may disagree on what that means. Strategies to cope with and avoid conflict can reproduce norms and at times exacerbate the tensions and accompanying inequities underpinning conventional interpersonal practices. We may assume to know how best to use technologies for our individual interest. We break unwritten social rules because it is technically possible to do so. We even do so, at times, with ambivalent awareness of contradictions of how we intervene in the communication environment. And yet, where possible, we can and do find opportunities to care for others by navigating these mediated opportunities for interpersonal life; over time such practices contribute to the repair of what we call connection in everyday life.

CONCLUSION

To Count and Be Counted

We must not let media stand in for us. The interventions of institution-alized economic and political power through commercially oriented mediations of interpersonal life and productivity-oriented mediations of working life consistently fail to consider the insights of everyday experience or the social bases of knowledge produced amid communication. This is not merely oversight. It is a central component of a particular worldview, a set of ideological assumptions that privilege entrenched, economically oriented institutional power over the lived experiences of individuals. Amid change and crisis, society continues to overlook everyday life as a site for negotiating social change, where, in connection, we find a way both to count and to be counted.[1]

The myths of "natural" and autonomous laws conjured amid the early statistical enumeration of populations; post-WWII Western economic powers hailing the unknowable wisdom of the market; Big Data's procla-mation of the veracity of machine learning and behavioral predictions—each of these represents an ideological veil for political-economic incursions at the scale of populations, focused on ways to categorize and enumerate people without considering individuals themselves or the contextual realities of their everyday experiences.

There are particular parallels and, arguably, a real historical con-flation between neoliberal theories of the market as a self-regulating force and the data-driven algorithmic management underpinning plat-form operations.[2] Commercial imperatives of platform governance are increasingly similar to neoliberal governance, benefiting from an ethos of equality reduced to the opportunity to compete, despite structural in-equality. The resulting polarization and conflict among individuals and groups online is a driver of that competition, further exacerbated by the replication of biases inherent to content online and other data sets that machine learning depends on.[3] Search engines and social-media sites are, functionally, elements of the frictionless neoliberal marketplace, where competition among individuals, expression, and content in cir-culation becomes a trusted, unknowable, yet biased arbiter of change.[4] Platforms for everyday productivity, interpersonal communication, and self-promotion have translated how we present ourselves to and commu-nicate with each other into measurable, quantifiable practices, requiring new rigors for professional accountability, alongside public, searchable spaces that give hints to our successes and failures.[5] With advances in generative artificial intelligence heralding a new horizon for the digital revolution, we can expect further ideological elisions to mask the biases already identified among these systems.

Historically, computation was thought to be patently limited to single purposes or to be a risky endeavor producing unexpected outcomes at scale.[6] Politically, statistics were never meant to tell us the whole truth about a population but were rather marshaled for economic manage-ment, contributing to a reconstitution of everyday life in market terms.[7] John Durham Peters outlines how there is a "safety in the universal and impersonal" of statistical quantification, while others see its "dehuman-izing indifference" and a manipulability toward particular ends.[8] There is a corresponding, presumed infallibility to market forces when cast as the sum total of human desires; even the unknown and incalculable are curiously sublimated into economic signals and interactions that are said to govern economies beyond the reach of analysis, governance, or regulation. Such myths are marshaled to dazzle and confuse, to justify and excuse, to stand in for and refute our sense of how and why every-day connection needs to be repaired. These myths are deployed to mask systemic asymmetries and to justify persistent inequities under the nar-rowly defined guise of fair economic competition.

Tech Disruption as a Commercial Imperative

Move fast and break things.

—Mark Zuckerberg, Facebook Founder, CEO of Meta[9]

Disruption, the mantra of Silicon Valley and tech start-ups worldwide, often involves fragmentation and reorganization of existing social and economic relationships. Established intermediaries are bypassed. Engagement between everyday individuals is mediated and thereby transformed by technologies that connect us as users but are designed to produce data-driven, commercial-marketing insights. Workflows are supported through partial automation by platforms, facilitating the management, indexing, and storage of communication in parallel with the production of new standards of professional practices and alongside corresponding metrics through which efficiency, commitment, professionalism, and success begin to be judged. Across numerous industries, the rationalization of workflows is ever more integrated into technological solutions. The platformization of knowledge work, communication management, and cultural production deploys hierarchies that standardize and thereby reduce the spaces for play, creativity, and entrepreneurialism such that they more directly correspond to the circulatory and productive potential of digital labor.[10]

When technological disruptions seek to manufacture opportunities for social change, calculable risks are already part of the economic equation, while the uncertainties that breed crises are systematically overlooked—at least in the short term. The everyday realities of vulnerable users were not publicly recognized by the platform until a whistleblower leaked Facebook research about the detrimental effects of Instagram on teens, and young girls in particular, in addition to the connection of real-world violence to hate speech coursing through the WhatsApp messaging service.[11] For the German sociologist Ulrich Beck, risk has long been a central aspect of contemporary society. Modernity itself is defined by the continuous engagement in preventative measures, avoidance, and crisis management, emanating from the consequences of past solutions, present infrastructure, and attempts to induce particular futures.[12] The unintended consequences of technological disruption cannot be managed by innovation alone, be they social polarization and bullying, the democratic deficit of silent majorities among the amplification of populist rhetoric, unprecedented industry sector dominance, or the increasing blight of economic precarity.

Failure is enrolled within technological infrastructures; it is planned for, and unexpected crises are exploited as opportunities to be built on, without any promise of their prevention in the first place. Today, even the industry of accident prevention analyzes crash simulations, while flight recorders—the "black box" so sought after following airplane crashes— produce reams of mechanical, analog, and digital data, systems designed to effectively map the anatomy of each and every technological failure.[13] Similarly, the economic engines that stimulate social acceleration of communication today are designed to map and generate data such that the production of social crises can be marshaled for additional techno- logical interventions.

While Facebook has shied away from its motto promising disruption, I prefer to consider the often-overlooked removal of Google's serendip- itous "I'm Feeling Lucky" button from their search-engine interface, struck because this shortcut to the most popular result bypassed their paid-for search results and meant they lost out on nearly $100 million in revenue annually. As then Google CEO Marissa Mayer outlined: "It's possible to become too dry, too corporate, too much about making money. I think what's delightful about 'I'm Feeling Lucky' is that it reminds you there are real people here."[14] Google's sidestepping of this reminder, as with their abandonment of their one-time code-of-conduct motto "don't be evil," captures the tech industry's clear prioritization of commercial imperatives above the social consequences and crises that the platform industry has consistently and reliably produced.

The Inequities of Political-Economic and Tech Regulation

And, you know, there's no such thing as society.
—*Margaret Thatcher*[15]

A pair of global political-economic crises, the Great Recession of 2008/2009 and the COVID-19 global pandemic frame the decade of social change at the center of this book. At their outsets, both events were her- alded as death knells of neoliberalism, the political and economic order that has come to define much of the Western and global economy over the last forty years and that is written into technologies governance, the makeup of global economic-institutional and legal frameworks, and the tensions and pressures that have come to define everyday life.

Risk, or *rischio*, from its origins in thirteenth-century Mediterranean trade, has always been understood as the monetary translation of chance into terms of possible profits and possible losses.[16] Risk represents the space of economic opportunity. Today it is embedded within predetermined categories of data collection, prediction, and behavioral change, yet the distribution of risk in the near-institutionalized powers of the platform and digital-advertising industries skews heavily toward social impacts that are considered external to the economic gambits of privately held and publicly listed companies.

Risk is what is calculable beforehand, through the limited framing of how and when gains and losses are comparable.[17] What occurs outside of risk's economic calculus are externalities separate from the planned and defined economic exchange—ones emanating from uncertainties that were not considered pertinent. Sometimes these externalities disrupt existing market sectors, founding new industries such as those that have sprung from the data-collection, -mining, and -brokerage of Silicon Valley actors. But social externalities of economic risk are difficult to express in economic terms alone. The growing climate crisis, the erosion of trust in democratic institutions, rising inequality, increasing economic insecurity, and more, are thought to reside outside the limited calculations of specific commercial endeavors—a collective social cost accrued over time that individuals and communities must navigate themselves. The rest of the famous quote above, from one of neoliberalism's early standard-bearers in 1987, reminds us that, under neoliberalism, economic crisis is a social crisis to which governance turns a blind eye: "There are individual men and women and there are families. And no government can do anything except through people, and people must look after themselves first."

Historically, the emergence of what would become the foundation of today's liberal democracies fostered a space within which early forms of political rights emerged as the precondition for a functioning economy, both tempering but also contributing to the absolute power of the state.[18] The challenge to political freedoms under fascism and communism, and the wholesale statist capture of economies, would see early neoliberalism articulated as an interwar response, to emerge more coherently in the postwar period, in contradistinction to the universal economic rights central to the economic-welfare state and the Keynesian state that spent to weather the boom and bust of economic cycles.[19] Neoliberalism's forceful emergence in the US and UK in the late 1970s and 1980s would come to define the manner in which economic interests mediate technological intervention today, contributing to the precarity that now characterizes working life for many.

Liberal governance became equated with the statistical management of the population as a whole, fostered in part by a partial retreat of the state to afford a degree of individualized freedom among citizens—now responsible for their own success as autonomous units of the economy.[20] The asymmetry between this domestic art of governance and wider geopolitics—in the British case, colonial commonwealth governance—was historically manifest in the distinction between rights for citizens at home and the lack of those same rights for colonial subjects. Over the last seventy years, this asymmetry took a new form in the global imbalances of where and to what extent neoliberal economic interventions have been applied through globalized free trade. Today, the contemporary manifestation of such structural inequality resides in the economic force of platform imperialism and data-colonialism that reinstates the economic subservience of populations—now digital markets—and the diminishment of individual rights, increasingly neglected in our roles as users whose autonomy can be reoriented and mediated toward the commercial production of data.[21]

Neoliberalism would see a shift in everyday autonomy from political to economic freedom. The common and popular welfare of citizenry would then be rearticulated in economic terms—only to be guaranteed by the impersonality of market forces. The previously negotiated balance of rights and governance that underpins liberal democracies would tip heavily toward the maintenance of the economy at scale, casting responsibilities onto individuals for their own economic well-being in the guise of economic freedom of choice, within a landscape manufactured by policies permitting the retreat of governmental support and deregulation of employment contexts, and limiting any sense of true autonomy over one's ability and position vis-à-vis economic empowerment. In other words, neoliberalism deprioritizes political rights in order to prioritize forms of economic freedom, not of equitable participation but from the regulation of competition that would ensue.[22] In this landscape, shifts

in the framing of corporate or state responsibility represent opportunistic, ideological maneuvers that shift any sense of rights—user, employee,
citizen rights—to the institutional rights of powerful actors maintaining
their privileged positions through competitive flexibility and considered
in turn to ensure the functioning of national and Western economies by
securing their geopolitical power and the status quo of global inequality.

The contemporary political landscape governing (or not governing)
Big Tech can be reduced to ideological leanings of three forms of neoliberalism debated among the pre- and postwar neoliberal theorists in
the twentieth century, hinging on interpretations of what a functioning
economy looks like. These interpretations are consequential specifically
for their precluding or permissiveness of individual agency and social
sources of knowledge. The first prioritizes limiting the wholesale capture
of the market accrual of political-economic power; the second prioritizes
unfettered circulation of market signals: economic information that provides for the competitive independence of opportunity among all actors.
A third seeks, instead, the accrual of data for flexible interventions, responding not to statistical truths of market functioning but to observable data mapping the reactive landscape of capricious and changing
outcomes from given interventions.[23] These diverging interpretations of
neoliberalism hinge on what can and cannot be known, again pointing
to the utility of modeling and statistical inference and to what degree the
market, or indeed social life itself, can be captured, enclosed, put to the
service of economic growth—questions that have spurred the growth of
a particular type of platform neoliberalism since the 1990s.

Regulating against the Excess of Power

Where the market is considered knowable, the responsibility of political
actors is to limit the excessive and destabilizing concentrations of powerful economic actors who hinder the proper functioning of quality, which
is market competition. There has been a political movement within the
US and China to reign in the growing economic power of sector-specific
monopolies and the cross-sector oligopoly of giant tech conglomerates.
Political economist Matthew Crain examines how the platform and data
brokerage industries in the West "appropriate transparency values . . . to
deflect the threat of government regulation. . . . Commercial monitoring is legitimized under a rubric of consumer choice."[24] Only recently,

in the US context, has there been a shift away from antitrust rulings predicated on the singular economic marker of whether consumer prices have increased and toward a more holistic understanding of both the social and economic consequences when competition is stifled.[25] These forms of regulation, however, still fall short of the idea of a "social-market economy," characterized by market-facilitating regulatory checks that are separate and distinct from, but complemented by, social interventions providing degrees of economic security such as housing policy and unemployment income.[26] Such interventions are often limited to governance within national jurisdictions beyond which both the language and legal mechanisms become largely absent.

Looking to the European Economic Community and more recent actions of the World Trade Organization, we see the fostering of regional, multistate blocks where unregulated trade is enclosed and managed within apparatuses of political and legal power. From this perspective, the global imbalances produced by the transnational operations of major tech companies remain limited to the scale of national polities and economies. There has been increasing interest by a consortium of EU countries to reclaim taxes by instituting policies focused on where platform-user and advertising profits are accrued rather than where the multinational company is incorporated. This shift has been accompanied by an increasing push toward national data-sovereignty legislation, equally focused on the migration of a resource—in this case user data—beyond the national economies where the user resides. The political scientist Quinn Slobodian warns that interventions sought at the transnational scale are often beyond the democratic accountability of the nation-states, where the powers of organized labor and civil society are limited, amounting to a degree of legal pragmatism: a technocratic rule sometimes devoid of local contexts, experience, and everyday, social-life insight.[27]

Society does not neatly break down into the domains of economic or scientific intervention that operate in isolation from lived contexts. Indeed, there are numerous institutionalized avenues for renegotiating balance between freely functioning market relations and types of socially oriented regulatory interventions. While international bodies are not just focused on internet governance, their work intersects with and contributes to its regulation by engaging with intellectual property, and the infrastructure of numerous multilateral institutions that coordinate jurisdiction and sovereignty of monetary and legal standards, and negotiate commercial and other transactions among private actors and between persons and states.[28] As numerous knowledge-work scholars have decried since the outset of the information revolution, this global space for technocratic governance needs the reach of civil society and labor advocacy to be effective in bringing social issues to the transnational scale of regulation. Consider the vast disparities in the types of labor on which our digital lives depend—beyond aspirational workers of advanced economies and including computer-based service workers, technology-producing manufacturing sectors, and the labor contexts of transport and resource-extraction, alongside the global ecological crises resulting from such industrial pressures.[29]

Circulation over Structural Inequality

In the prewar period, international economic institutions set out to manage the world economy through global statistics and data-based interventions they believed could capture the totality of the market. By 1945 the economist Fredrich Hayek retheorized the economy in terms of a structural totality—"the whole acts as one market"—that contained the unknowable "sum total of all individual decisions everywhere." The limits of individual knowledge became the basis on which certain economic rights were secured as long as the free flow of exchange and resources accommodated the unfettered circulation of market signals. Online spaces of mediated interaction, even the peer-production model of Wikipedia—a not-for-profit arguably untainted by the marshaling of user engagement toward commercial-value production—ascribe to group-oriented aggregations of value and truth: a market-style assumption that the best information will rise to the top, assessments that are deemed otherwise inaccessible to any given individual or, for that matter, to non-technologically mediated collective negotiation. Where previously un-calculated externalities emerge, such as the degradation of interpersonal engagement, online hate-speech, explicit content, and misinformation, platforms respond with new layers of communicative control. Yet both the automated forms of moderation and the leagues of often poorly paid human content moderators simply represent additional sets of voices—with their inherent, inevitable misinterpretation and biases—detached from the social and cultural context that informs the local, situated integrity of what is appropriate behavior.[30] As Philip Mirowski argues in his examination of neoliberal thought, the so-called wisdom of the crowds suffers from a cacophony of voices seeking to negotiate what is common by mediating contradictions between divergent and sometimes extreme outliers—the neoliberal faith in the marketplace of ideas reduced the truth to whatever is validated by circulation—that is, whatever sells.[31]

First came the incompleteness of statistical intervention, then the invisibility and unknowability of the market economy and the market-place of ideas alike, and finally the self-stylized scale of social life as a marketplace, governed by a "homeostatic self-equilibrating system."[32] Geopolitically, these ideas would prove to be an opportunistic shift, with "free trade" maintaining global imbalances after seventy-seven countries demanded a "right to development" by pointing to the manner in which domestic policies of the Global North entrenched existing structural in-equalities. Following the Great Recession, however, populist movements would consolidate contradictions between domestic governance and in-ternational trade through a focus on national sovereignty and economic protectionism, away from the subjugation of Western neoliberal institu-tions. Political sociologist Paulo Gerbaudo calls this "neo-statism," a dan-gerous culmination of the neoliberal era, progressing into chilling new geopolitical realities defined domestically by populist fear and techno-cratic or authoritarian systems of isolation and control.[33] COVID-19 and Russia's 2022 full invasion of Ukraine would disrupt economic global supply chains along a similar trajectory. Western sanctions against the Russian Federation would effect a partial decoupling of global media systems, with the greater balkanization of the internet being mirrored economically in the competitive race between G7 countries and China to consolidate every step of the tech supply chain—from rare earth minerals to semiconductor manufacturing.

When the economic clout of Big Tech conglomerates allows them to govern entire sectors of the digital economy, the rights of users, which are largely nonexistent under platforms' terms of service and algorithmi-cally moderated community standards, begin to echo the contradiction of neoliberalism's "double truth": framing all political questions in eco-nomic terms to facilitate rigid hierarchies. On the one hand, Big Tech conglomerates maintain a position of cross-sector dominance, effectively governing app and digital marketplaces, with the platformization of nu-merous sectors further subsumed within their economic ecosystems. On the other hand, everyday individuals—as users, knowledge workers, and gig-economy contractors—are subjected to unbridled competition, with its masked inequalities and perpetuated precarity.

The first computer-aided statistical modeling of the global economy, the Club of Rome's "The Limits to Growth," would additionally point to the unsustainable and catastrophic consequences of global consumption, an ominous harbinger of our contemporary climate crisis. Yet such consequences do not fit neatly into the circulatory paradigm defined by deregulation and competition. The realities of how the early tech sector developed, now better understood through economic and historical analysis, reveal the inherent paradoxes of neoliberalism. Within liberal market economies throughout the 1970s and 1980s, in contradiction to the popular neoliberal maxim about a weak and limited state, forceful government intervention secured rigid spaces where well-managed contours of market competition contributed to sector dominance of emerging tech giants, at home and abroad. The economist S. K. Vogel calls this "marketcraft," whereby free-market reform for the purpose of increased competition is not a matter of deregulation but of recrafting existing regulation—"freer markets and more rules."[34] In his comparison of the US and Soviet management of industrial innovation, Benjamin Peters upends another common myth by pointing to commercial collaboration, public-private partnerships, and government subsidies at the foundation of the US information revolution, in contrast to the competition, fragmentation, and institutional infighting that undermined Soviet attempts.[35] The extent to which data-brokerage firms use publicly collected information to dominate the hierarchy of digital advertising—becoming proprietary once it is combined with or reprocessed as commercial data—represents another way the private-public foundation of the data-mining industry belies its neoliberal values.[36]

The Great Recession offers the clearest example of the ideological pitfalls of this free-market fallacy, where the US and, indeed, the global financial sectors demonstrated a consolidated degree of what is called regulatory capture: the resources and power of organizational networks within a particular industry allow these industries to force favorable regulatory conditions across a number of international jurisdictions, often only redressed following cascades of crises beyond the sector in question—which is exactly what happened when the Great Recession rippled across the global economy.[37] More than a decade later, the import of the tech sector on global economic geopolitical power all but ensures a market capture of innovations in adjacent industries and the regulatory capture of democratic governments attempting to manage a more equitable economic landscape for their citizens.

Economic Interventions Precluding Individual Agency

The data economy as a whole today is not only considered unknowable, but its signals are also illegible to the everyday individual. All an individual has is personal and professional insight. In the 1970s, Hayek's prioritization of information circulation would be transformed through an emphasis on the precognitive and prerational nature of signals within the market system, thereby diminishing any space of agency or free will that an individual market actor might have. Troublingly, this diminishment of individual agency within a globally ascendant economic ideology occurred in parallel with the successive independence movements of countries representing the majorities of global populations, just as they were wresting control from transnational colonial systems of economic and political domination.[38] Western platforms operate today from a positivist position that similarly overwrites agency of those affected: the totality of data-driven processes is unknown, certainty in observable data that occurs only through formal mathematical modeling defined in terms of iterative interventions and failures, similar to the aforementioned flight recorders capturing every detail of airplane crashes.

This undervaluation of the individual and interpersonal contribution to social change is a predecessor to today's platform imperialism, where dominant tech giants from the US or China compete to capture global user data, enrolled into the systems of targeted advertising or voice- and facial-recognition applications, in addition to the capture of regional platform and app industries, dependent on and subject to types of platform governance by major tech firms.[39] Computer scientists sometimes proselytize about extreme behavioralist approaches, what the academic and entrepreneur Alex Pentland refers to as a type of "social physics," metaphorically applying particular laws of interaction for intended outcomes. The approach has been criticized for its overemphasis on environments of behavioral cues and an absence of the thinking, feeling human actor.[40] In her assessment of Silicon Valley as the engine of what she calls surveillance capitalism, Shoshana Zuboff points to the logic within Pentland's early work that assesses aggregate behavior of beaver populations through the enumeration of environmental changes (beaver dams and the resulting ponds) as observable within satellite imagery.[41] This god's-eye view is not only detached from individual practice and the local contexts of each pond but also dependent on the quantification of indirect traces of behavior rather than behavior itself. Individual actors are below any threshold of detectability; only their gross engagement with the environment is legible.[42] Inverting this logic, whether it's statistically minded economic policy or databased interventions into particular types of online behavior, provides a useful sense of how systematic changes to an environment are meant to determine what can be expected, from rational economic decisions to the desire patterns of platform engagement and use, where both individual and aggregate data positions comparable behavior against a database's innumerable comparable situations.

This erasure of individuals contributes to data-driven platform interventions on behavior that fails to capture much of what is valued by individuals and written into interpersonal social life. From its outset, early data collection of web-based behavior contributed to individually specific profiles, users' "data doubles," which were tied to browser histories or credit scores. The collection was so effective that elements of "pseudorandomness" would have to be purposefully introduced to algorithmic recommendations and targeted ads to reduce the creepy factor of commercial nudges too consistent with our behavior, too indicative of how closely we are monitored for the purposes of influencing our decision-making.[43] While government regulation and industry actors alike enforce new privacy controls on user data, regarded as a step in the right direction, aggregate data are applied in such a granular manner toward the targeted user or customer that the mathematical anonymity of the individual becomes a moot point. Embracing the database-level granularity not just of individual practices but of constituent variables within any instance of individual behavior begins to resemble the divisibility of individual agency into precognitive, prerational signals that lie beyond human reflection.[44] This "hollowing out of the social" is a central facet of what Nick Couldry and Ulises Mejias call data colonialism.[45] Data-based proxies for the experience and interactions that are the social fabric of everyday life contribute both to the extraction of economic resources and to technological mediation of social situations and practices reconstituted to better facilitate that very extraction. Economic interventions no longer seek to capture the economy as a whole but the totality of social life, extending digital collection of data throughout the remaining space of everyday life while reframing individual choice and autonomy in terms of predictable behavior, in intensified circuits of user practices afforded by and intervened on by data-driven environmental cues.

The neoliberal permissiveness of entrenched market power in the West faces moral and political crises in its hesitancy to regulate the tech industry, which comes from a desire to maintain commercial competition abroad, with ascendant tech giants essentially forming a centrally organized, authoritarian capitalism. The political instability and economic insecurity that accompanied COVID-19 have made it clear that liberal democracy is being tested, both through an attempt at correcting its establishment principles (never fully realized) and through social critique pushing for a certain kind of more radical change.

While the balkanization of the internet among dominant tech companies reduces the diversity of global populations to the capture of data-oriented advertising markets and their patterns of platform use, the technocratic vision of behavioralist intervention reduces the complexity of everyday interpersonal life to the productive spaces of user-data collection. As the antitrust legal scholar Lina Khan, appointed chair of the US Federal Trade Commission in 2021, frames the situation: "If markets are leading us in directions that we, as a democratic society, decide are not compatible with our vision of liberty or democracy, it is incumbent upon government to do something." Khan adds: "This isn't just about antitrust. It's about values."[46]

The Value in Social Practices

**Change is happening. There are many ways
to start moving in the right way.**
—Jane Goodall[47]

If there is one resounding lesson that emerged from the clamor of recent crises, it is that change is possible, at a swift and sweeping collective scale previously unknown to many. The sudden halting and reorganizing—nearly overnight in many countries—of work, commerce, education, and entertainment has upended widely held assumptions about the impossibility of large-scale responsive change to the social organization of everyday life. The abruptness of governmental intervention in tandem with collective social cooperation challenged the apparently incontrovertible nature of the staid conventions of our social and economic worlds. Our collective responses to COVID-19 indicate the complex matrices of social and economic practices as they map onto our changing relationships with technology. This relationship, however, is often erroneously simplified within grand, deterministic framings, removing the disconnected practices and realities of everyday life from the equation.

Both the Great Recession and the COVID-19 pandemic were turning points, crises unprecedented in living memory for many, that forced the reconsideration of how we cope and manage with the pressures of everyday life. Such disruption offers a glimpse at what could be, an aperture for understanding how social change does, in fact, occur and how radically we can renegotiate the status quo. In the West, these moments of seismic reconsideration in governance and economics have not been seen since the end of WWII and the inflationary crisis of 1979–80, both, in hindsight, distinct milestones in the reordering of political-economic policy and contributing to long-term transitions of the everyday spaces within which we negotiate what it is to be members of a society. In early 2022, inflation rates in the US reached heights not seen since that crisis forty years ago.[48] What follows in the wake of this once-in-a-century global pandemic depends on how we navigate social change amid economic turmoil and what we learn in connection with each other.

When society fixates on one of its era's predominant innovations, there is a direct and oversimplified assumption of causality where shifts in social practice are linked to the latest in a long line of overlapping, integrated communication technologies, be they computers, smart phones, email, Facebook, X (formerly Twitter), Instagram, and onward, to Snapchat and TikTok. A "natural" linearity of technological development gets projected onto our understanding of the past to the present, where each innovation ushers in the next set of inevitable steps, new societal moments, outside the influence of regulation and public interest, as well as individual or collective action. A pair of further oversimplifications puts both credit and blame on the distant world of Silicon Valley entrepreneurs or the abstracted machinations of the market economy, relinquishing the role of everyday experience and practices. It is easier to make the screen, device, or social-media platform and associated companies solely accountable for why and how we make use of them. Forgotten is how we reflect on connection, negotiate new forms of engagement at the level of metacommunication, or find new uses of technology through degrees of disconnection—and how, more often than not, we do so together.

Also forgotten: the economic dimensions of connection and disconnection, captured in the reproducibility of the status quo, and the individual benefits of adhering to pressures, expectations, and conventions, even where they seem contradictory and arbitrary, because they are accepted as contributing to a common good. This book has sought to excavate the fields of social practices and interpersonal life, to better understand the way levers of political-economic control—whether of commercial institutions that design and govern communication platforms or of the institutional domain of employment—produce tensions that make individual benefit seem incommensurate with contributing to something more, to participating in social change.

We develop disconnected tactics in response to these levers of political-economic power to escape our entire lives being rearticulated in terms of productivity as defined by data-collection industries and the daily pressures of our working life. Amid the gears of technological and normative pressures that prescribe how we must connect as professionals and as people, too, we develop coping strategies to escape the negative consequences of being seen as anything but the idealized media-literate user or the fully committed employee. Illouz highlights how "emotional ambiguity, ambivalence, and lack of clarity" represent competent comping mechanisms when faced with "contradiction-ridden social situations."[49] When it becomes too difficult to be present—to be connected—as friend, family member, a partner, or simply as ourselves—then these levers of disconnection and control in everyday life serve as tests of our capacity to justify participating in and contributing to the reproduction of those normative pressures or to justify seeking something different.

It is not a coincidence that the book ends on individual justifications on which collective social change hinges. The early career adults at the center of this book enjoy socioeconomic privileges that come with university education and find themselves supported by universal health care systems and economic safety nets guaranteed across the UK and Canadian welfare states. As the reader is well aware, many of these participants in the knowledge, creative, and digital sectors struggle at the start of their professional lives; others eke out new ways to manage precarity in the second or third decades of their working lives. They seek upward career mobility with economic stability, but there are those who are wholly excluded from such opportunities, a growing disconnected generation who may not always find any room for maneuverability against the strictures of economic insecurity. Others featured in this book find themselves excelling in high-profile freelance careers, the idealized disconnected practitioner sensitive to pressures of maintaining the necessary professional veneer, which gives them a vantage point for understanding how things could be done better, for themselves and others. These are unevenly distributed and radically divergent perspectives on uncertainty. There is uncertainty with plausible options and outcomes, permitting hope, and there is fearful uncertainty, with few expectations and little space for agency.[50]

Where time and connection are so structured by the strategies of commercial institutions, the tactical forging of reparative practices through disconnection, surveillance, authenticity, and metacommunication help us find ways to ensure there is something human about how we connect and disconnect with each other—that there is some space for that type of social value while still managing to make a living. Such practices wrest open social spaces for renegotiation, ameliorating the pressures and inequities of the status quo. The everyday individual costs of constant connection, and collective opportunities for social change, are made real and negotiated in how we practice communication.

Temporal Overload and the Uncertainty of Everyday Communication

The practice of everyday life is sculpted in time and uncertainty. Our everyday lives are overwhelmed by the potential for interaction—and are prone to communication overload. Interactions are temporally remediated as tasks: the flow of everyday communication is consuming and quantifiable; interpersonal engagement is reframed in limited, temporally bounded instances; sociality is defined by efficiency and completion. Interpersonal life, then, becomes something to be managed: how many known tasks remain unaddressed alongside a specter of unexpected potential interaction? These are the temporal contingencies of connection, and they cannot be disentangled from the disconnected experiences of economic uncertainty—for instance, proving oneself in an entry-level position, struggling through the maintenance of freelance contracts, or managing the job hunt while still being able to pay the rent. The pressures of economic and career insecurity come to define our relative autonomy—or lack thereof—within constant connection and the degrees of control that others have to stipulate how and when we can step away from our desk, log out of email, or put our phones down, to find time for ourselves and those we care about, even when that means connecting through media use.

Only recently has the dissolution of work boundaries—that blurring of personal and professional times of day afforded by constant connection—been considered a political question in terms of disconnection. While protection of weekends, compensation for overtime, and other temporal limits to the working week have long been considered successes of labor regulation, the intensification of work and its extension into the times and spaces beyond the formal workday is now, finally, under scrutiny. This is the first of many political and economic tests seeking to renegotiate the unaccounted-for social detriments that have accompanied networked and platform technologies. In 2019, prior to the pandemic, the World Health Organization codified a new occupational phenomenon, "burnout," where unmanaged, chronic workplace stress contributes to exhaustion, cynicism, and mental distancing, reducing professional efficacy.[51] Since then, in France, Portugal, and the Canadian province of Ontario, workers have achieved a "right to disconnect" through legislation that bars out-of-hours workplace communication or insists on explicit policies regarding emails and calls.[52] Despite this policy success, the shift to working from home during the pandemic opened additional anxieties about the intensities of working life and the scrutiny of workplace surveillance. The right to disconnection is more often than not a pressure specific to white-collar knowledge work. Economic insecurity characterizes so many of the professions hit hardest by the pandemic, including those in between contracts, faced with furloughs, or managing health and ability challenges who would be best served by a basic safety net, be it substantial reconsideration of living wages or the implementation of Universal Basic Income.[53] The shuttering of so many small businesses during the pandemic—restaurants, artist spaces, more—highlighted the precarity of numerous shift and part-time workers, while pointing to a need to redress remuneration across so many frontline sectors: transport, sanitation, health care, education.

The anxiety that motivates our compulsion for constant connection also motivates the insecurities and pressures of working life, both of which are sublimated into fears of communication overload, the foundation for our disconnected sociality. These fears have translated into the moment-to-moment, task-by-task management of our communication environments, parsed further within platforms, before any considered communicative engagement with others. While platform technologies mediate connection by affording more efficient, partial forms of engagement—a refracted, productivity-oriented sociality centered on managing the communication environment rather than mutual relationality—the political-economic pressures of working life force the economization of our attention in this manner.

This changing landscape has led to new intimacies of copresence and mutual media use: sincere reevaluations of how we conduct ourselves watching a movie with our parents, putting our phones down before the kids are asleep, and also whiling away an hour after work making videos for friends, keeping our social-media streaks alive, or staying up late in a group chat or during video-game play, with headsets on. The potential for communication overload has contributed to an emerging acceptance of asynchronous modes of communication, partial disconnections that forge spaces for social connection that are more meaningful than work's proscriptive sociality. The more legible these practices become, the more attuned we are to the diverse ways we can connect and disconnect, with degrees of presence and absence carrying intrinsic meanings, negotiating social change through interpersonal practices at the level of metacommunication.

Disconnection and the Labor of Constant Connection

Each platform's mediation of social and productive practices through interface design, algorithmic logic, and multisited infrastructures of data production only tells a part of the story. Focusing only on users and use centers technological design and the (commercial) solutions it offers, ignoring the ways we relate to media through disengagement, subversion, disconnection, migration, and whatever else lies beyond any single platform. Far from shunning the valuable insights of quantitative and network-facilitated sociological insights into how we engage with and relate to one another, this book begins with a look at the embodied, time-consuming work of maintaining constant connection and its impact on our physically situated social realities, thereby refusing to limit the scope of investigating communication in terms of online user practices alone. My goal has been to ground a critical examination of how we negotiate the role of technology in our lives beyond the detached perspective of networked totalities—and instead in situational contexts that commit us to our near-compulsive practices of maintaining constant connection.[54]

While embracing the contributions of humans to understanding technologically driven social change, the subsuming extremes of the tech industry offer valuable insights into more quotidian media use for interpersonal communication. The games industry and the wider interpretative communities of gamers serve as a model for user-centered collective negotiation while also serving as a warning about the extent to which normative power will be policed. Beyond the operating systems of any particular platform, player communities carry with them the creative tradition of fan cultures in their appropriation, redesign, and subverting of games as technical and cultural systems. Gamers' empowerment as a vocal set of consumers is forged through the public sphere of blogs and forums—both branded marketing spaces and also wholly independent from and at times at odds with commercial interests.[55] Within the confines of gaming platforms, gamers are participatory users who understand their participation in cocreating online spaces, and, as such, game developers take their grievances seriously—such as those relating to automated regulation of player behavior alongside other terms of service—with industry and commercial bodies often having to mediate.[56] Despite the widespread popularity of gaming among women, the games industry has long been criticized for its gendered barriers and reductive stereotypes, reproduced and amplified in game-play design. The wave of online harassment, doxing of personal information, and real-world threats to female game developers known as "Gamergate" serves as a reminder that discrimination is a social, not only technological, reality. As our engagement with online spaces has intensified through mobile connection, wearable technologies have enrolled our bodies into regimes of self- and socially oriented surveillance. Voice-recognition interfaces extend into the home spaces through smart speakers, carrying with them the inequality of normative assumptions, such as the gendering of AI-driven virtual assistants that uncritically reinforce traditional divisions of domestic and professional labor.[57]

Throughout this book, I have referenced Norbert Elias's historical work and applied his understanding of the intertwined nature of interpersonal practices. What we have yet to consider is the wider trajectory and political-economic context of what he called "the civilizing process": the ways subjects of late medieval Europe, over time, mutually attuned and increasingly constrained their actions in everyday life for the benefit of mitigating strife and social conflicts, despite, for example, class differences.[58] This self-regulating behavior involved the stabilization of norms of etiquette in the everyday domain of social life, from using napkins and forks to avoiding tempers that led to brawls and murder. Over centuries, Elias argues, this secured the monopolization of violence among institutionalized powers of the monarchy, courts, and their enforcers. Today, in the to-and-fro of individualized user preferences, alongside divergent strategies for time management and practices of disconnection, in the division and discord sowed online alongside new affinities and affiliations, what powers then are being monopolized through the steady, media-driven rearticulation of interpersonal life, toward a type of managed sociality, the disconnected sociality of constant connection?

To answer this, we need only look at what connects the autonomy of upwardly mobile executives, the managerial surveillance of administrative staff and service workers, the rigors of managing communication overload at work, the necessary reputational work of policing how we engage with coworkers or in our self-presentation online, and the inculcation of technological literacies that allow for both the antisocial imposition of individual preferences on others and the legibility of digital behaviors for prosocial support and care at the level of communication. Our compulsion to be constantly connected characterizes so many of these divergent practices. The capture of everyday social life in terms of labor—by simultaneous workers and users—represents the most pressing rearticulation of power today.

In practice, we individually manage our communication environments so that degrees of disconnection can persist and, indeed, be facilitated for ourselves and for others. This management affords a distance that recasts the norms of working life and platform-specific mediations as domain-specific constructs, focused on particular ends of productive labor, regardless of discomfort, anxiety, and inequities. Much of the social theorist Michel Foucault's historical work, what he called an archaeology of power, involved the role of institutional domains such as barracks, schools, and prisons for the purpose of internalizing self-discipline toward being productive citizens. Erving Goffman's study of interpersonal behavior in public life led him to the more extreme settings of mid-twentieth-century institutional control; indeed, he embedded himself as staff within a mental-health ward.[59] These closed institutions were defined by their totalizing tendency to encompass every aspect of life, where barriers to communicating beyond that space were accompanied by restriction of personal identity, limiting opportunities for certain ways of communicating and policing behavior in public and mortifying ways.

In addition to these proscriptive mediations of behavior toward a limited and circumscribed ideal, there are other parallels between such restrictive environments and contemporary working life, with its constant imperatives of connection. Identities are administratively mediated—trimmed and reprogrammed—to better fit their management amid blocks of others in similar situations. There is the breakdown of barriers between sleep, work, and play, such that a constant visibility accompanies this curtailment of identity and role. Of course, the extreme restrictions of incarceration are not the same as paid work or the voluntary use of communication platforms. But there is a degree of commonality between Foucault's and Goffman's subjects and working life's 24/7, connected-and-networked bleed into space and time. The totality of the institutional recreation of everyday life echoes the commercial desire of major platform conglomerates to offer a wholly connected totality within their multifaceted walled gardens: an ecosystem of services that capture entertainment, commerce, and professional and personal life alike.

As it stands today, our ability to manage our communication environments, to shift between degrees of connection and disconnection, where attention can be concerted or divided across a myriad of possible instantiations of digital presence and absence, stymies the totalizing tendencies of such institutional pressures.[60] Individual and interpersonal negotiations of wider, everyday communication environments transcend the scope of such total control. There remains an opening for users to socially negotiate their relationships with the free labor of data production inherent to media use, as governed within each platform, but also across the industry as a whole and, for those fortunate enough to have the privilege, to attain something resembling a work-life balance. The recent history of the internet has been one of greater and greater conglomerate control and diminishing spaces for user agency: for example, the proprietary closing of computer hardware and operating systems from amateur tinkering and community building; the rise of platform ecosystems and app marketplaces that have reduced the generative cultures of the early web; and formal industry relationships and platform templates that dictate aesthetics and forms.[61]

Contemporary technological reality points not only to enclosure of spaces for interpersonal interaction but also to expansive capture, where biometric, mobility, and spatially oriented technologies extend our engagement, while the promise of wholly online worlds of virtual reality—recently rebranded as the metaverse—attempt to supplant embodied social and professional interactions entirely. While we need only look to the dystopian futures of pop-culture entertainment to see our technological fears taken to their logical extremes, the social-distancing restrictions and strict lockdowns of the COVID-19 pandemic offer a more chilling example of what working from home could possibly look like if institutional governance of both employment and connection found common purpose in the capture of everyday life for the purposes of extractive labor. Unfortunately, that pop dystopia rings true for many, without the intercession of a coronavirus. Economic insecurity drives many toward labor-oriented situations without respite of disconnection from income-earning practices. Precariousness may force one to work numerous jobs—from multiple low-wage part-time positions to indiscriminate, pressure-filled gig-economy positions—but the lack of social support and a living wage dovetail with issues of transport, affordable housing, childcare, and disability accommodations. Even at the heights of corporate mobility, whether in the finance industry or the tech sectors of metropolitan centers and advanced economies, there is an internalized ethos of overwork that similarly monopolizes lives. Jack Ma, the founder of multinational platform conglomerate Alibaba Group, recently celebrated in his invocation of "996" work culture in the Chinese tech industry: 9:00 a.m. to 9:00 p.m., six days a week.[62]

The Radical Plasticity of Practice and the Justifications for Change

Let's all stop this downward plunge towards a very dysfunctional future.
—Tim Berners-Lee[63]

What is inherent in all communication practices is their constitution of social life: the very basis for relationships between humans. Lived social realities are woven from everyday practice; what is social can change and is always changing. In his excoriating 2020 critique of the cultures of practice—both online and within the tech industry—the World Wide Web's so-called inventor, Tim Berners-Lee, declared that "the web is not working," highlighting the "online harms facing women and girls—especially those of colour, from LGBTQ+ communities and other marginalized groups"—that are threatening society's efforts toward equality. Crucially, Berners-Lee's remaining optimism centered on the cross-sector power held by knowledge workers alongside the democratic rights of citizens to effect change:

> It's up to all of us to make the web work for everyone. That requires the attention of all those who shape technology, from CEOs and engineers to academics and public officials.
> I think we've got the ability and the motivation to try and do the right thing on both governments and companies so long as people, individuals—if necessary protesting in the street—hold them to account.

In less than two decades, we have grown so accustomed to constant connection that it has become integral to our very sense of participation in everyday life. Yet we have parsed its promises of absolute speeds, of unprecedented productivity, and of global reach to foster something more human in the spaces between connection and disconnection in everyday, situated lives—a communication environment of possibilities. In that time, we have struggled to cope with the vulnerabilities and insecurities that come with online exposure. We are learning more every day about the gross inequity of such experiences, contributing to a sensitivity and ability to listen in ways that produce a value-type of social knowledge about how we communicate: a knowledge that exists outside the commercial surveillance and the afforded mediations inherent in platform architecture. This knowledge founds and declares spaces of meta-communication where we communicate—the patterning and adjustment of practice—that are socially expressive, legible, and mutually negotiated toward something resembling repair.

There is malleability to what is social about interpersonal practices, a radical openness to the possibilities of what can be interpreted and recognized as social interaction or communication.[64] Learning from social negotiation inherent in the open-software movement of the 1990s offers insight that can help us to understand the impact of our communication-management practices, where recursive negotiation occurs among users, in "making, maintaining, and modifying" the possibility for communication that "constrains their everyday practical commitments" but also contributes to "their ability to . . . compose a common world."[65] Only realized in practice, interpersonal communication is a space of radical possibility—a connection that can only be discovered together.

Although probability and mathematical modeling cannot dictate values, there is an institutional tendency among our commercial and governing bodies to supplant human judgment and lived experience with the objective veneer of computation, which has constantly proven to reflect existing biases and to amplify inequality.[66] When the governance of how we know ourselves and know each other operates at scales beyond human experience, we lose the opportunity that social life affords to reflect, tinker, and learn from each other. Zuboff's critique of expanding commercial capture and enclosure of communication environments by surveillance- and data-driven interventions centers in on a crucial threat to our individual and collective "right to the future tense."[67] In his critique of limiting and partial epistemologies of Western economic and technological thinking, the social scientist and legal scholar Boaventura de Sousa Santos points out that "the world does not lack alternatives. It lacks alternative thinking about alternatives."[68] Yet the situatedness and relationality of how we can recognize knowledge effects a particular position in relation to everyday instantiations of power.[69] At the day-to-day level, there is a security in norms, a safety in the status quo, and a validation in conforming to and indeed asserting technologically or productivity-oriented procedural meritocracies. These are only partial sanctuaries. They serve to stand in place of the uncertain potential of truly mutual engagement, for power relies on the levers of normative corrections, of exclusion through limiting the diversity of how we know each other and communicate with each other. The normative frameworks of sociality throughout this book all involve a reduction of ways of connecting in order to learn about oneself and others. Where the median minimum of stability enjoyed by many may limit individual justifications for choosing to support social change, increases in individual literacy and public awareness about such self-interest (i.e., that it diminishes opportunities for common, shared progress) bring to light the inequalities that are testing the very fabric of social life and institutional life today.[70]

Practices are an inversion of the colloquial understanding of a rule: rather than single instances of a rule being obeyed, practices constitute know-how neither governing nor proscribing particular actions in a limiting way.[71] Social practices may have norms, but it is in the uncritical certainty in such conventions that we lose the depth and diversity that an openness to human connection fosters—forgetting that a degree of certainty for some comes at the cost of insecurity and censorship for others. For those who can retreat to the stability of procedural norms, to the efficiency of a managed sociality, there are consequences to this privilege, consequences that effect a closure of opportunities and a policing of conventions for others who must respond in kind for fear of destabilizing what little degree of social and, indeed, economic security they enjoy. The reflexivity necessary for understanding one's position within these matrices of everyday power is defined by a relationality with others. The change and multiplicity that this entails involve simultaneous recognition of diverse ways of knowing by some, which in turn support the breathing room necessary for other users to represent themselves and their world as their own, affording their own priorities the opportunity of bringing the past and an ongoing resilience into a present-oriented self-esteem and future-oriented participation in social change.[72] A global recession and pandemic, along with the degradation of democratic institutions and the devastation of the environment, are occurring alongside persistent calls for the wholesale recalibration of social and institutional life for something more equitable, more human. An ongoing existential emergency begs for a new common sense. The practices of everyday communication are also the politics of crafting limits to the platform and data industries—of negotiating spaces for individual and collective agency—as they continue to overlook the fact that there are real people here, and their voices deserve to count and to be counted.

NOTES

Preface

1. Throughout this book, quotations attributed to individuals without a corresponding source note are drawn from my field interviews, media diaries, and thinking-aloud protocol tasks undertaken with research participants between 2010 and 2020, as well as a pilot study in late 2009. All participant names have been anonymized. Personal details have been deidentified and in some cases partially aggregated or swapped where appropriate.

2. See Judy Wajcman, *Pressed for Time: The Acceleration of Life in Digital Capitalism* (Chicago: University of Chicago Press, 2015); and Victor M. González and Gloria Mark, "Managing Currents of Work: Multi-tasking among Multiple Collaborations," *ECSCW 2005* (Berlin: Springer-Verlag, 2005).

3. Alice E. Marwick and danah boyd, "Networked Privacy: How Teenagers Negotiate Context in Social Media," *New Media & Society* 16, no. 7 (2014).

4. Peter Vorderer et al., *Permanently Online, Permanently Connected: Living and Communicating in a POPC World* (New York: Routledge, 2017).

5. Nick Couldry and Andreas Hepp, *The Mediated Construction of Reality* (Cambridge: Polity, 2017).

6. See Marshall McLuhan, *The Gutenberg Galaxy: The Making of Typographic Man* (Toronto: University of Toronto Press, 1962); and John Perry Barlow, "A Declaration of the Independence of Cyberspace," *Electronic Frontier Foundation*, Feb. 8, 1996.

7. StatsCAN, "Canadian Internet Use Survey 2012," Nov. 26, 2013; StatsCAN,

243

"Canadian Internet Use Survey, 2020," July 22, 2021; PEW, "Internet/Broadband Fact Sheet," PEW Research Center, April 7, 2021.

8. Grant Blank, William H. Dutton, and Julia Lefkowitz, *Perceived Threats to Privacy Online: The Internet in Britain*. Oxford Internet Survey (Oxford: Oxford Internet Institute, University of Oxford, 2019).

9. Rich Ling, *Taken for Grantedness: The Embedding of Mobile Communication into Society* (Cambridge, MA: MIT Press, 2012).

10. "Half the Planet Is on Lockdown, but Not Every U.S. State Is, Even after Alabama Issues an Order," *New York Times*, April 28, 2020; BBC, "As It Happened: Coronavirus Deaths Pass 20,000," BBC.com, March 24, 2020.

11. Katie Hope, "Facebook Now Used by Half of World's Online Users," *BBC News*, July 29, 2015.

12. Giorgio Agamben, *States of Exception* (Chicago: University of Chicago Press, 2005); Rebecca Bramall, *The Cultural Politics of Austerity: Past and Present in Austere Times* (New York: Palgrave Macmillan, 2013).

13. Michael Burton, *The Politics of Austerity: A Recent History* (London: Palgrave MacMillan, 2016); Stephen Wilks, "Austerity and Outsourcing in Britain's New Corporate State," in *The Austerity State*, ed. Stephen McBride and Bryan M. Evans (Toronto: University of Toronto Press, 2017); Pat Armstrong, "Neoliberalism in Action: Canadian Perspectives," in *Neoliberalism and Everyday Life*, ed. Susan Braedley and Meg Luxton (Montreal: McGill-Queen's University Press, 2010).

14. Sherry Turkle, *Alone Together: Why We Expect More from Technology and Less from Each Other* (New York: Basic Books, 2011); Richard Sennett, *Together: The Rituals, Pleasures and Politics of Cooperation* (New Haven, CT: Yale University Press, 2012); Robert D. Putnam, *Bowling Alone: The Collapse and Revival of American Community* (New York: Simon & Schuster, 2000); Émile Durkheim, *The Division of Labour in Society*, trans. W. D. Halls (Basingstoke: Macmillan, 1984).

15. Norbert Elias, *The Norbert Elias Reader: A Biographical Selection* (Oxford: Blackwell, 1998).

16. See Catherine McKercher and Vincent Mosco, eds., *Knowledge Workers in the Information Society* (Plymouth, UK: Lexington Books, 2007); David Hesmondhalgh and Sarah Baker, *Creative Labour: Media Work in Three Cultural Industries* (Abingdon: Routledge, 2011); Ursula Huws, *Labor in the Global Digital Economy: The Cybertariat Comes of Age* (New York: New York University Press, 2014); Andreas Reckwitz, *The Invention of Creativity: Modern Society and the Culture of the New*, trans. Stephen Black (Cambridge: Polity, 2017).

17. The use of the word *society* throughout this work relates to the colloquial use of the word and is neither an embrace of the scalar distinction among micro, meso, and macro levels of society, on the one hand, nor of the "flat ontology" of social practices proposed in Theodore Schatzki, "Practice Theory as Flat Ontology," in *Practice Theory and Research: Exploring the Dynamics of Social Life*, ed. Gert Spaargaren, Don Weenink, and Machiel Lamers (London: Routledge, 2016). For recent discussions of these uneasy ontological distinctions in relation to the

sociological use of practice-oriented research, see Kenzie Burchell, Olivier Dries-sens, and Alice Mattoni, "Practicing Media—Mediating Practice: Introduction," *International Journal of Communication* 14 (2020).

Introduction

1. Ludwig Wittgenstein, *Philosophical Investigations*, trans. G. E. M. Anscombe (New York: Macmillan, 1953); Theodore R. Schatzki, *Social Practices: A Wittgensteinian Approach to Human Activity and the Social* (New York: Cambridge University Press, 1996).

2. Peter L. Berger and Thomas Luckmann, *The Social Construction of Reality: A Treatise in the Sociology of Knowledge* (New York: First Anchor, 1967); Couldry and Hepp, *Mediated Construction*, 21.

3. James R. Beniger, *The Control Revolution: Technological and Economic Origins of the Information Society* (Cambridge, MA: Harvard University Press, 1986).

4. Max Weber, *The Protestant Ethic and the Spirit of Capitalism,* trans. Talcott Parsons (London and New York: Routledge, 2001); Guenther Roth and Claus Wittich, eds. *Economy and Society: An Outline of Interpretative Sociology* (Berkeley: University of California Press, 2013).

5. David Shariatmadari, "A Year of 'Permacrisis,'" *Collins Dictionary*, Nov. 1, 2022.

6. Sonia Livingstone and Peter Lunt, "Representing Citizens and Consumers in Media and Communications Regulation," *Annals of the American Academy of Political and Social Science* 611, no. 1 (2007).

7. Shoshana Zuboff, *The Age of Surveillance Capitalism: The Fight for a Human Future at the New Frontier of Power* (New York: PublicAffairs, 2018).

8. José van Dijck, Thomas Poell, and Martijn de Waal, *The Platform Society: Public Values in a Connective World* (New York: Oxford University Press, 2018).

9. Yann Moulier Boutang, *Cognitive Capitalism*, trans. Ed Emery (Cambridge: Polity, 2012).

10. My research here also parallels Bourdieu's stylistic and methodological approach in *Weight of the World*, specifically in his extended exposition of interview data and in his attempt, as Couldry outlines, to take seriously individual experience prior to conceptualization of social structures as Bourdieu so often did in his previous work. I echo this shift in my prioritization of the "phenomenological" and "grounded theory" methodology here that stays close to the data, grounding any theory building in fieldwork first and foremost. See Maurice Merleau-Ponty, *Phenomenology of Perception* (London: Routledge, 1962); Shaun Moores, "Media Uses and Everyday Environmental Experience: A Positive Critique of Phenomenological Geography," *Participations* 3, no. 2 (2006); Tim Markham and Scott Rodgers, eds., *Conditions of Mediation: Phenomenological Perspectives on Media* (New York: Peter Lang, 2017); Barney G Glaser and Anselm L Strauss, *Discovery of Grounded Theory: Strategies for Qualitative Research* (London: Routledge, 2017).

11. Paul du Gay and Glenn Morgan, eds., *New Spirits of Capitalism? Crises, Justifications, and Dynamics* (Oxford: Oxford University Press, 2013).

12. Luc Boltanski and Ève Chiapello, *The New Spirit of Capitalism*, trans. Gregory Elliott (London: Verso, 2018).

13. Luc Boltanski, *The Making of a Class: Cadres in French Society*, trans. Arthur Goldhammer (Cambridge: Cambridge University Press; Paris: Éditions de la maison des sciences de l'homme, 1987).

14. Ève Chiapello and Norman Fairclough, "Understanding the New Management Ideology: A Transdisciplinary Contribution from Critical Discourse Analysis and New Sociology of Capitalism," *Discourse & Society* 13, no. 2 (2002).

15. Edgar Cabanas and Eva Illouz, "The Making of a 'Happy Worker': Positive Psychology in Neoliberal Organizations," in *Beyond the Cubicle: Job Insecurity, Intimacy, and the Flexible Self*, ed. Alliison Pugh (Oxford: Oxford University Press, 2017).

16. Chiapello and Fairclough, "Understanding the New Management."

17. See Emile Durkheim, "Anomie and the Moral Structure of Industry," in *Emile Durkheim: Selected Writings*, ed. Antony Giddens (Cambridge: Cambridge University Press, 1972).

18. Pierre Bourdieu et al., *The Weight of the World: Social Suffering in Contemporary Society* (Stanford, CA: Stanford University Press, 1999).

19. Richard Sennett, *The Corrosion of Character: The Personal Consequences of Work in the New Capitalism* (New York: Norton, 1998).

20. Nick Couldry, "The Individual Point of View: Learning from Bourdieu's 'The Weight of the World,'" *Cultural Studies ↔ Critical Methodologies* 5, no. 3 (2005).

21. Bourdieu et al., *The Weight*, 61.

22. Bourdieu et al., 263.

23. Bourdieu et al., 265.

24. Michael Bull, *Sound Moves: iPod Culture and Urban Experience* (London: Routledge, 2007).

25. Du Gay and Morgan, *New Spirits*.

26. Luc Boltanski and Laurent Thévenot, *On Justification: Economies of Worth*, trans. Catherine Porter (Princeton, NJ: Princeton University Press, 2006).

27. The UK-based fieldwork was piloted in late 2009 (included) with an immediate first phase in early 2010, another over the winter of 2010–11, and a third phase in winter 2011–12, effectively representing the years of instability immediately following the Great Recession. The methods of the Canadian-based fieldwork were piloted in 2016 (not included) and conducted each Spring in 2017–20, representing the years leading up to and including the COVID-19 pandemic. The UK-based fieldwork represents extensive in-depth multimethod engagement with thirty-five individuals over multiple weeks each, complemented by a secondary set of diagnostic studies with eighty-eight individuals conducted in Canada.

28. Kenzie Burchell, "Tasking the Everyday: Where Mobile and Online Communication Take Time," *Mobile Media & Communication* 3, no. 1 (2015).

29. Nick Couldry and Andreas Hepp, "Conceptualizing Mediatization: Contexts, Traditions, Arguments," *Communication Theory* 23, no. 3 (2013); Roger

Silverstone, "The Sociology of Mediation and Communication," in *The Sage Handbook of Sociology* (London: Sage, 2005); Peter Lunt and Sonia Livingstone, "Is 'Mediatization' the New Paradigm for Our Field? A Commentary on Deacon and Stanyer (2014, 2015) and Hepp, Hjarvard and Lundby (2015)," *Media, Culture & Society* 38, no. 3 (2016).

30. J. Wajcman, "Feminist Theories of Technology," *Cambridge Journal of Economics* 34, no. 1 (2010).

31. Christian Pentzold and Andreas Bischof, "Making Affordances Real: Socio-material Prefiguration, Performed Agency, and Coordinated Activities in Human-Robot Communication," *Social Media + Society* 5, no. 3 (2019).

32. Andrew Feenberg, *Questioning Technology* (London: Routledge, 1999); Wiebe E. Bijker, *Of Bicycles, Bakelites, and Bulbs: Toward a Theory of Sociotechnical Change* (Cambridge, MA: MIT Press, 1997); Donald A. MacKenzie and Judy Wajcman, *The Social Shaping of Technology* (Milton Keynes: Open University Press, 1999); Elanor Sandry, "Taking Social Machines beyond the Ideal Human-like Other," in *A Networked Self and Human Augmentics, Artificial Intelligence, Sentience*, ed. Zizi Papacharissi (New York: Routledge, 2019).

33. Bruno Latour, *Reassembling the Social: An Introduction to Actor-Network-Theory* (Oxford: Oxford University Press, 2007); see also Nick Couldry, "Recovering Critique in an Age of Datafication," *New Media & Society* 22, no. 7 (2020).

34. Annemarie Mol, "Actor-Network Theory: Sensitive Terms and Enduring Tensions," special issue, *Kölner Zeitschrift für Soziologie und Sozialpsychologie* 50 (2010): 253.

35. Tero Karppi, *Disconnect: Facebook's Affective Bonds* (Minneapolis: University of Minnesota Press, 2018).

36. In terms of connection, affect scholars highlight something "more than" can be captured in the defining of emotion or given form of social engagement; it precedes that reflection, just as it precedes any particular instantiation of collective identity: see Zizi Papacharissi, *A Networked Self Identity, Community, and Culture on Social Network Sites* (New York: Routledge, 2010); and Karppi, *Disconnect.*

37. Thomas Poell, David Nieborg, and José van Dijck, "Platformisation," *Internet Policy Review* 8, no. 4 (2019), 3.

38. James J. Gibson, *The Ecological Approach to Visual Perception* (Boston: Houghton Mifflin, 1979), 127 (italics in the original).

39. Tarleton Gillespie, "The Politics of 'Platforms,'" *New Media & Society* 12, no. 3 (2010).

40. Sabine Trepte et al., "A Cross-Cultural Perspective on the Privacy Calculus," *Social Media + Society* 3, no. 1 (2017); Kate Mannell, "Plural and Porous: Reconceptualizing the Boundaries of Mobile Messaging Group Chats," *Journal of Computer-Mediated Communication* 25, no. 4 (2020).

41. Mark Andrejevic, "Surveillance in the Digital Enclosure," *Communication Review* 10, no. 4 (2007); Wendy Hui Kyong Chun, *Updating to Remain the Same: Habitual New Media* (Cambridge, MA: MIT Press, 2016).

42. Joseph Turow, *The Daily You: How the New Advertising Industry Is Defining Your Identity and Your Worth* (New Haven, CT: Yale University Press, 2011); Nick Couldry and Joseph Turow, "Advertising, Big Data, and the Clearance of the Public Realm," *International Journal of Communication* 8, no. 1 (2014).

43. José van Dijck, *The Culture of Connectivity: A Critical History of Social Media* (Oxford: Oxford University Press, 2013).

44. Van Dijck, Poell, and Waal, *The Platform Society*.

45. Karin Wahl-Jorgensen, "The Emotional Architecture of Social Media," in *A Networked Self and Platforms, Stories, Connections*, ed. Zizi Papacharissi (New York: Routledge, 2018).

46. danah boyd, "Social Network Sites as Networked Publics," in *A Networked Self: Identity, Community and Culture on Social Network Sites*, ed. Zizi Papacharissi (New York: Routledge, 2011); Zizi Papacharissi, *Affective Publics: Sentiment, Technology, and Politics* (Oxford: Oxford University Press, 2015).

47. Thomas Poell, Sudha Rajagopalan, and Anastasia Kavada, "Publicness on Platforms: Tracing the Mutual Articulation of Platform Architectures and User Practices," in *A Networked Self and Platforms, Stories, Connections*, ed. Zizi Papacharissi (New York: Routledge, 2018); Zach Edwards, "Breitbart.com Is Partnering with RT.com & Other Sites via Mislabeled Advertising Inventory," *Medium*, July 22, 2022.

48. Andreas Hepp and Nick Couldry, "Introduction: Media Events in Globalized Media Cultures," in *Media Events in a Global Age*, ed. Nick Couldry, Andreas Hepp, and Friedrich Krotz (London: Routledge, 2009).

49. Henry Jenkins, *Convergence Culture: Where Old and New Media Collide* (New York: New York University Press, 2006); Zizi Papacharissi, "Introduction," in *A Networked Self and Love*, ed. Zizi Papacharissi (New York: Routledge, 2018).

50. Daniel Kreiss, "A Networked Self in the Age of Identity Fundamentalism," in *A Networked Self and Platforms, Stories, Connections*, ed. Zizi Papacharissi (New York: Routledge, 2018).

51. Ben Light, *Disconnecting with Social Networking Sites* (Houndmills, Basingstoke, Hampshire: Palgrave Macmillan, 2014), 150.

52. Michael Petit, "Digital Disaffect," in *Networked Affect*, ed. Ken Hillis, Susanna Paasonen, and Michael Petit (Cambridge, MA: MIT Press, 2015), 177.

53. Tim Markham, "Subjective Recognition in a Distracted World," in *Making Time for Digital Lives: Beyond Chronotopia*, ed. Anne Kaun, Christian Pentzold, and Christine Lohmeier (Lanham, MD: Rowman & Littlefield, 2020), 16.

54. Greg Goldberg, *Antisocial Media: Anxious Labor in the Digital Economy* (New York: New York University Press, 2017), 9.

55. Anne Kaun, Christine Lohmeier, and Christian Pentzold, "Introduction: Making Time for Digital Lives: Sketching the Field and History of Resisting Dominant Temporal Regimes," in *Making Time for Digital Lives: Beyond Chronotopia*, ed. Anne Kaun, Christian Pentzold, and Christine Lohmeier (Lanham, MD: Rowman & Littlefield, 2020), 1.

56. Light, *Disconnecting*.

57. G. T. Marx, "A Tack in the Shoe: Neutralizing and Resisting the New Surveillance," *Journal of Social Sciences* 59, no. 2 (2003); Finn Brunton and Helen Nissenbaum, *Obfuscation: A User's Guide for Privacy and Protest* (Cambridge, MA: MIT Press, 2016).

58. Light, *Disconnecting*.

59. Peter Nagy and Gina Neff, "Imagined Affordance: Reconstructing a Keyword for Communication Theory," *Social Media + Society* 1, no. 2 (2015); Lee Humphreys, Veronika Karnowski, and Thilo von Pape, "Smart Phones as Metamedia: A Framework for Identifying the Niches Structuring Smartphone Use," *International Journal of Communication* 12 (2018).

60. Aure Schrock (as Andrew Richard Schrock), "Communicative Affordances of Mobile Media: Portability, Availability, Locatability and Multimediality," *International Journal of Communication* 9 (2015); Kate Mannell, "A Typology of Mobile Messaging's Disconnective Affordances," *Mobile Media & Communication* 7, no. 1 (2019). For earlier discussions of "media switching," see Rich Ling and Jonathan Donner, *Mobile Communication* (Cambridge: Polity, 2010); Ilana Gershon, "Breaking Up Is Hard to Do: Media Switching and Media Ideologies," *Journal of Linguistic Anthropology* 20, no. 2 (2010).

61. Erving Goffman, *Relations in Public: Microstudies of the Public Order* (New York: Basic Books, 1971).

62. Humphreys, Karnowski, and von Pape, "Smart Phones as Metamedia."

63. Mirca Madianou and Daniel Miller, *Migration and New Media: Transnational Families and Polymedia* (London: Routledge, 2013); Mirca Madianou, "Smartphones as Polymedia," *Journal of Computer-Mediated Communication* 19, no. 3 (2014).

64. Erving Goffman, *Frame Analysis: An Essay on the Organization of Experience* (New York: Harper & Row, 1974).

65. Mizuko Ito and Daisuke Okabe, "Technosocial Situations: Emergent Structuring of Mobile E-mail Use," in *Personal, Portable, Pedestrian: Mobile Phones in Japanese Life*, ed. Mizuko Ito, Daisuke Okabe, and Misa Matsuda (Cambridge, MA: MIT Press, 2005); Kazys Varnelis and Anne Friedberg, "Place: Networked Place," in *Networked Publics*, ed. Kazys Varnelis (Cambridge, MA: MIT Press, 2008); Giovanna Mascheroni and Jane Vincent, "Perpetual Contact as a Communicative Affordance: Opportunities, Constraints, and Emotions," *Mobile Media & Communication* 4, no. 3 (2016).

66. Peter Vorderer, Nicola Krömer, and Frank M. Schneider, "Permanently Online—Permanently Connected: Explorations into University Students' Use of Social Media and Mobile Smart Devices," *Computers in Human Behavior* 63 (2016); Jessica Klein, "The Darkly Soothing Compulsion of 'Doomscrolling,'" *BBC Worklife*, March 3, 2021; Frank M. Schneider and Selina Hitzfeld, "I Ought to Put Down That Phone but I Phub Nevertheless: Examining the Predictors of Phubbing Behavior," *Social Science Computer Review* 39, no. 6 (2021).

67. Gina Neff and Peter Nagy, "Agency in the Digital Age: Using Symbiotic Agency to Explain Human-Technology Interaction," in *A Networked Self and*

Human Augmentics, Artificial Intelligence, Sentience, ed. Zizi Papacharissi (New York: Routledge, 2019).

68. Couldry and Hepp, *Mediated Construction*, 21.

69. Berger and Luckmann, *Social Construction of Reality*, 66.

70. Theodore R. Schatzki, *The Site of the Social: A Philosophical Account of the Constitution of Social Life and Change* (University Park: Pennsylvania State University Press, 2002). See also Laurent Thévenot, "Pragmatic Regimes Governing the Engagement with the World," in *The Practice Turn in Contemporary Theory*, ed. Theodore R. Schatzki, Karin Knorr Cetina, and Eike von Savigny (London: Routledge, 2001), 15; Joseph Rouse, "Two Concepts of Practices," in *The Practice Turn in Contemporary Theory*, ed. Theodore R. Schatzki, Karin Knorr Cetina, and Eike von Savigny (London: Routledge, 2001); John Postill, "Introduction: Theorising Media and Practice," in *Theorising Media and Practice*, ed. Birgit Bräuchler and John Postill (New York: Berghahn, 2010); Burchell, Driessens, and Mattoni, "Practicing Media—Mediating Practice"; and Christian Pentzold, "Jumping on the Practice Bandwagon: Perspectives for a Practice-Oriented Study of Communication and Media," *International Journal of Communication* 14, no. 1 (2020).

71. See Fabienne Brugère, "Common Sense," in *Dictionary of Untranslatables: A Philosophical Lexicon*, ed. Barbara Cassin, Steven Rendall, and Emily S. Apter (Princeton, NJ: Princeton University Press, 2014).

72. Étienne Balibar, Barbara Cassin, and Sandra Laugier, "Praxis," in *Dictionary of Untranslatables: A Philosophical Lexicon*, ed. Barbara Cassin, Steven Rendall, and Emily S. Apter (Princeton, NJ: Princeton University Press, 2014), 820.

73. Theodore R. Schatzki, "Introduction: Practice Theory," in *The Practice Turn in Contemporary Theory*, ed. Theodore R. Schatzki, Karin Knorr Cetina, and Eike von Savigny (London: Routledge, 2001), 5; Andreas Reckwitz, "Toward a Theory of Social Practices," *European Journal of Social Theory* 5, no. 2 (2002): 253.

74. Thévenot, "Pragmatic Regimes," 15.

75. For an extended discussion of critical digital labor see Fuchs's application of Dallas Smythe's notion of the audience as a productive set of actors in the context of digital-media use as a type of community and data-producing labor. Christian Fuchs, "Dallas Smythe Today—The Audience Commodity, the Digital Labour Debate, Marxist Political Economy and Critical Theory," *tripleC: Communication, Capitalism & Critique* 10, no. 2 (2012); Christian Fuchs and Sebastian Sevignani, "What Is Digital Labour? What Is Digital Work? What's Their Difference? And Why Do These Questions Matter for Understanding Social Media," *tripleC: Communication, Capitalism & Critique* 11, no. 2 (2013).

76. Norbert Elias, *Time: An Essay* (London: Wiley-Blackwell, 1992), 21; du Gay and Morgan, *New Spirits*.

77. Balibar, Cassin, and Laugier, "Praxis," 824–26.

78. Ann Swidler, "What Anchors Cultural Practices," in *The Practice Turn in*

Contemporary Theory, ed. Theodore R. Schatzki, Karin Knorr Cetina, and Eike von Savigny (London: Routledge, 2001), 85.

79. Schatzki, *Social Practices*, 98.

80. Norbert Elias, *The Civilizing Process: Sociogenetic and Psychogenetic Investigations*, rev. ed., trans. Edmund Jephcott (Malden, MA: Blackwell, 2000), 367.

81. Elias, 452.

82. Elias, 383.

83. Ling, *Taken for Grantedness*.

84. Roger Silverstone, Eric Hirsch, and David Morely, "Information and Communication Technologies and the Moral Economy of the Household," in *Consuming Technologies: Media and Information in Domestic Spaces*, ed. Roger Silverstone and Eric Hirsch (London: Routledge, 2003); Leslie Haddon, "Roger Silverstone's Legacies: Domestication," *New media & society* 9, no. 1 (2007); Sonia Livingstone, "On the Material and the Symbolic: Silverstone's Double Articulation of Research Traditions in New Media Studies," *New Media & Society* 9, no. 1 (2007).

85. Nick Couldry, "Theorising Media as Practice," *Social Semiotics* 14, no. 2 (2004): 121, 125.

86. Anne Kaun, "Ways of Seeing Digital Disconnection: A Negative Sociology of Digital Culture," *Convergence* 27, no. 6 (2021).

87. Maria Bakardjieva, "New Paradigm or Sensitizing Concept: Finding the Proper Place of Practice Theory in Media Studies," *International Journal of Communication* 14 (2020).

88. Peter Lunt provides close examination of the interactionist basis of "practice theory" that draws Goffman into an otherwise Bourdieusian lineage in Peter Lunt, "Beyond Bourdieu: The Interactionist Foundations of Media Practice Theory," *International Journal of Communication* 14 (2020).

89. Annemarie Mol, "Good Taste," *Journal of Cultural Economy* 2, no. 3 (2009); Eva Illouz, "On Rationality and Passions," in *Communication of Love: Mediatized Intimacy from Love Letters to SMS*, ed. Eva Lia Wyss (Bielefeld: Transcript, 2014).

90. Kaun, Lohmeier, and Pentzold, "Introduction: Making Time" (see n. 60 above).

91. Ilana Gershon, *Down and Out in the New Economy: How People Find (or Don't Find) Work Today* (Chicago: University of Chicago Press, 2017).

92. Cabanas and Illouz, "Making of a 'Happy Worker.'"

93. Georg Simmel, "The Metropolis and Mental Life," in *The Blackwell City Reader*, ed. Gary Bride and Sophie Watson (Malden, MA: Blackwell, 2002).

94. Ilana Gershon, "Calling the Irrational Unmanageable Neoliberal Self," in *A Networked Self and Love*, ed. Zizi Papacharissi (New York: Routledge, 2018), 13.

95. Erving Goffman, *The Presentation of Self in Everyday Life* (New York: Doubleday, 1959).

96. K. Anders Ericsson and Herbert A. Simon, *Protocol Analysis: Verbal Reports as Data* (Cambridge, MA: MIT Press, 1984); Michael A. Shapiro, "Think-Aloud and Thought-List Procedures in Investigating Mental Processes," in

Measuring Psychological Responses to Media Messages, ed. Annie Lang (New York: Lawrence Erlbaum, 1994).

97. This follows Lunt and Livingstone's suggestion that "mediatization research might usefully re-interpret the many existing findings of mediation research by re-locating and integrating them within a historical frame." Lunt and Livingstone, "Is 'Mediatization' the New Paradigm?" 719.

98. Burchell, "Tasking the Everyday."

99. Kenzie Burchell, "Finding Time for Goffman: When Absence Is More Telling Than Presence," in *Conditions of Mediation: Phenomenological Perspectives on Media*, ed. Tim Markham and Scott Rodgers (New York: Peter Lang, 2017).

Chapter 1. Economies of Communication Management

1. Ian Hacking, *The Taming of Chance* (Cambridge: Cambridge University Press, 1990).

2. See Merlin Sheldrake, *Entangled Life: How Fungi Make Our Worlds, Change Our Minds & Shape Our Futures* (New York: Random House, 2020), 70–71.

3. Gibson, *Ecological Approach*, 127 (italics in the original).

4. Ian Hutchby, "Technologies, Texts and Affordances," *Sociology* 35, no. 2 (2001); Nagy and Neff, "Imagined Affordance"; Pentzold and Bischof, "Making Affordances Real."

5. Mol, "Actor-Network Theory"; Zuboff, *Age of Surveillance Capitalism*.

6. See Quinn Slobodian, *Globalists: The End of Empire and the Birth of Neoliberalism* (Cambridge, MA: Harvard University Press, 2018).

7. Zygmunt Bauman, *Liquid Modernity* (Cambridge: Polity, 2000); Zygmunt Bauman and Leonidas. Donskis, *Moral Blindness: The Loss of Sensitivity in Liquid Modernity* (Chichester: Polity, 2013); Zygmunt Bauman and David Lyon, *Liquid Surveillance: A Conversation* (Cambridge: Polity, 2013).

8. Lee Rainie and Barry Wellman, *Networked: The New Social Operating System* (Cambridge, MA: MIT Press, 2012).

9. Hacking, *The Taming of Chance*; Tim Jordan, *Information Politics: Liberation and Exploitation in the Digital Society* (London: Pluto, 2015), 44.

10. Jordan, *Information Politics*, 39.

11. David B. Nieborg and Thomas Poell, "The Platformization of Cultural Production: Theorizing the Contingent Cultural Commodity," *New Media & Society* 20, no. 11 (2018).

12. Couldry and Hepp, *Mediated Construction*.

13. Joost Rietveld, Joe N. Ploog, and David B. Nieborg, "The Coevolution of Platform Dominance and Governance Strategies: Effects on Complementor Performance Outcomes," *Academy of Management Discoveries* 6, no. 3 (2020).

14. Michael Dieter et al., "Multi-situated App Studies: Methods and Propositions," *Social Media + Society* 5, no. 2 (2019): 12.

15. Theodore R. Schatzki, "Keeping Track of Large Phenomena," *Geographische Zeitschrift* 104, no. 1 (2016); Burchell, Driessens, and Mattoni, "Practicing Media–Mediating Practice."

16. Tiziana Terranova, *Network Culture: Politics for the Information Age* (London: Pluto, 2004), 9.

17. Couldry and Hepp, *Mediated Construction*, 35.

18. Nick Couldry, *Media, Society, World: Social Theory and Digital Media Practice* (Cambridge: Polity, 2012), 16–17.

19. Couldry and Hepp, *Mediated Construction*, 55.

20. Schatzki, "Introduction: Practice Theory," 9 (see introduction, n. 78 above).

21. Kenneth J. Gergen, *The Saturated Self: Dilemmas of Identity in Contemporary Life* (New York: Basic Books, 1991).

22. Hartmut Rosa, *Social Acceleration: A New Theory of Modernity*, trans. Jonathan Trejo-Mathys (New York: Columbia University Press, 2013), 233 (italics in the original).

23. I draw here on Rosa's assertion of the "temporalization of time," aligning with Castell's notion of "timeless time" in the network society, in contrast to the temporalization of life thought in terms of sequential biographies. Manuel Castells, *Communication Power* (Oxford: Oxford University Press, 2013), 35,50; Rosa, *Social Acceleration*, 233.

24. Melissa Gregg, *Counterproductive: Time Management in the Knowledge Economy* (Durham, NC: Duke University Press, 2018).

25. William Gibson, "The Science in Science Fiction," interview by Brooke Gladstone, *Talk of the Nation*, NPR, Nov. 30, 1999.

26. Keith Tribe, "Liberalism and Neoliberalism in Britain, 1930–1980," in *The Road from Mont Pèlerin: The Making of the Neoliberal Thought Collective*, ed. Philip Mirowski and Dieter Plehwe (Cambridge, MA: Harvard University Press, 2009), 81–82.

27. Bryan M. Evans and Stephen McBride, "The Austerity State: An Introduction," in *The Austerity State*, ed. Stephen McBride and Bryan M. Evans (Toronto: University of Toronto Press, 2017).

28. Gershon, *Down and Out*.

29. Gerard William Boychuk, Rianne Mahon, and Stephen McBride, "Conclusion," in *After '08: Social Policy and the Global Financial Crisis*, ed. Gerard William Boychuk, Rianne Mahon, and Stephen McBride (Vancouver: UBC Press, 2015); Heather Whiteside, "Austerity Budgets and Public Sector Retrenchment: Crisis Era Policy Making in Canada, the United Kingdom, and Australia," in *After '08: Social Policy and the Global Financial Crisis*, ed. Gerard William Boychuk, Rianne Mahon, and Stephen McBride (Vancouver: UBC Press, 2015).

30. Tribe, "Liberalism and Neoliberalism."

31. Christopher Hood and Rozana Himaz, *A Century of Fiscal Squeeze Politics: 100 Years of Austerity, Politics, and Bureaucracy in Britain* (Oxford: Oxford University Press, 2017).

32. Bent Boel, *The European Productivity Agency and Transatlantic Relations, 1953–1961* (Copenhagen: Museum Tusculanum Press/University of Copenhagen, 2003), 28.

33. Boltanski, *Making of a Class*.

34. Boel, *The European Productivity Agency*, 28.

35. See Google Ngram analysis of usage of management in English language books from 1800 to 2019 "Management." *Google Ngram Viewer*, 2019. Tellingly, the preceding archaic usage of *management* denoted "trickery" or "deceit." "Management," *Oxford English Dictionary*, 2020.

36. Shoshana Zuboff, *In the Age of the Smart Machine: The Future of Work and Power* (New York: Basic Books, 1988), 100.

37. Zuboff, *Age of the Smart Machine*; Shoshana Zuboff, "The White-Collar Body in History," in *Rise of the Knowledge Worker*, ed. James W. Cortada (Boston: Butterworth-Heinemann, 1998).

38. Weber, *The Protestant Ethic*.

39. The 1954 European Productivity Agency and Organization for Economic Cooperation and Development (OECD/OECE) report "OECE les problèmes de gestion des entreprises" went so far as to explicitly outline the need to instruct Europeans on "the direct relationships between a high level of productivity and the use of sound methods in the area of human relations." See OECD/OECE 1954 as cited in Boltanski, *Making of a Class*, 100.

40. British labor laws and the noninterventionist approach to deregulation did not result in a lawless labor market but rather a basic "floor of rights" for individual employees from which individual contracts and collective bargaining could proceed, the laissez-faire "freedom to contract." See Lord Wedderburn, "Deregulation and Labour Law in Britain and Western Europe," *Hofstra Labor and Employment Law Journal* 6, no. 1 (1988).

41. Wedderburn, "Deregulation and Labour Law."

42. Wendy Brown, *Undoing the Demos: Neoliberalism's Stealth Revolution* (New York: Zone, 2015), 65.

43. Daniel Bell, *The Coming of Post-Industrial Society: A Venture in Social Forecasting* (New York: Basic Books, 1976).

44. Peter F. Drucker, *Landmarks of Tomorrow* (New York: Harper, 1957).

45. McKercher and Mosco, *Knowledge Workers*.

46. Enda Brophy and Greig de Peuter, "Immaterial Labor, Precarity, and Recomposition," in *Knowledge Workers in the Information Society*, ed. Catherine McKercher and Vincent Mosco (Plymouth: Lexington Books, 2007), 179.

47. Mark Deuze, "Convergence Culture in the Creative Industries," *International Journal of Cultural Studies* 10, no. 2 (2007); Mark Banks, Rosalind Gill, and Stephanie Taylor, eds., *Theorizing Cultural Work: Labour, Continuity and Change in the Cultural and Creative Industries* (London: Routledge, 2013).

48. Reckwitz, *The Invention of Creativity*, 89.

49. Alessandro Gandini, *The Reputation Economy: Understanding Knowledge Work in Digital Society* (London: Palgrave MacMillan, 2016); Brooke Erin Duffy, *(Not) Getting Paid to Do What You Love: Gender, Social Media, and Aspirational Work* (New Haven, CT: Yale University Press, 2017); Brooke Erin Duffy and Urszula Pruchniewska, "Gender and Self-Enterprise in the Social Media Age: A Digital Double Bind," *Information, Communication & Society* 20, no. 6 (2017).

50. Phoebe Harris Elefante and Mark Deuze, "Media Work, Career Management, and Professional Identity," *Northern Lights* 10, no. 1 (2012); Boltanski and Chiapello, *New Spirit of Capitalism*, 112.

51. For ethnographic accounts from Australia, Europe, and the US, see Rosalind Gill, " 'Life Is a Pitch': Managing the Self in New Media Work," in *Managing Media Work*, ed. Mark Deuze (London: Sage, 2010); and Melissa Gregg, *Work's Intimacy* (Cambridge: Polity, 2013).

52. Hélène Vérin, "Entrepreneur," in *Dictionary of Untranslatables: A Philosophical Lexicon*, ed. Barbara Cassin, Steven Rendall, and Emily S. Apter (Princeton, NJ: Princeton University Press, 2014), 265.

53. Zuboff, "The White-Collar Body."

54. Gregg, *Counterproductive*.

55. Sara Ahmed, *Living a Feminist Life* (Durham, NC: Duke University Press, 2017), 85.

56. Boltanski, *Making of a Class*, 17.

57. Carrie M. Lane, "Unemployed Tech Workers' Ambivalent Embrace of the Flexible Ideal," in *Beyond the Cubicle: Job Insecurity, Intimacy, and the Flexible Self*, ed. Allison J. Pugh (Oxford: Oxford University Press, 2017).

58. Lane, 76.

59. Gershon, *Down and Out*.

60. David Hesmondhalgh and Sarah Baker, "Sex, Gender, and Work Segregation in the Cultural Industries," in *Gender and Creative Labour*, ed. Bridget Conor, Rosalind Gill, and Stephanie Taylor (Oxford: Wiley Blackwell, 2015), 33.

61. Sennett, *Together*, 117.

62. Bell, *Coming of Post-Industrial Society*, 126, 162.

63. Eva Illouz, *Cold Intimacies: The Making of Emotional Capitalism* (Cambridge: Polity, 2007).

64. McKercher and Mosco, *Knowledge Workers*.

65. Zuboff, *Age of the Smart Machine*.

66. Ilana Gershon, "Media Ideologies: An Introduction," *Journal of Linguistic Anthropology* 20, no. 2 (2010); Gregg, *Counterproductive*.

67. Boutang, *Cognitive Capitalism*, 66.

68. Jyotsna Kapur, " 'New' Economy/Old Labor: Creativity, Flatness, and Other Neoliberal Myths," in *Knowledge Workers in the Information Society*, ed. Catherine McKercher and Vincent Mosco (Plymouth: Lexington Books, 2007), 166–67.

69. Huws, *Labor*, 136.

70. Mary L. Gray and Siddharth Suri, *Ghost Work: How to Stop Silicon Valley from Building a New Global Underclass* (Boston: Houghton Mifflin Harcourt, 2019); Tarleton Gillespie, *Custodians of the Internet: Platforms, Content Moderation, and the Hidden Decisions That Shape Social Media* (New Haven, CT: Yale University Press, 2018).

71. Fritz Machlup, "Knowledge Production and Occupational Structure (I)," in *Rise of the Knowledge Worker*, ed. James W. Cortada (Boston: Butterworth-Heinemann, 1998), 74.

72. Linchuan Qiu Jack, "Network Labour and Non-elite Knowledge Workers in China," *Work Organisation, Labour & Globalisation* 4, no. 2 (2010); Sarah T. Roberts, "Commercial Content Moderation: Digital Laborers' Dirty Work," in *Intersectional Internet: Race, Sex, Class and Culture Online*, ed. Safiya Umoja Noble and Brendesha M. Tynes (New York: Peter Lang, 2016).

73. Marlen van den Ecker and Sebastian Sevignani, "Media and Communication in Digital Capitalism: Critical Perspectives," *Global Dialogue* 10, no. 2 (2020).

74. danah boyd and Kate Crawford, "Cultural Critical Questions for Big Data," *Information, Communication & Society* 15, no. 5 (2012).

75. Anne Helmond, "The Platformization of the Web: Making Web Data Platform Ready," *Social Media + Society* 1, no. 2 (2015).

76. Langdon Winner, *Autonomous Technology: Technics-Out-of-Control as a Theme in Political Thought* (Cambridge, MA: MIT Press, 1977); Clive Norris and Gary Armstrong, *The Maximum Surveillance Society: The Rise of CCTV* (Oxford: Berg, 1999); Kevin D Haggerty and Richard V. Ericson, "The Surveillant Assemblage," *British Journal of Sociology* 51, no. 4 (2000).

77. Mark Andrejevic, "Automating Surveillance," *Surveillance & Society* 17, no. 1/2 (2019).

78. David B. Nieborg, "Apps of Empire: Global Capitalism and the App Economy," *Games and Culture* (2020).

79. Helmond, "Platformization of the Web"; Nieborg and Poell, "Platformization of Cultural Production"; Nick Couldry and Ulises A. Mejias, "Data Colonialism: Rethinking Big Data's Relation to the Contemporary Subject," *Television & New Media* 20, no. 4 (2019).

80. Nieborg and Poell, "Platformization of Cultural Production"; Robert Gorwa, "What Is Platform Governance," *Information, Communication & Society* 22, no. 6 (2019).

81. Nieborg and Poell, "Platformization of Cultural Production," 4277.

82. Taina Bucher, *If/Then: Algorithmic Power and Politics* (New York: Oxford University Press, 2018).

83. Matthew Crain, "The Limits of Transparency: Data Brokers and Commodification," *New Media & Society* 20, no. 1 (2018).

84. For an early review of the US and Western data brokerage industries, see FTC, *Data Brokers: A Call for Transparency and Accountability* (Washington, DC: Federal Trade Commission, 2014). For the UK context, see ICO, *Big Data, Artificial Intelligence, Machine Learning and Data Protection* (Wilmslow, Cheshire: Information Commissioner's Office, 2017); ICO, *Update Report into Adtech and Real Time Bidding* (Wilmslow, Cheshire: Information Commissioner's Office, 2019).

85. Daniel Knapp, personal correspondence, 2023.

86. Fuchs, "Dallas Smythe Today."

87. Mark Andrejevic, *Automated Media* (London: Routledge, 2020).

88. David M. Berry, *The Philosophy of Software: Code and Mediation in the Digital Age* (New York: Palgrave Macmillan, 2011).

89. Greg Siegel, *Forensic Media: Reconstructing Accidents in Accelerated Modernity* (Durham, NC: Duke University Press, 2014).

90. Dieter, "Multi-situated App Studies."

91. Poell, Rajagopalan, and Kavada, "Publicness on Platforms," 53.

92. Hood and Himaz, *Century of Fiscal Squeeze*, 120.

93. For discussion of the brief Keynesian moment of economic recovery following the crash, see Rianne Mahon, Gerard William Boychuk, and Stephen McBride, introduction to *After '08: Social Policy and the Global Financial Crisis*, ed. Gerard William Boychuk, Rianne Mahon, and Stephen McBride (Vancouver: UBC Press, 2015), 4–5.

94. Like the nationalization of struggling banks at the outset of the Great Recession, the 2020 pandemic saw emergency measures to shore up rail companies, effecting a renationalization process of rail in Britain. ONS, *Public Sector Finances, UK: July 2020* (Newport: Office of National Statistics, 2020).

95. Sennett, *Together*; Stephen McBride and Sorin Mitrea, "Internalizing Neoliberalism and Austerity," in *The Austerity State*, ed. Stephen McBride and Bryan M. Evans (Toronto: University of Toronto Press, 2017).

96. Bourdieu et al., *The Weight*, 64.

97. McBride and Mitrea, "Internalizing Neoliberalism and Austerity," 102.

Chapter 2. Managing Time

1. Jason Farman, *Delayed Response: The Art of Waiting from the Ancient to the Instant World* (New Haven, CT: Yale University Press, 2018), 48.

2. Christoph Klimmt et al., "The Permanently Online and Permanently Connected Mind: Mapping the Cognitive Structures behind Mobile Internet Use," in *Permanently Online, Permanently Connected: Living and Communicating in a POPC World*, ed. Peter Vorderer et al. (New York: Routledge, 2017).

3. Robert Larose, Junghyun Kim, and Wei Peng, "Social Networking: Addictive, Compulsive, Problematic, or Just Another Media Habit?," in *A Networked Self: Identity, Community and Culture on Social Network Sites*, ed. Zizi Papacharissi (New York: Routledge, 2011).

4. Goldberg, *Antisocial Media*; Ethan Tussey, *The Procrastination Economy: The Big Business of Downtime* (New York: New York University Press, 2018).

5. Olivier Klein, "Social Perception of Time, Distance and High Speed Transportation," *Time & Society* 13, no. 2/3 (2004); Barbara Adam, "Time," *Theory, Culture & Society* 23, no. 2–3 (2006); Theodore R Schatzki, "Timespace and the Organization of Social Life," in *Time, Consumption and Everyday Life: Practice, Materiality and Culture*, ed. Elizabeth Shove, Frank Trentmann, and Richard R. Wilk (Oxford: Berg, 2009).

6. Elias, *Time*, 3, 39–44.

7. Elias, 1, 2.

8. Elias, 12.

9. Helga Nowotny, *Time: The Modern and Postmodern Experience*, trans. Neville Plaice (Cambridge: Polity, 1994), 40.

10. Noel King, "An Expert Has the Answers to Daylight Saving Time Conundrum," *Morning Edition*, NPR, June 2, 2021.

11. Jonathan Finn, *Beyond the Finish Line: Images, Evidence, and the History of the Photo-Finish* (Montreal: McGill-Queen's University Press, 2020).

12. Theodore R. Schatzki, "Peripheral Vision: The Sites of Organizations," *Organization Studies* 26, no. 3 (2005).

13. Farman, *Delayed Response*, 53.

14. See Hartmut Rosa for examination of this shift from "ontologically relative" to "time-relative" aspects of assessment and decision-making in Rosa, *Social Acceleration*, 233. Rosa draws from Luhman's examination of this relational transformation as from the "schema of being" to that of the "schema of time" in Niklas Luhmann, *Theory of Society* (Stanford, CA: Stanford University Press, 2012).

15. Elias, *Time: An Essay*, 101.

16. Amelia Acker, "Born Networked Records: A History of Short Message Service Format" (PhD diss., UCLA, 2014).

17. Anne Kaun and Fredrik Stiernstedt, "Facebook Time: Technological and Institutional Affordances for Media Memories," *New Media & Society* 16, no. 7 (2014).

18. Christian Pentzold and Manuel Menke, "Conceptualizing the Doings and Sayings of Media Practices: Expressive Performance, Communicative Understanding, and Epistemic Discourse," *International Journal of Communication* 14 (2020).

19. Taina Bucher, "Want to Be on the Top? Algorithmic Power and the Threat of Invisibility on Facebook," *New Media & Society* 14, no. 7 (2012).

20. Esther Weltevrede, Anne Helmond, and Carolin Gerlitz, "The Politics of Real-Time: A Device Perspective on Social Media Platforms and Search Engines," *Theory, Culture & Society* 31, no. 6 (2014).

21. Min Zhang and Yiqun Liu, "A Commentary of TikTok Recommendation Algorithms in *MIT Technology Review* 2021," *Fundamental Research* 1, no. 6 (2021); Zhengwei Zhao, "Analysis on the 'Douyin (Tiktok) [*sic*] Mania' Phenomenon Based on Recommendation Algorithms," *E3S Web of Conferences* 235 (2021).

22. Trung T. Phan, "The Secret Sauce behind TikTok's Recommendation Algorithm," *The Hustle*, Sept. 29, 2020; Pengda Wang, "Recommendation Algorithm in TikTok: Strengths, Dilemmas, and Possible Directions," *International Journal of Social Science Studies* 10, no. 5 (2022).

23. Ignacio Siles, Luciana Valerio-Alfaro, and Ariana Meléndez-Moran, "Learning to Like TikTok. And Not: Algorithm Awareness as Process," *New Media & Society* 0, no. 0 (2022).

24. Hamza Shaban, "Facebook, Instagram, WhatsApp Suffered a Global Outage. What Happened?" *Washington Post*, March 14, 2019.

25. Elias, *Time*.

26. Elizabeth Shove, "Everyday Practice and the Production and Consumption of Time," in *Time, Consumption and Everyday Life: Practice, Materiality and*

Culture, ed. Elizabeth Shove, Frank Trentmann, and Richard R. Wilk (Oxford: Berg, 2009), 19.

27. Martin Hand, "Persistent Traces, Potential Memories," *Convergence* 22, no. 3 (2016); Martin Hand and Michelle Gorea, "Digital Traces and Personal Analytics: iTime, Self-Tracking, and the Temporalities of Practice," *International Journal of Communication* 11 (2017).

28. Schrock, "Communicative Affordances"; Taina Bucher and Anne Helmond, "The Affordances of Social Media Platforms," in *The Sage Handbook of Social Media* (London: Sage, 2018).

29. Eviatar Zerubavel, *Hidden Rhythms: Schedules and Calendars in Social Life* (Chicago: University of Chicago Press, 1981).

30. David Pascal, "Anxiety," in *Dictionary of Untranslatables: A Philosophical Lexicon*, ed. Barbara Cassin, Steven Rendall, and Emily S. Apter (Princeton, NJ: Princeton University Press, 2014), 37.

31. Helga Nowotny, *The Cunning of Uncertainty* (Cambridge: Polity, 2016).

32. Quoted in David and Pascal, "Anxiety," 38.

33. Annette M. Markham, "The Ontological Insecurity of Disconnecting," in *Reckoning with Social Media*, ed. Aleena Chia, Ana Jorge, and Tero Karppi (Lanham, MD: Rowman & Littlefield, 2021), 41.

34. Julia Ticona, "Strategies of Control: Workers' Use of ICTs to Shape Knowledge and Service Work," *Information, Communication & Society* 18, no. 5 (2015): 514; Tussey, *The Procrastination Economy*.

35. Robert Hassan, "Network Time," in *24/7: Time and Temporality in the Network Society*, ed. Robert Hassan and Ronald E. Purser (Stanford, CA: Stanford University Press, 2007).

36. Elias, *Time*, 15.

37. Goffman, *Relations in Public*.

38. Elias, *Time*, 37.

39. See JoAnne Yates, "From Press Book and Pigeonhole to Vertical Filing: Revolution in Storage and Access Systems for Correspondence," *Journal of Business Communication* 19, no. 3 (1982): 7.

40. Lisa. Gitelman, *Paper Knowledge: Toward a Media History of Documents* (Durham, NC: Duke University Press, 2014).

41. Goffman, *Presentation of Self*.

42. Christoph Bagger and Stine Lomborg, "Overcoming Forced Disconnection," in *Reckoning with Social Media*, ed. Aleena Chia, Ana Jorge, and Tero Karppi (Lanham, MD: Rowman & Littlefield, 2021), 168.

43. G. F. Corporaal and V. Lehdonvirta, *Platform Sourcing: How Fortune 500 Firms Are Adopting Online Freelancing Platforms* (Oxford: Oxford Internet Institute, University of Oxford, 2017).

44. Gandini, *The Reputation Economy*.

45. Edward P. Thompson, "Time, Work-Discipline, and Industrial Capitalism," *Past & Present* 38 (1967): 60.

46. Kenzie Burchell, "Infiltrating the Space, Hijacking the Platform: Pussy

Riot, Sochi Protests, and Media Events," *Participations* 12, no. 1 (2015): 38.

47. Yates, "Press Book and Pigeonhole."

48. Irma Rochmawati, "User Interface Design of Mobile Photo Editors," *Advances in Social Science, Education and Humanities Research* 225 (2018); Vikram Mohanty and Genèvieve Patterson, "When Content Decides Where You Belong: Investigating Micro Communities on VSCO" (AAAI Conference on Human Computation, virtual, Nov. 14–18, 2021).

49. Jennifer R. Whitson, "Gaming the Quantified Self," *Surveillance & Society* 11, no. 1/2 (2013).

50. Gregg, *Counterproductive*; Melissa Gregg, "From Careers to Atmospheres," in *Working and Organizing in the Digital Age*, ed. Stephan M. Schaefer et al. (Lund, Sweden: Pufendorf Institute for Advanced Studies, Lund University, 2018).

51. Elias, *Time*, 14.

52. Burchell, "Tasking the Everyday"; Burchell, "Finding Time for Goffman"; Karin Fast, "The Disconnection Turn: Three Facets of Disconnective Work in Post-Digital Capitalism," *Convergence* 27, no. 6 (2021): 1617.

53. Ilana Gershon, "Neoliberal Agency," *Current Anthropology* 52, no. 4 (2011): 539.

54. Merleau-Ponty, *Phenomenology of Perception*.

55. Hassan, "Network Time."

56. Merleau-Ponty, *Phenomenology of Perception*, 416.

57. Elias, *Time*, 29.

Chapter 3. Managing Connection

1. Tim Markham, "Subjective Recognition," 20.

2. Emile Durkheim, *The Division of Labor in Society*, trans. W. D. Halls (New York: Free Press, 1984).

3. Durkheim, 368–70.

4. Richard Sennett, *The Uses of Disorder: Personal Identity & City Life* (New York: Knopf, 1970).

5. Simmel, "Metropolis and Mental Life," 15.

6. Erving Goffman, *Behavior in Public Places: Notes on the Social Organization of Gatherings* (New York: Free Press, 1963), 83; Louise Eley and Ben Rampton, "Everyday Surveillance, Goffman, and Unfocused Interaction," *Surveillance & Society* 18, no. 2 (2020).

7. Kenzie Burchell, "Everyday Communication Management and Perceptions of Use," *Convergence* 23, no. 4 (2017).

8. Kenneth J. Gergen, "The Challenge of Absent Presence," in *Perpetual Contact: Mobile Communication, Private Talk, Public Performance*, ed. James E. Katz and Mark A. Aakhus (Cambridge: Cambridge University Press, 2002.

9. Gergen, 231.

10. Scott McQuire, *The Media City: Media, Architecture and Urban Space* (Los Angeles: Sage, 2008), 25.

11. Goffman, *Behavior in Public Places*, 63.

12. Christian Licoppe, "'Connected' Presence: The Emergence of a New Repertoire for Managing Social Relationships in a Changing Communication Technoscape," *Environment and Planning D: Society and Space* 22, no. 1 (2004).

13. Burchell, "Finding Time for Goffman," 187.

14. Joshua. Meyrowitz, *No Sense of Place: The Impact of Electronic Media on Social Behavior* (New York: Oxford University Press, 1985); Kaun, "Ways of Seeing" (see introduction, n. 90 above).

15. Karppi, *Disconnect*, 24.

16. Goffman, *Behavior in Public Places*, 89; Ruth Rettie, "Mobile Phone Communication: Extending Goffman to Mediated Interaction," *Sociology* 43, no. 3 (2009).

17. In terms of today's communication environment, constant attentiveness and availability across numerous hypermediated forms of presence—texts, likes, comments, Snaps or Stories, and video calls—have become an idealized norm of mutual interpersonal intimacy. J. David Bolter and Richard Grusin, *Remediation: Understanding New Media* (Cambridge, MA: MIT Press, 1999); Henry Jenkins and Richard A. Grusin, "A Remediated, Premeditated, and Transmediated Conversation with Richard Grusin," *Confessions of an Aca-Fan: The Official Weblog of Henry Jenkins* (blog), 2011, https://henryjenkins.org/blog/2011/03/a_remediated_premediated_and_t_2.html.

18. Mizuko Ito, Daisuke Okabe, and Ken Anderson, "The Reconstruction of Space and Time: Mobile Communication Practices," in *Portable Objects in Three Global Cities: The Personalization of Urban Places*, ed. Rich Ling and Scott W. Campbell (New Brunswick, NJ: Transaction, 2009).

19. Ito and Okabe, "Technosocial Situations"; Kate Crawford, "Following You: Disciplines of Listening in Social Media," *Continuum* 23, no. 4 (2009): 252.

20. Tetsuro Kobayashi and Jeffrey Boase, "Tele-cocooning: Mobile Texting and Social Scope," *Journal of Computer-Mediated Communication* 19, no. 3 (2014): 682.

21. Sarah Cefai and Nick Couldry, "Mediating the Presence of Others: Reconceptualising Co-presence as Mediated Intimacy," *European Journal of Cultural Studies* 22, no. 3 (2019): 11, 21.

22. Travis Kadylak et al., "Disrupted Copresence: Older Adults' Views on Mobile Phone Use during Face-to-Face Interactions," *Mobile Media & Communication* 6, no. 3 (2018); Leonard Reinecke et al., "Permanently Online and Permanently Connected: Development and Validation of the Online Vigilance Scale," *PLoS One* 13, no. 10 (2018); Xiaochun Xie et al., "Parents' Phubbing Increases Adolescents' Mobile Phone Addiction: Roles of Parent-Child Attachment, Deviant Peers, and Gender," *Children and Youth Services Review* 105 (2019); Schneider and Hitzfeld, "I Ought to Put Down That Phone" (see introduction, n. 71 above).

23. This particular phase of fieldwork took place just prior to the launch of Wi-Fi on the London Underground subway network in July 2012.

24. Nowotny, *Time*.

25. Carol Ekinsmyth, "Mothers' Business, Work/Life and the Politics of 'Mumpreneurship,'" *Gender, Place & Culture* 21, no. 10 (2014).

26. Almudena Sevilla et al., *How Are Mothers and Fathers Balancing Work and Family under Lockdown* (London: Institute for Fiscal Studies, 2020).

27. Hesmondhalgh and Baker, "Sex, Gender, and Work Segregation."

28. DBEI, *Business Population Estimates for the UK and the Regions 2020* (Department for Business, Energy & Industrial Strategy, 2020).

29. Melissa Mazmanian, Wanda J. Orlikowski, and JoAnne Yates, "The Autonomy Paradox: The Implications of Mobile Email Devices for Knowledge Professionals," *Organization Science* 24, no. 5 (2013): 1141–42.

30. Stephanie Taylor, "A New Mystique? Working for Yourself in the Neoliberal Economy," in *Gender and Creative Labour*, ed. Bridget Conor, Rosalind Gill, and Stephanie Taylor (Oxford: Wiley Blackwell, 2015).

31. Ekinsmyth, "Mothers' Business," 1238.

32. Bagger and Lomborg, "Overcoming Forced Disconnection," 173.

33. Gershon, *Down and Out*, 239.

34. Lisa A. Schur, Mason Ameri, and Douglas Kruse, "Telework after Covid: A 'Silver Lining' for Workers with Disabilities," *Journal of Occupational Rehabilitation* 30, no. 4 (2020); Lisa Schur and Douglas L. Kruse, "Coronavirus Could Revolutionize Work Opportunities for People with Disabilities," *The Conversation*, March 5, 2020.

35. Yang Wang and Sun Sun Lim, "ICTs and Transnational Householding: The Double Burden of Polymedia Connectivity for International 'Study Mothers,'" in *Research Handbook on International Migration and Digital Technology*, ed. Marie McAuliffe (Cheltenham, UK: Edward Elgar, 2021).

36. Larissa Hjorth, Ingrid Richardson, and William Balmford, "Careful Surveillance and Pet Wearables: At Home with Animals." *The Conversation*, Sept. 4, 2016.

37. Larissa Hjorth et al., *Digital Media Practices in Households: Kinship through Data* (Amsterdam: Amsterdam University Press, 2020), 55.

38. Madianou, "Smartphones as Polymedia."

39. Ticona, "Strategies of Control."

40. Hjorth, Richardson, and Balmford, "Careful Surveillance"; Hjorth, *Digital Media Practices*.

41. Larissa Hjorth and Ingrid Richardson, *Gaming in Social, Locative, and Mobile Media* (London: Palgrave Macmillan UK, 2014).

42. Mihaly Csikszentmihalyi, *Flow: The Psychology of Optimal Experience* (New York: Harper & Row, 1990); Garry Crawford, Victoria K. Gosling, and Ben Light, "The Social and Cultural Significance of Online Gaming," in *Online Gaming in Context: The Social and Cultural Significance of Online Games*, ed. Garry Crawford, Victoria K. Gosling, and Ben Light (New York: Routledge, 2011).

43. Burchell, "Everyday Communication Management."

44. Tina L. Taylor, *Play between Worlds: Exploring Online Game Culture* (Cambridge, MA: MIT Press, 2009), 28.

45. Taina Bucher, *Facebook* (New York: Polity, 2021), 121.

46. Ben Highmore, *Ordinary Lives: Studies in the Everyday* (London: Routledge, 2011), 184.

47. Petit, "Digital Disaffect"; Bruce Sterling, "Transcript of Reboot 11 Speech, Copenhagen," Wired.com, July 25, 2009.

48. Tim Markham, "Subjective Recognition," 16, 17.

49. Craig Robertson, "Learning to File: Reconfiguring Information and Information Work in the Early Twentieth Century," *Technology and Culture* 58, no. 4 (2017): 964.

50. Christian Licoppe, "The 'Crisis of the Summons': A Transformation in the Pragmatics of 'Notifications,' from Phone Rings to Instant Messaging," *Information Society* 26, no. 4 (2010).

51. Gregg, "From Careers to Atmospheres"; Gregg, *Work's Intimacy*.

52. Doug Pyper and Feargal McGuinness, "Briefing Paper Zero-Hour Contracts Number 06553," House of Commons Library, August 17, 2018.

53. Julia Ticona, "The Future of Work: The Digital Hustle," *Pacific Standard*, June 14, 2017.

54. Jodi Dean, *Democracy and Other Neoliberal Fantasies: Communicative Capitalism and Left Politics* (Durham, NC: Duke University Press, 2009); Brooke Erin Duffy, "The Romance of Work: Gender and Aspirational Labour in the Digital Culture Industries," *International Journal of Cultural Studies* 19, no. 4 (2016).

55. Brad Hershbein and Lisa B. Kahn, "Do Recessions Accelerate Routine-Biased Technological Change? Evidence from Vacancy Postings," *NBER Working Paper* 22762 (2016).

56. Duffy, "The Romance of Work."

57. Leslie Regan Shade and Jenna Jacobson, "Hungry for the Job: Gender, Unpaid Internships and the Creative Industries," in *Gender and Creative Labour*, ed. Bridget Conor, Rosalind Gill, and Stephanie Taylor (Oxford: Wiley Blackwell, 2015).

58. Brooke Erin Duffy and Becca Schwartz, "Digital 'Women's Work?': Job Recruitment Ads and the Feminization of Social Media Employment," *New Media & Society* 20, no. 8 (2018).

59. Rasmus Helles, "Mobile Communication and Intermediality," *Mobile Media & Communication* 1, no. 1 (2013).

60. Aleena Chia, Ana Jorge, and Tero Karppi, "Introduction: Reckoning with Social Media in the Pandemic Denouement," in *Reckoning with Social Media*, ed. Aleena Chia, Ana Jorge, and Tero Karppi (Lanham, MD: Rowman & Littlefield, 2021).

61. Tussey, *The Procrastination Economy*.

62. Nick Couldry, "New Online News Sources and Writer-Gatherers," in *New Media, Old News: Journalism & Democracy in the Digital Age*, ed. Natalie Fenton (London: Sage, 2010); Tim Markham, "Subjective Recognition," 14.

63. Kaun, Lohmeier, and Pentzold, "Introduction: Making Time," 2 (see introduction, n. 60 above).

Chapter 4. Practicing Surveillance

1. Mark Andrejevic, "The Work of Watching One Another: Lateral Surveillance, Risk, and Governance," *Surveillance & Society* 2, no. 4 (2004); Alice Marwick, "The Public Domain: Surveillance in Everyday Life," *Surveillance & Society* 9, no. 4 (2012).

2. David Lyon, ed., *Theorizing Surveillance: The Panopticon and Beyond* (New York: Routledge, 2006); Mark B. Andrejevic, "Surveillance and Alienation in the Online Economy," *Surveillance & Society* 8, no. 3 (2011); Anne Helmond, David B. Nieborg, and Fernando N. van der Vlist, "The Political Economy of Social Data," —*#SMSociety17: Proceedings of the 8th International Conference on Social Media & Society* (2017).

3. Chun, *Updating to Remain.*

4. Melissa Gregg, "Inside the Data Spectacle," *Television & New Media* 16, no. 1 (2015).

5. Burchell, "Tasking the Everyday."

6. Mark Andrejevic, "Work of Watching One Another"; Anders Albrechtslund, "Online Social Networking as Participatory Surveillance," *First Monday* 13, no. 3 (2008); Marwick, "The Public Domain."

7. Greg Elmer, "Panopticon-Discipline-Control," in *Routledge Handbook of Surveillance Studies*, ed. Kirstie Ball, Kevin Haggerty, and David Lyon (London: Routledge, 2012); Colin J. Bennett et al., *Transparent Lives: Surveillance in Canada* (Edmonton: Athabasca University Press, 2014).

8. Nick. Couldry, *Listening beyond the Echoes: Media, Ethics, and Agency in an Uncertain World* (Boulder, CO: Paradigm, 2006).

9. Crawford, "Following You."

10. Marwick, "The Public Domain."

11. Alfred Schütz, *Collected Papers: The Problems of Social Reality* (Dordrecht: Martinus Nijoff, 2012), 11.

12. Goffman, *The Presentation of Self*, 160–61.

13. Merleau-Ponty, *Phenomenology of Perception.*

14. Schütz, *Collected Papers.*

15. W. H. Dutton and Grant Blank, *Next Generation Users: The Internet in Britain* (Oxford: Oxford Internet Institute, University of Oxford, 2011); William H. Dutton and Grant Blank, *Cultures of the Internet: Five Clusters of Attitudes and Beliefs among Users in Britain* (Oxford: Oxford Internet Institute, University of Oxford, 2013); StatsCAN, "The Use of Media to Follow the News and Current Affairs: Spotlight on Canadians: Results from the General Social Survey," Feb. 15, 2016; Blank, Dutton, and Lefkowitz, *Perceived Threats.*

16. Madianou, "Smartphones as Polymedia."

17. Gershon, "Breaking Up."

18. Berry, *The Philosophy of Software*; BBC News, "The Vocabularist: What's the Root of the Word Computer?," Feb. 2, 2016.

19. David B. Nieborg, "Crushing Candy: The Free-to-Play Game in Its Connective Commodity Form," *Social Media + Society* 1, no. 2 (2015).

20. Berry, *The Philosophy of Software*, 14.

21. Daniel Rosenberg, "Data before the Fact," in *"Raw Data" Is an Oxymoron*, ed. Lisa Gitelman (Cambridge, MA: MIT Press, 2013), 33.

22. Tyler Butler Reigeluth, "Why Data Is Not Enough: Digital Traces as Control of Self and Self-Control," *Surveillance & Society* 12, no. 2 (2014).

23. Reigeluth, 245.

24. Reigeluth, 254.

25. Cliff Lampe, Nicole B. Ellison, and Charles W. Steinfield, "A Face(book) in the Crowd: Social Searching vs. Social Browsing," *CSCW '06: Proceedings of the 2006 20th Anniversary Conference on Computer Supported Cooperative Work* (2006).

26. Nicole S. Cohen, "The Valorization of Surveillance: Towards a Political Economy of Facebook," *Democratic Communiqué* 22, no. 1 (2008); Bucher, "Want to Be on the Top?" (see chap. 2n19 above); John Cheney-Lippold, *We Are Data: Algorithms and the Making of Our Digital Selves* (New York: New York University Press, 2017).

27. Wahl-Jorgensen, "Emotional Architecture of Social Media" (see introduction, n. 50 above).

28. Tama Leaver, Tim Highfield, and Crystal Abidin, *Instagram: Visual Social Media Cultures* (Cambridge: Polity, 2020).

29. Dhiraj Murthy, *Twitter*, 2nd ed. (Cambridge: Polity, 2018); Leaver, Highfield, and Abidin, *Instagram*; Bucher, *Facebook*.

30. Walter Benjamin, "Little History of Photography," in *Selected Writings of Walter Benjamin*, vol. 2, *1927–1934*, ed. Michael W. Jennings, Howard Eiland, and Gary Smith (Cambridge, MA: Belknap, 1999), 512.

31. Daniel Knapp, "The Social Construction of Computational Reality: Reclaiming Agency under Conditions of Pervasive Surveillance" (PhD diss., London School of Economics and Political Science, 2016); Siles, Valerio-Alfaro, and Meléndez-Moran, "Learning to Like TikTok."

32. Philip Khan, "Photography Changes How We Communicate," in *Photography Changes Everything* (Washington, DC: Smithsonian Institute, 2012), 176.

33. Stine Lomborg, Lina Dencik, and Hallvard Moe, "Methods for Datafication, Datafication of Methods: Introduction to the Special Issue," *European Journal of Communication* 35, no. 3 (2020).

34. Leaver, Highfield, and Abidin, *Instagram*, 205.

35. Sarah Kember and Joanna Zylinska, *Life after New Media* (Cambridge, MA: MIT Press, 2012), 72.

36. Bolter and Grusin, *Remediation*, 233.

37. Helles, "Mobile Communication and Intermediality"; Karppi, *Disconnect*; Mannell, "A Typology."

38. Couldry and Hepp, "Conceptualizing Mediatization"; Andreas Hepp, *Cultures of Mediatization*, trans. Keith Tribe (Cambridge; Malden, MA: Polity, 2013); Andreas Hepp and Friedrich. Krotz, "Mediatized Worlds—Understanding Everyday Mediatization," in *Mediatized Worlds*, ed. Andreas Hepp and Friedrich Krotz (London: Palgrave Macmillan UK, 2014).

39. David Lyon, "Surveillance as Social Sorting: Computer Codes and Mobile Bodies," in *Surveillance as Social Sorting: Privacy, Risk and Automated Discrimination*, ed. David Lyon (New York: Routledge, 2002).

40. Van Dijck, *Culture of Connectivity*, 31.

41. Zuboff, *Age of Surveillance Capitalism*.

42. Mark Andrejevic, *iSpy: Surveillance and Power in the Interactive Era* (Lawrence: University of Kansas Press, 2007), 220.

43. Lampe, Ellison, and Steinfield, "Face(book) in the Crowd."

44. Christopher M. Kelty, *Two Bits: The Cultural Significance of Free Software* (Durham, NC: Duke University Press, 2008); Crawford, Gosling, and Light, "Social and Cultural Significance"; Aphra Kerr, Stefano DePaoli, and Max Ketainge, "Surveillant Assemblages of Governance in Massively Multiplayer Online Games: A Comparative Analysis," *Surveillance & Society* 12, no. 3 (2014); Sebastian Kubitschko, "Acting on Media Technologies and Infrastructures: Expanding the Media as Practice Approach," *Media, Culture & Society* 40, no. 4 (2018).

45. Albrechtslund, "Online Social Networking"; Burchell, "Everyday Communication Management."

Chapter 5. Practicing Authenticity

1. Goffman, *The Presentation of Self*, 23.

2. Eva Illouz, "Emotional Capital, Therapeutic Language, and the Habitus of 'the New Man,'" in *Sexualized Brains: Scientific Modeling of Emotional Intelligence from a Cultural Perspective*, ed. Nicole Christine Karafyllis and Gotlind Ulshöfer (Cambridge, MA: MIT Press, 2008).

3. Illouz, 158.

4. Trine Syvertsen and Gunn Enli, "Digital Detox: Media Resistance and the Promise of Authenticity," *Convergence* 26, no. 5–6 (2020).

5. Michel Foucault, *Discipline and Punish: The Birth of the Prison* (New York: Random House, 1977).

6. V. P. Pecora, "The Culture of Surveillance," *Qualitative Sociology* 25, no. 3 (2002).

7. Jon Dovey, *Freakshow: First Person Media and Factual Television* (London: Pluto, 2000).

8. Joshua Gamson, *Freaks Talk Back: Tabloid Talk Shows and Sexual Nonconformity* (Chicago: University of Chicago Press, 1998).

9. Brenda R. Weber, *Reality Gendervision: Sexuality and Gender on Transatlantic Reality Television* (Durham, NC: Duke University Press, 2014), 19.

10. Gershon, *Down and Out*, 5.

11. Cabanas and Illouz, "Making of a 'Happy Worker,'" 33.

12. Gershon, *Down and Out*, 15.

13. Goffman, *The Presentation of Self*.

14. Weber, *Reality Gendervision*.

15. Erving. Goffman, *Asylums; Essays on the Social Situation of Mental Patients and Other Inmates* (Garden City, NY: Anchor, 1961).

16. Goffman, 61–63.

17. Leaver, Highfield, and Abidin, *Instagram*.

18. Eric W. Rothenbuhler, "The Church of the Cult of the Individual," in *Media Anthropology*, ed. Eric W. Rothenbuhler and Mihai Coman (Thousand Oaks, CA: Sage, 2005), 94.

19. Alexander R. Galloway, "Social Realism in Gaming," *Game Studies* 4, no. 1 (2004); Rachel E. Dubrofsky and Megan M. Wood, "Gender, Race, and Authenticity: Celebrity Women Tweeting for the Gaze," in *Feminist Surveillance Studies*, ed. Rachel E. Dubrofsky and Shoshana Amielle Magnet (Durham, NC: Duke University Press, 2015); Taina Bucher, "Cleavage-Control: Stories of Algorithmic Culture and Power in the Case of the YouTube 'Reply Girls,'" in *A Networked Self and Platforms, Stories, Connections*, ed. Zizi Papacharissi (New York: Routledge, 2018).

20. Rothenbuhler, "Church of the Cult," 94.

21. Nic Newman et al., *Reuters Institute Digital News Report 2021*, 10th ed. (Oxford: Reuters Institute for the Study of Journalism, 2021).

22. Goffman, *Asylums*, 161; Ian Hacking, "Between Michel Foucault and Erving Goffman: Between Discourse in the Abstract and Face-to-Face Interaction," *Economy and Society* 33, no. 3 (2004).

23. Whitney Phillips and Ryan M. Milner, *The Ambivalent Internet: Mischief, Oddity, and Antagonism Online* (Cambridge: Polity, 2017).

24. Brooke Erin Duffy and Elizabeth Wissinger, "Mythologies of Creative Work in the Social Media Age: Fun, Free, and 'Just Being Me,'" *International Journal of Communication* 11 (2017).

25. Duffy, *(Not) Getting Paid*.

26. Shenila Khoja-Moolji and Alyssa D. Niccolini, "Watch Me Speak: Muslim Girls' Narratives and Postfeminist Pleasures of Surveillance," in *Expanding the Gaze: Gender and the Politics of Surveillance*, ed. Emily van der Meulen and Robert Heynen (Toronto: University of Toronto Press, 2016).

27. Hille Koskela, "Webcams, TV Shows and Mobile Phones: Empowering Exhibitionism," *Surveillance & Society* 2, no. 2/3 (2004); Gill, "'Life Is a Pitch.'"

28. Eva Illouz, *The End of Love: A Sociology of Negative Relations* (New York: Oxford University Press, 2019), 100.

29. Arlie Russell Hochschild, *The Managed Heart: Commercialization of Human Feeling*, 3rd ed. (1983; Berkeley: University of California Press, 2012).

30. Goffman, *The Presentation of Self*, 123.

31. Darin G. Johnson et al., "Social-Cognitive and Affective Antecedents of Code Switching and the Consequences of Linguistic Racism for Black People and People of Color," *Affective Science* (2021).

32. Nisha Nair, Deborah Cain Good, and Audrey J. Murrell, "Microaggression Experiences of Different Marginalized Identities," *Equality, Diversity and Inclusion* 38, no. 8 (2019).

33. Michel Pialoux and Stéphane Beaud, "Permanent and Temporary Workers," in *The Weight of the World: Social Suffering in Contemporary Society*, ed.

Pierre Bourdieu et al. (Stanford, CA: Stanford University Press, 1999); Monica Heller, "Code-Switching and the Politics of Language," in *The Bilingualism Reader*, ed. Li Wei, 2nd ed. (New York: Routledge, 2007).

34. Marwick and boyd, "Networked Privacy."

35. Winfield and Murrell as cited in Kimberly Adams, "For Many Black Employees, Working from Home Can Provide Relief from Inequitable Workplaces," *Marketplace Morning Report*, June 8, 2021, Marketplace.org.

36. Mikaela Pitcan, Alice E. Marwick, and danah boyd, "Performing a Vanilla Self: Respectability Politics, Social Class, and the Digital World," *Journal of Computer-Mediated Communication* 23, no. 3 (2018).

37. Hadiya Roderique, "The Workplace Social Networks of Professional Parents" (PhD diss., Rotman School of Management, University of Toronto, 2020).

38. Belle Rose Ragins, "Disclosure Disconnects: Antecedents and Consequences of Disclosing Invisible Stigmas across Life Domains," *Academy of Management Review* 33, no. 1 (2008).

39. Shani Orgad, "The Transformative Potential of Online Communication," *Feminist Media Studies* 5, no. 2 (2005).

40. Mikayla Gordon Wexler and Christopher Dole, "Giving Care a Platform: The Use of Instagram by Mothers of Children with Chronic Illness," *Medicine Anthropology Theory* 9, no. 3 (2022).

41. Katie Warfield and Courtney Demone, "Writing the Body of the Paper: Three New Materialist Methods for Examining the Socially Mediated Body," in *A Networked Self and Human Augmentics, Artificial Intelligence, Sentience*, ed. Zizi Papacharissi (New York: Routledge, 2019).

42. Sabine Trepte, "Social Media, Privacy, and Self-Disclosure: The Turbulence Caused by Social Media's Affordances," *Social Media + Society* 1 (2015).

43. Chun, *Updating to Remain*.

44. Trepte et al., "A Cross-Cultural Perspective."

45. Owen Bowcott and Kevin Rawlinson, "Romanian Whose Messages Were Read by Employer 'Had Privacy Breached,'" *Guardian Online*, Sept. 5, 2017.

46. danah boyd, *It's Complicated: The Social Lives of Networked Teens* (New Haven, CT: Yale University Press, 2014).

47. Ahmed, *Living a Feminist Life*.

48. G. A. Fine, "Small Groups and Culture Creation: The Idioculture of Little League Baseball Teams," *American Sociological Review* 44, no. 5 (1979); Rich Ling, *New Tech, New Ties* (Cambridge, MA: MIT Press, 2008); Dawn R. Gilpin, "Working the Twittersphere: Microblogging as Professional Identity Construction," in *A Networked Self: Identity, Community and Culture on Social Network Sites*, ed. Zizi Papacharissi (New York: Routledge, 2011).

49. Berger and Luckmann, *Social Construction of Reality*, 55.

50. Susanne Ekman, "Authenticity at Work: Questioning the New Spirit of Capitalism from a Micro-sociological Perspective," in *New Spirits of Capitalism? Crises, Justifications, and Dynamics*, ed. Paul du Gay and Glenn Morgan (Oxford: Oxford University Press, 2013).

51. Mark Deuze, Phoebe Elefante, and Brian Steward, "Media Work and the Recession," *Popular Communication* 8, no. 3 (2010); Mark Deuze, "Professional Identity and Media Work," in *Theorizing Cultural Work: Labour, Continuity and Change in the Cultural and Creative Industries*, ed. Mark Banks, Rosalind Gill, and Stephanie Taylor (London: Routledge, 2013).

52. Pialoux and Beaud, "Permanent and Temporary Workers."

53. Simone Browne, *Dark Matters: On the Surveillance of Blackness* (Durham, NC: Duke University Press, 2015).

54. bell hooks as cited in Browne, *Dark Matters*, 57, 62.

55. Boltanski, *Making of a Class*.

56. Sennett, *Together*, 187.

57. Gregg, *Counterproductive*, 5.

58. Shani Orgad and Rosalind Gill, *Confidence Culture* (Durham, NC: Duke University Press, 2022).

59. Sara Ahmed, "Killing Joy: Feminism and the History of Happiness," *Signs* 35, no. 3 (2010).

60. Illouz, "On Rationality and Passions," 28.

61. Berger and Luckmann, *Social Construction of Reality*.

62. Bagger and Lomborg, "Overcoming Forced Disconnection."

63. Asha Tomlinson, Lisa Mayor, and Nazim Baksh, "Being Black on Campus: Why Students, Staff and Faculty Say Universities Are Failing Them," *CBC Fifth Estate*, Feb. 24, 2021.

64. Bagger and Lomborg, "Overcoming Forced Disconnection," 176.

65. Gamson, *Freaks*; Kath Browne and Andrew McCartan, "Sexuality and Queer Geographies," in *International Encyclopedia of Human Geography* (Amsterdam: Elsevier, 2020).

66. Helen Kim, *Making Diaspora in a Global City* (New York: Routledge, 2014).

67. Jun-E Tan, "The Leap of Faith from Online to Offline: An Exploratory Study of Couchsurfing.org," *Trust and Trustworthy Computing International Conference Proceedings* (2010); Stefanie Duguay, "'The More I Look Like Justin Bieber in the Pictures, the Better': Queer Women's Self-Representation on Instagram," in *A Networked Self and Platforms, Stories, Connections*, ed. Zizi Papacharissi (New York: Routledge, 2018); Erika Polson, "'Doing' Local: Place-Based Travel Apps and the Globally Networked Self," in *A Networked Self and Platforms, Stories, Connections*, ed. Zizi Papacharissi (New York: Routledge, 2018).

68. Richard Jenkins, "Identity, Surveillance and Modernity," in *Routledge Handbook of Surveillance Studies*, ed. Kirstie Ball, Kevin Haggerty, and David Lyon (New York: Routledge, 2012), 159.

69. Ian Hacking, "Making Up People," *London Review of Books*, August 17, 2006, 233.

70. Anthony Giddens, *Modernity and Self-Identity: Self and Society in the Late Modern Age* (Stanford, CA: Stanford University Press, 1991).

71. Annette M. Markham, "Ontological Insecurity," 45, 47.

72. Daniel Dayan and Elihu Katz, *Media Events: The Live Broadcasting of His-*

tory (Cambridge, MA: Harvard University Press, 1992); N. K. Rivenburgh, "In Pursuit of a Global Image: Media Events as Political Communication," in *Media Events in a Global Age*, ed. Nick Couldry, Andreas Hepp, and Friedrich Krotz (London: Routledge, 2010); Daniel Dayan, "Beyond Media Events: Disenchantment, Derailment, and Disruption," in *Media Events in a Global Age*, ed. Nick Couldry, Andreas Hepp, and Friedrich Krotz (London: Routledge, 2010); Hepp and Couldry, "Introduction"; Burchell, "Infiltrating the Space"; Kenzie Burchell, "'Take My Picture': The Media Assemblage of Lone-Wolf Terror Events, Mobile Communication, and the News," in *The Routledge Companion to Media and Humanitarian Action*, ed. Robin Andersen and Purnaka L. de Silva (New York: Routledge, 2017); Kenzie Burchell, "Reporting, Uncertainty, and the Orchestrated Fog of War: A Practice-Based Lens for Understanding Global Media Events," *International Journal of Communication* 14 (2020).

73. Poell, Rajagopalan, and Kavada, "Publicness on Platforms."

74. Lee Humphreys, *The Qualified Self: Social Media and the Accounting of Everyday Life* (Cambridge, MA: MIT Press, 2018).

75. Poell, Rajagopalan, and Kavada, "Publicness on Platforms"; Amy Ross Arguedas et al., *Echo Chambers, Filter Bubbles, and Polarisation: A Literature Review* (Oxford: Reuters Institute for the Study of Journalism, 2022).

76. Mark Granovetter, "The Strength of Weak Ties," *American Journal of Sociology* 78, no. 6 (1973); Mark Granovetter, "The Strength of Weak Ties: A Network Theory Revisited," *Sociological Theory* 1 (1983).

77. Ronald S. Burt, "The Social Capital of Structural Holes," in *New Directions in Economic Sociology*, ed. Mauro F. Guillén, Randall Collins, Paula England, and Marshall Meyer (New York: Russell Sage, 2001); Rich Ling, "Trust, Cohesion and Social Networks: The Case of Quasi-Illicit Photos in a Teen Peer Group," Hungarian Academy of Sciences, Conference on Mobile Communications (2008).

78. Mario Tronti, *Workers and Capital*, trans. D. Broder (London: Verso, 2019); Terranova, *Network Culture*; Trebor Scholz, *Digital Labor: The Internet as Playground and Factory* (Abingdon: Routledge, 2012).

79. Nancy K. Baym, "Connect with Your Audience! The Relational Labor of Connection," *Communication Review* 18, no. 1 (2015).

80. Pierre Bourdieu, "The Forms of Capital," in *Handbook of Theory and Research for the Sociology of Education*, ed. J. G. Richardson (New York: Greenwood Press, 1986).

81. Rodney Benson and Erik Neveu, eds., *Bourdieu and the Journalistic Field* (Cambridge: Polity, 2005).

82. Illouz, *Cold Intimacies*.

83. Pierre Bourdieu, *Distinction*, trans. Paul Kegan (London: Routledge, 1984).

84. Douglas Zytko et al., "Dating Apps Are Used for More Than Dating," *Proceedings of the ACM on Human-Computer Interaction* 6, no. GROUP (2022).

85. Silverstone, "Sociology of Mediation."

86. boyd, "Social Network Sites."

87. Pierre Bourdieu, *Outline of a Theory of Practice*, trans. Richard Nice (Cambridge: Cambridge University Press, 1977), 167.

88. Ahmed, *Living a Feminist Life*, 115.

89. Schütz, *Collected Papers*.

90. As Couldry assesses, Bourdieu examines the structuring nature of individual actions as "locally improvised actions of individuals that are based upon 'dispositions' those individuals have acquired . . . a person's available set of dispositions (or 'habitus') of possibilities for action, by constraining the resources she has to act in situations she encounters." Couldry, "Individual Point of View," 5 (see introduction, n. 20 above).

91. Gershon, *Down and Out*.

92. Bourdieu, *Outline of a Theory*.

93. Bauman, *Liquid Modernity*, 20.

94. Erving Goffman, *Stigma: Note on the Management of Spoiled Identity* (New York: Touchstone, 1986).

95. Ian Hacking, "Making Up People," in *Reconstructing Individualism: Autonomy, Individuality, and the Self in Western Thought*, ed. Thomas C. Heller, Morton Sosna, and David E. Wellbery (Stanford, CA: Stanford University Press, 1986).

96. Sara Ahmed, *On Being Included: Racism and Diversity in Institutional Life* (Durham, NC: Duke University Press, 2012).

97. Susan Leigh Star, "Power, Technology, and the Phenomenology of Conventions: On Being Allergic to Onions," in *Boundary Objects and Beyond: Working with Leigh Star*, ed. Geoffrey C. Bowker et al. (Cambridge, MA: MIT Press, 2015).

98. Ahmed, *Living a Feminist Life*.

99. Bourdieu, *Distinction*.

100. Goffman, *Asylums*, 61; Ahmed, *On Being Included*, 175.

101. Albert O. Hirschman, *Exit, Voice, and Loyalty: Responses to Decline in Firms, Organizations, and States* (Cambridge, MA: Harvard University Press, 1970); Zeena Feldman, "Quitting Digital Culture," in *Reckoning with Social Media*, ed. Aleena Chia, Ana Jorge, and Tero Karppi (Lanham, MD: Rowman & Littlefield, 2021), 117.

102. Goffman, *Asylums*; Ahmed, "Killing Joy"; T. L. Cowan, "Transfeminist Kill/Joys," *TSQ: Transgender Studies Quarterly* 1, no. 4 (2014); Star, "Power, Technology," 266.

Chapter 6. Practicing Metacommunication

1. Emmanuel Levinas as quoted in Tim Markham, "Subjective Recognition," 31.

2. See Zuboff, "The White-Collar Body," 200.

3. Fuchs and Sevignani, "What Is Digital Labour?"

4. Alessandro Gandini, "Digital Labour: An Empty Signifier," *Media, Culture & Society* 43, no. 2 (2021).

5. Sigrid Kannengießer and Sebastian Kubitschko, "Acting on Media: Influ-

encing, Shaping and (Re)configuring the Fabric of Everyday Life," *Media and Communication* 5, no. 3 (2017).

6. Sebastian Kubitschko, "The Role of Hackers in Countering Surveillance and Promoting Democracy," *Media and Communication* 3, no. 2 (2015).

7. Asen O. Ivanov, "Evaluative Practice in a Broadcasting Newsroom Archive: Culture, Context, and Understanding in Practice," *International Journal of Communication* 14 (2020).

8. Hilde C. Stephansen, "Conceptualizing the Role of Knowledge in Acting on Media," in *Citizen Media and Practice: Currents, Connections, Challenges*, ed. Hilde C. Stephansen and Emiliano Treré (London: Routledge, 2020).

9. Sherry Turkle, "Always-On/Always-on-You: The Tethered Self," in *Handbook of Mobile Communication Studies*, ed. James E. Katz (Cambridge, MA: MIT Press, 2008), 124.

10. Zuboff, *Age of the Smart Machine*.

11. Gershon, "Media Ideologies."

12. Bourdieu, *Outline of a Theory*, 164.

13. Berger and Luckmann, *Social Construction of Reality*, 56.

14. Illouz, "On Rationality and Passions," 27.

15. Ling and Donner, *Mobile Communication*, 146.

16. David K. Lewis, *Convention: A Philosophical Study* (Cambridge, MA: Harvard University Press, 1969).

17. Lewis, 12.

18. Boutang, *Cognitive Capitalism*.

19. Lisa Nakamura, "Racism, Sexism, and Gaming's Cruel Optimism," in *Gaming Representation: Race, Gender, and Sexuality in Video Games*, ed. Jennifer Malkowski and TreaAndrea M. Russworm (Bloomington: Indiana University Press, 2017).

20. Ruha Benjamin, *Race after Technology: Abolitionist Tools for the New Jim Code* (Cambridge: Polity, 2019).

21. Christian Sandvig et al., "When the Algorithm Itself Is a Racist: Diagnosing Ethical Harm in the Basic Components of Software," *International Journal of Communication* (2016).

22. Bagger and Lomborg, "Overcoming Forced Disconnection," 174.

23. Rogers Brubaker, "Rethinking Classical Theory," *Theory and Society* 14, no. 6 (1985).

24. Lewis, *Convention*.

25. Goffman, *Asylums*; Boltanski and Chiapello, *New Spirit of Capitalism*.

26. Feldman, "Quitting Digital Culture," 103–4.

27. Goldberg, *Antisocial Media*; Karppi, *Disconnect*; Magdalena Kania-Lundholm, "Why Disconnecting Matters," in *Reckoning with Social Media*, ed. Aleena Chia, Ana Jorge, and Tero Karppi (Lanham, MD: Rowman & Littlefield, 2021).

28. This offers an adaptation or rather extension of Silverstone's "double articulation" of media, in practice and in discourse, as part of the domestication process.

See Roger Silverstone and Eric Hirsch, introduction to *Consuming Technologies: Media and Information in Domestic Spaces*, ed. Roger Silverstone and Eric Hirsch (London: Routledge, 2003); Silverstone, Hirsch, and Morely, "Information and Communication Technologies"; Silverstone, "Sociology of Mediation"; Haddon, "Roger Silverstone's Legacies"; and Livingstone, "On the Material and the Symbolic."

29. Dean, *Democracy*; Alice Mattoni, *Media Practices and Protest Politics: How Precarious Workers Mobilise* (London: Routledge, 2016).

Conclusion: To Count and Be Counted

1. In English, "to 'count' is both to matter and to be subject to an arithmetical calculus." Judith Butler and Athena Athanasiou, *Dispossession: The Performative in the Political* (Cambridge: Polity, 2013), 100.

2. Slobodian, *Globalists*, 223; Marion Fourcade and Jeffrey Gordon, "Learning like a State: Statecraft in the Digital Age," *Journal of Law and Political Economy* 1 (2020).

3. Joy Buolamwini and Timnit Gerbru, "Gender Shades: Intersectional Accuracy Disparities in Commercial Gender Classification," *Proceedings of Machine Learning Research* 81 (2018).

4. Elizabeth J. Van Couvering, "Search Engine Bias: The Structuration of Traffic on the World-Wide Web" (PhD diss., London School of Economics and Political Science, 2009); Safiya Umoja Noble, *Algorithms of Oppression: How Search Engines Reinforce Racism* (New York: New York University Press, 2018).

5. Nicole S. Cohen, "Entrepreneurial Journalism and the Precarious State of Media Work," *South Atlantic Quarterly* 114, no. 3 (2015); Maggie Reid, "Entrepreneurial Journalism and Ubiquitous Media," in *Mobile and Ubiquitous Media: Critical and International Perspectives*, ed. Michael S. Daubs and Vincent R. Manzerolle (New York: Peter Lang, 2018).

6. A. M. Turing, "Computing Machinery and Intelligence," *Mind* 49 (1950); Christopher Hollings, Ursula Martin, and Adrian C. Rice, *Ada Lovelace: The Making of a Computer Scientist* (Oxford: Bodleian Library, 2018). See also Elizabeth A. Wilson, *Affect and Artificial Intelligence* (Seattle: University of Washington Press, 2010).

7. Hacking, *The Taming of Chance*.

8. John Durham Peters, " 'The Only Proper Scale of Representation': The Politics of Statistics and Stories," *Political Communication* 18, no. 4 (2001).

9. Quoted in Taneja, Hemant Taneja, "The Era of 'Move Fast and Break Things' Is Over," *Harvard Business Review*, Jan. 22, 2019.

10. Boutang, *Cognitive Capitalism*.

11. CBC Radio, "Canada Could Lead a Coalition to Force Change at Facebook, Says Whistleblower Frances Haugen," *The Current*, Jan. 14, 2022.

12. Ulrich Beck, *Risk Society: Towards a New Modernity* (London: Sage, 1992).

13. Siegel, *Forensic Media*, 30.

14. Quoted in Nicholas Carlson, " 'I'm Feeling Luck' Button Costs Google $110 Million per Year," Gawker.com, Nov. 20, 2007.

15. Margaret Thatcher, "Margaret Thatcher: A Life in Quotes," *Guardian Online*, April 8, 2013.

16. Nowotny, *The Cunning of Uncertainty*, 65–66.

17. Nowotny, *The Cunning of Uncertainty*, 70.

18. Michel Foucault, *The Essential Foucault: Selections from Essential Works of Foucault, 1954–1984* (New York: New Press, 2003); Michel Foucault, *The Birth of Biopolitics: Lectures at the Collège de France, 1978–79*, trans. Graham Burchell (New York: Picador, 2008).

19. Tribe, "Liberalism and Neoliberalism."

20. Foucault, *The Essential Foucault*.

21. For critiques of the data-colonialism thesis, see Nick Couldry and Ulises Ali Mejias, "The Decolonial Turn in Data and Technology Research: What Is at Stake and Where Is It Heading," *Information, Communication & Society* (2021); Robert Mejia and Ergin Bulut, "The Cruel Optimism of Casual Games: Neocolonialism, Neoliberalism, and the Valorization of Play," *Critical Studies in Media Communication* 36, no. 2 (2019).

22. Nick Couldry and Ulises Ali Mejias, *The Costs of Connection: How Data Is Colonizing Human Life and Appropriating It for Capitalism* (Stanford, CA: Stanford University Press, 2019).

23. Nazmi Tolga TUNCER, "F. A. Hayek and Ordoliberalism: A Comparative Study," *Socyoekonomi Society* 20, no. 20 (2013).

24. Crain, "The Limits of Transparency," 90.

25. Lisa Khan, "Amazon's Antitrust Paradox," *Yale Law Journal* 126, no. 710 (2017).

26. Thomas Lemke, " 'The Birth of Bio-Politics': Michel Foucault's Lecture at the Collège de France on Neo-liberal Governmentality," *Economy and Society* 30, no. 2 (2001).

27. Slobodian, *Globalists*.

28. Robin Mansell, *Imagining the Internet: Communication, Innovation, and Governance* (Oxford: Oxford University Press, 2012).

29. James W. Cortada, ed., *Rise of the Knowledge Worker: Resources for the Knowledge-Based Economy* (Boston: Butterworth-Heinemann, 1998); Malcolm Waters, "Daniel Bell and the Post-Industrial Society," in *Rise of the Knowledge Worker*, ed. James W. Cortada (Boston: Butterworth-Heinemann, 1998); Ursula Huws, *Reinventing the Welfare State: Digital Platforms and Public Policies* (London: Pluto, 2020).

30. Sarah T. Roberts, *Behind the Screen: Content Moderation in the Shadows of Social Media* (New Haven, CT: Yale University Press, 2019); Susan Leigh Star and Geoffrey C. Bowker, *Sorting Things Out: Classification and Its Consequences* (Cambridge, MA: MIT Press, 1999).

31. Philip Mirowski and Dieter Plehwe, eds., *The Road from Mont Pèlerin: The Making of the Neoliberal Thought Collective* (Cambridge, MA: Harvard University Press, 2009).

32. Jan Tumlir, "Need for an Open Multilateral Trading System," *World Economy* 6, no. 4 (1983), quoted in Slobodian, *Globalists*, 222.

33. Paolo Gerbaudo, *The Great Recoil: Politics after Populism and Pandemic* (New York: Verso, 2021).

34. Steven Kent Vogel, *Marketcraft: How Governments Make Markets Work* (Oxford: Oxford University Press, 2018).

35. Benjamin Peters, *How Not to Network a Nation: The Uneasy History of the Soviet Internet* (Cambridge, MA: MIT Press, 2016).

36. Crain, "The Limits of Transparency."

37. Vogel, *Marketcraft.*

38. Slobodian, *Globalists*, 270.

39. Such market dominance speaks to a "rentierization" of national and transnational economies. See Brett Christophers, "The Rentierization of the United Kingdom Economy," *Environment and Planning A: Economy and Space* (2019): 5–6.

40. Alex Pentland, *Social Physics: How Good Ideas Spread—The Lessons from a New Science* (New York: Penguin, 2014).

41. Zuboff, *Age of Surveillance Capitalism*, 418.

42. Eyal Weizman, *Forensic Architecture: Violence at the Threshold of Detectability* (Brooklyn, NY: Zone, 2017).

43. Adam Rutherford and Hannah Fry, "The Random Request." *The Curious Cases of Rutherford and Fry* (blog), BBC Radio 4, Sept. 6, 2018.

44. Gilles Deleuze, "Postscript on the Societies of Control," *October* 59 (1992): 5.

45. Couldry and Mejias, *The Costs of Connection.*

46. Rana Foroohar, "Lisa Khan: 'This Isn't Just about Antitrust. It's about Values,'" *Financial Times*, March 29, 2019.

47. Jonathan Watts, "Jane Goodall: 'Change Is Happening. There Are Many Ways to Start Moving in the Right Way,'" *Guardian Online*, Jan. 3, 2021.

48. BLS, "Consumer Price Index—January 2022," *Bureau of Labor Statistics*, Feb. 10, 2022.

49. Illouz, "Emotional Capital," 159.

50. Boaventura de Sousa Santos, *The End of the Cognitive Empire: the Coming of Age of Epistemologies of the South* (Durham, NC: Duke University Press, 2018), 293.

51. WHO, "Burn-Out an 'Occupational Phenomenon': International Classification of Diseases," *World Health Organization*, May 28, 2019.

52. Government of Canada, "Disconnecting from Work-Related E-communications Outside of Work Hours," *Employment and Social Development Canada*, Jan. 2019; Ope Akanbi, "The Right to Disconnect: Why Legislation Doesn't Address the Real Problems with Work." *The Conversation*, Nov. 15, 2021.

53. Huws, *Reinventing the Welfare State*; Gerbaudo, *The Great Recoil.*

54. Kristian Møller and Maja Nordtug, "Platformed Bodies," *Journal of Media and Communication Research* 71 (2021).

55. Jenkins, *Convergence Culture*; Gillian Rose, *Visual Methodologies: An Introduction to Researching with Visual Materials* (London: SAGE Publications Ltd, 2016).

56. Kerr, DePaoli, and Ketainge, "Surveillant Assemblages of Governance."

57. Hand and Gorea, "Digital Traces"; Jenny Kennedy, *Digital Domesticity: Media, Materiality, and Home Life* (New York: Oxford University Press, 2020).

58. Norbert Elias, *The Civilizing Process: The Development of Manners* (New York: Urizen, 1978).

59. Goffman, *Asylums*; Foucault, *Discipline and Punish*; Hacking, "Between Michel Foucault and Erving Goffman."

60. Eviatar Zerubavel, *Taken for Granted: The Remarkable Power of the Unremarkable* (Princeton, NJ: Princeton University Press, 2018).

61. Jonathan Zittrain, *The Future of the Internet: And How to Stop It* (New Haven, CT: Yale University Press, 2008).

62. Lin Qiqing and Raymond Zhong, "'996' Is China's Version of Hustle Culture. Tech Workers Are Sick of It," *New York Times [online]*, April 29, 2019, https://www.nytimes.com/2019/04/29/technology/china-996-jack-ma.html.

63. Rory Cellan-Jones, "Tim Berners-Lee: 'Stop Web's Downward Plunge to Dysfunctional Future,'" *BBC News*, March 11, 2019 [00:50–01:10 minutes]; Ian Sample, "Internet 'Is Not Working for Women and Girls,' Says Berners-Lee," *The Guardian*, March 11, 2020.

64. Helga Nowotny, *An Orderly Mess* (Budapest: Central European University Press, 2017).

65. Christopher M Kelty, *Two Bits: The Cultural Significance of Free Software* (Durham, NC: Duke University Press, 2008), 28–29.

66. Hacking, *The Taming of Chance*, 4, 7.

67. Zuboff, *Age of Surveillance Capitalism*.

68. Santos, *End of the Cognitive Empire*, 294–95.

69. Doreen Massey, *For Space* (London: Sage, 2005); Cynthia Wang, "A Slice of Time: An Exploration of Temporal Capital and Its Relationships to Economics, Culture, and Society in a Technological and Digital Age," *Gnovis* 13, no. 2 (2013); Sarah Sharma, *In the Meantime: Temporality and Cultural Politics* (Durham, NC: Duke University Press, 2014).

70. Du Gay and Morgan, *New Spirits*.

71. Balibar, Cassin, and Laugier, "Praxis" (see introduction, n. 77 above).

72. Santos, *End of the Cognitive Empire*, 296.

INDEX

Note: page numbers followed by n refer to notes, with note number.

Printed in the USA
CPSIA information can be obtained
at www.ICGtesting.com
JSHW021255200624
65111JS00002B/2

9 781503 639799